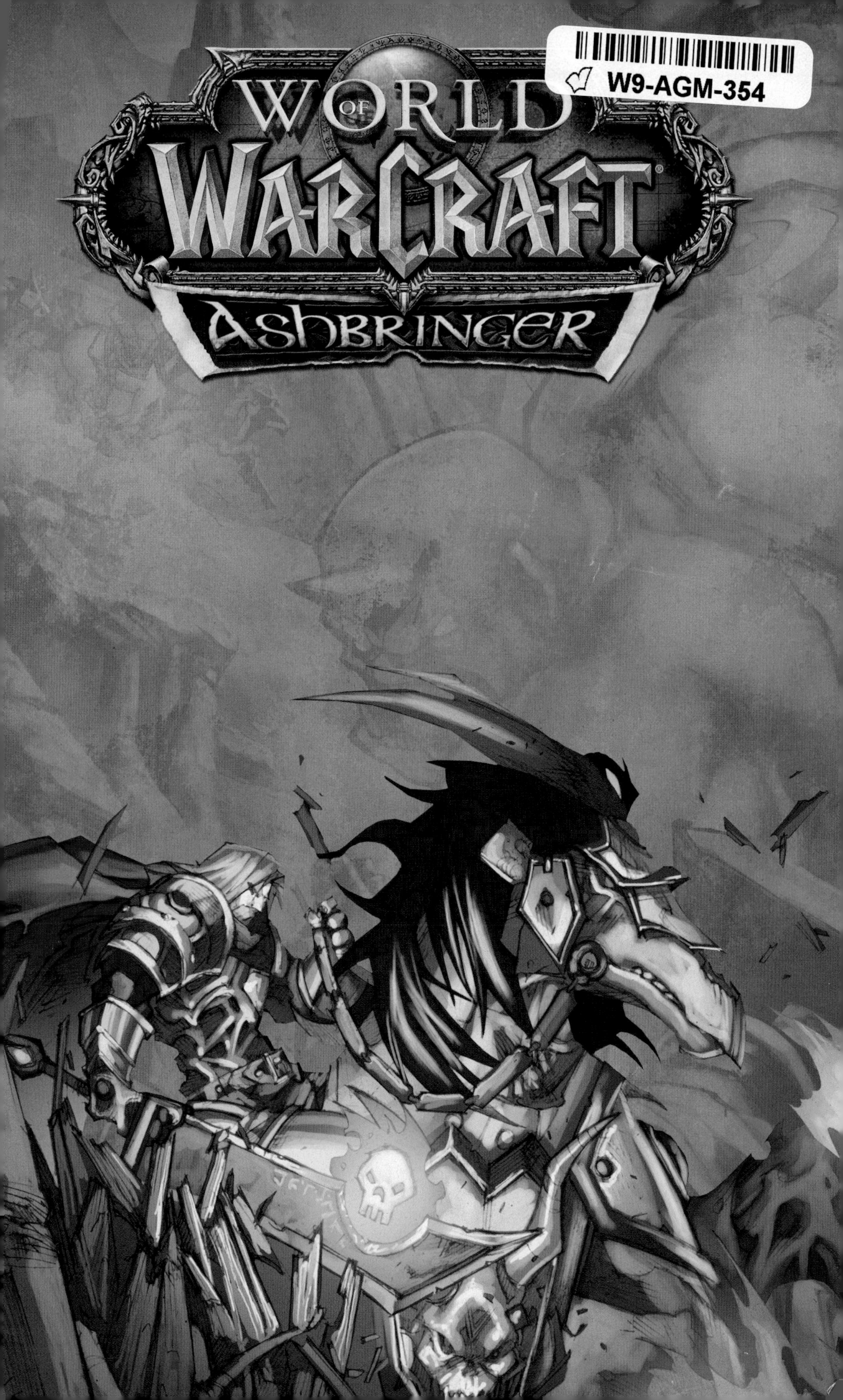
WORLD OF WARCRAFT®
ASHBRINGER

Writer: Micky Neilson
Artists: Ludo Lullabi and Tony Washington
Letterer: Wes Abbott

Story Consultants: Chris Metzen and Alex Afrasiabi
Collected Edition Cover and Original Series Covers by Chris Robinson
Original Series Variant Covers by Ludo Lullabi and Tony Washington

For Blizzard Entertainment:

Chris Metzen	Senior VP—Creative Development
Jeff Donias	Director—Creative Development
Micky Neilson	Story Consultation and Development
Glenn Rane	Art Director
Cory Jones	Director—Global Business Development and Licensing
Jason Bischoff	Associate Licensing Manager
Additional Development:	Samwise Didier, Evelyn Fredericksen, Ben Brode, Sean Wang
Blizzard Special Thanks:	Brian Hsieh, Gina Pippin

For DC Comics:

Jim Lee	Editorial Director
Hank Kanalz	VP – General Manager & Editor – Original Series
Sarah Gaydos	Assistant Editor – Original Series
Kristy Quinn	Editor
Ed Roeder	Art Director
Paul Levitz	President & Publisher
Richard Bruning	SVP – Creative Director
Patrick Caldon	EVP – Finance & Operations
Amy Genkins	SVP – Business & Legal Affairs
Gregory Noveck	SVP – Creative Affairs
Steve Rotterdam	SVP – Sales & Marketing
Cheryl Rubin	SVP – Brand Management

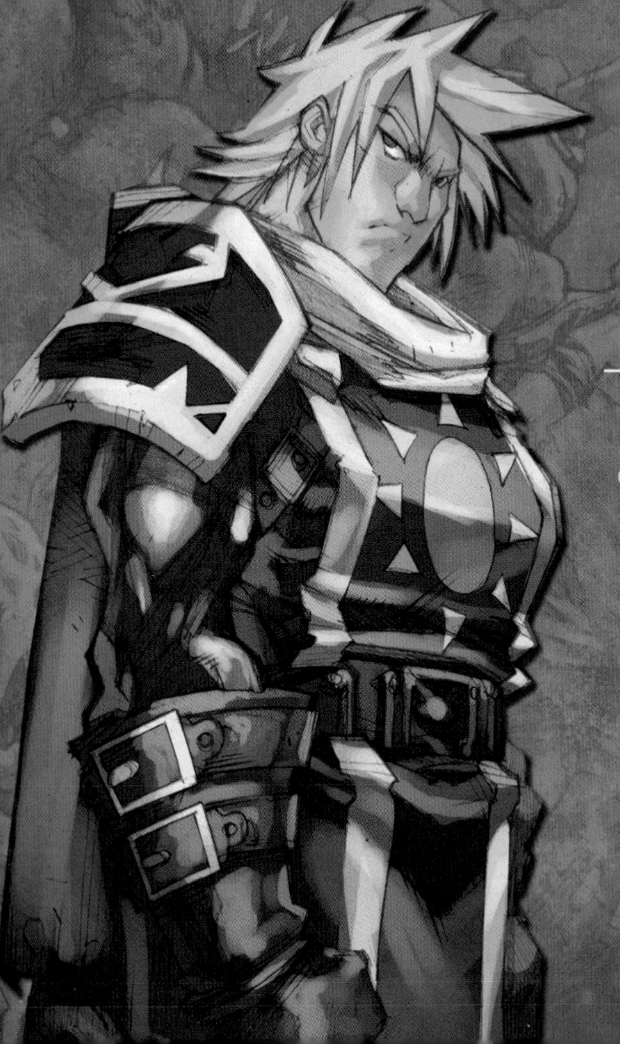

SUSTAINABLE FORESTRY INITIATIVE
Certified Chain of Custody
Promoting Sustainable Forest Management
www.sfiprogram.org

Fiber used in this product line meets the sourcing requirements of the SFI program.

www.sfiprogram.org
NSF-SFICOC-C0001801

WORLD OF WARCRAFT: ASHBRINGER, published by WildStorm Productions, an imprint of DC Comics, 888 Prospect St, Suite 240, La Jolla, CA 92037.

Printed by RR Donnelley, Roanoke, VA, USA. 3/17/10

DC Comics, a Warner Bros. Entertainment Company.

Softcover ISBN: 978-1-4012-2342-7

LICENSED BLIZZARD ENTERTAINMENT PRODUCT

Cast of Characters

HIGHLORD ALEXANDROS MOGRAINE

A courageous and devoted commander within the Knights of the Silver Hand. He directs his forces with steadfast determination and unwavering faith.

RENAULT AND DARION MOGRAINE

Alexandros' only sons. Their mother died when Darion was born. Following that tragic loss, each of them struggles to find his own identity.

FAIRBANKS

A loyal and devoted friend of the Mograine family. He is Alexandros' trusted advisor and right hand in all diplomatic matters.

SAIDAN DATHROHAN

A devout paladin, respected leader, and honorable warrior. Dathrohan is a man of strength and conviction to whom all paladins look for guidance.

GENERAL ABBENDIS AND LADY BRIGETTE ABBENDIS

Though both are occupied with scouring evil from the world, General Abbendis is just as often engaged in controlling his willful daughter's behavior.

ISILLIEN AND DOAN

Isillien the priest and Doan the mage work to maintain the "purity" of the Order of the Silver Hand.

MAXWELL TYROSUS

An outspoken devotee of the Light, Maxwell's views of what is best for the Order are not always shared by the majority of his companions.

CHAPTER I

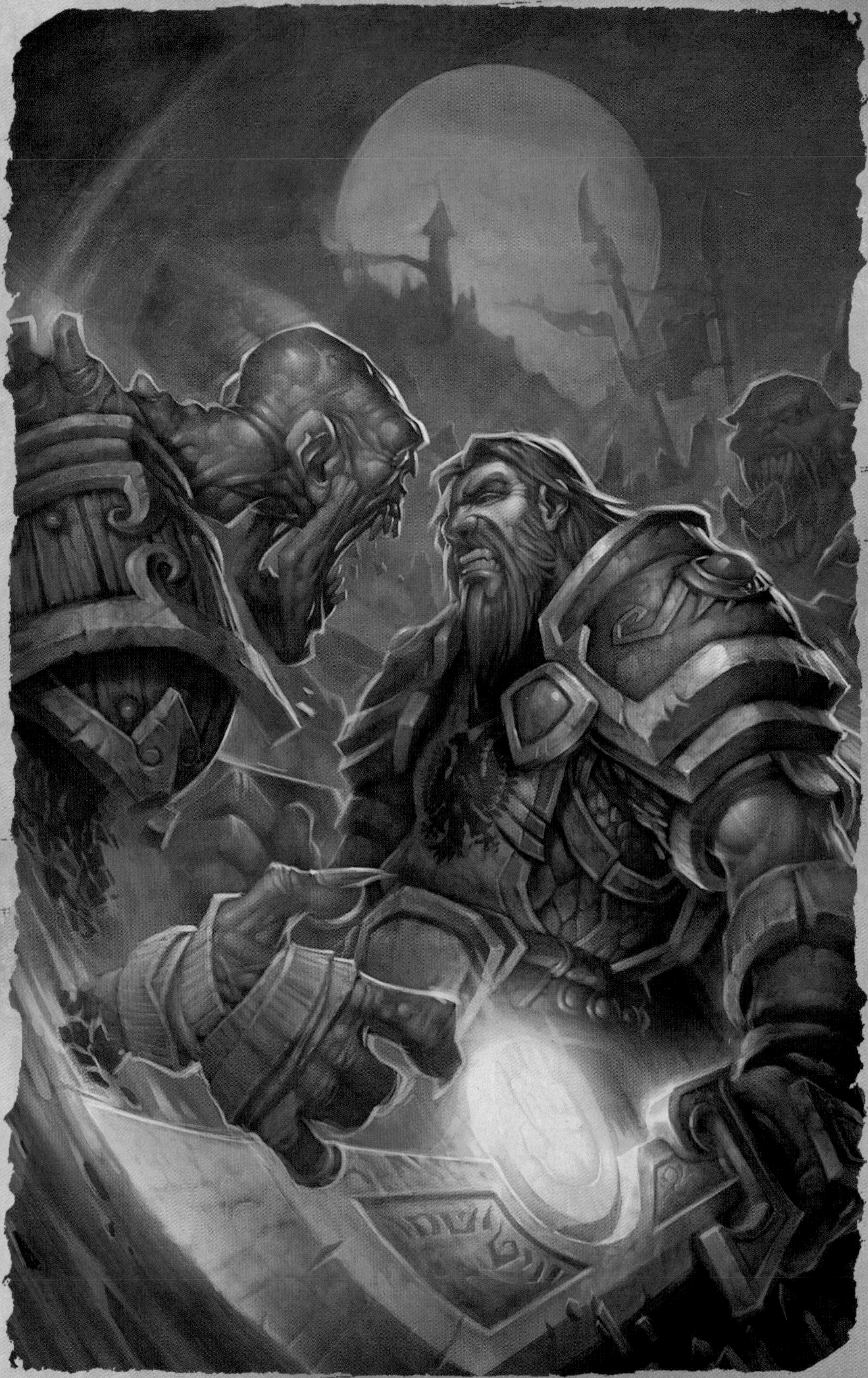

Cover by Chris Robinson

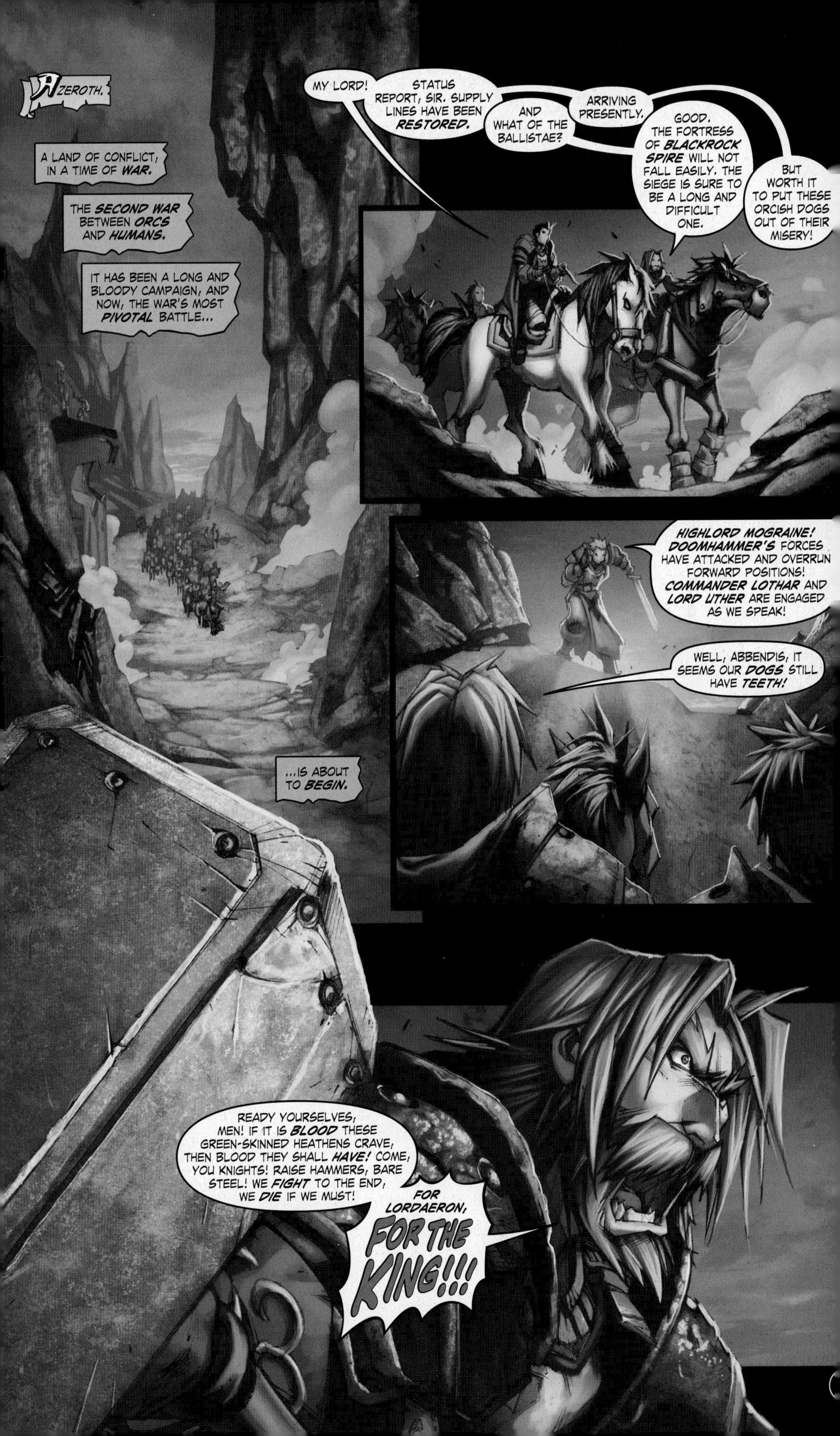

AZEROTH.
A LAND OF CONFLICT, IN A TIME OF WAR.
THE SECOND WAR BETWEEN ORCS AND HUMANS.
IT HAS BEEN A LONG AND BLOODY CAMPAIGN, AND NOW, THE WAR'S MOST PIVOTAL BATTLE...
...IS ABOUT TO BEGIN.
MY LORD!
STATUS REPORT, SIR. SUPPLY LINES HAVE BEEN RESTORED.
AND WHAT OF THE BALLISTAE?
ARRIVING PRESENTLY.
GOOD. THE FORTRESS OF BLACKROCK SPIRE WILL NOT FALL EASILY. THE SIEGE IS SURE TO BE A LONG AND DIFFICULT ONE.
BUT WORTH IT TO PUT THESE ORCISH DOGS OUT OF THEIR MISERY!
HIGHLORD MOGRAINE! DOOMHAMMER'S FORCES HAVE ATTACKED AND OVERRUN FORWARD POSITIONS! COMMANDER LOTHAR AND LORD UTHER ARE ENGAGED AS WE SPEAK!
WELL, ABBENDIS, IT SEEMS OUR DOGS STILL HAVE TEETH!
READY YOURSELVES, MEN! IF IT IS BLOOD THESE GREEN-SKINNED HEATHENS CRAVE, THEN BLOOD THEY SHALL HAVE! COME, YOU KNIGHTS! RAISE HAMMERS, BARE STEEL! WE FIGHT TO THE END, WE DIE IF WE MUST!
FOR LORDAERON, FOR THE KING!!!

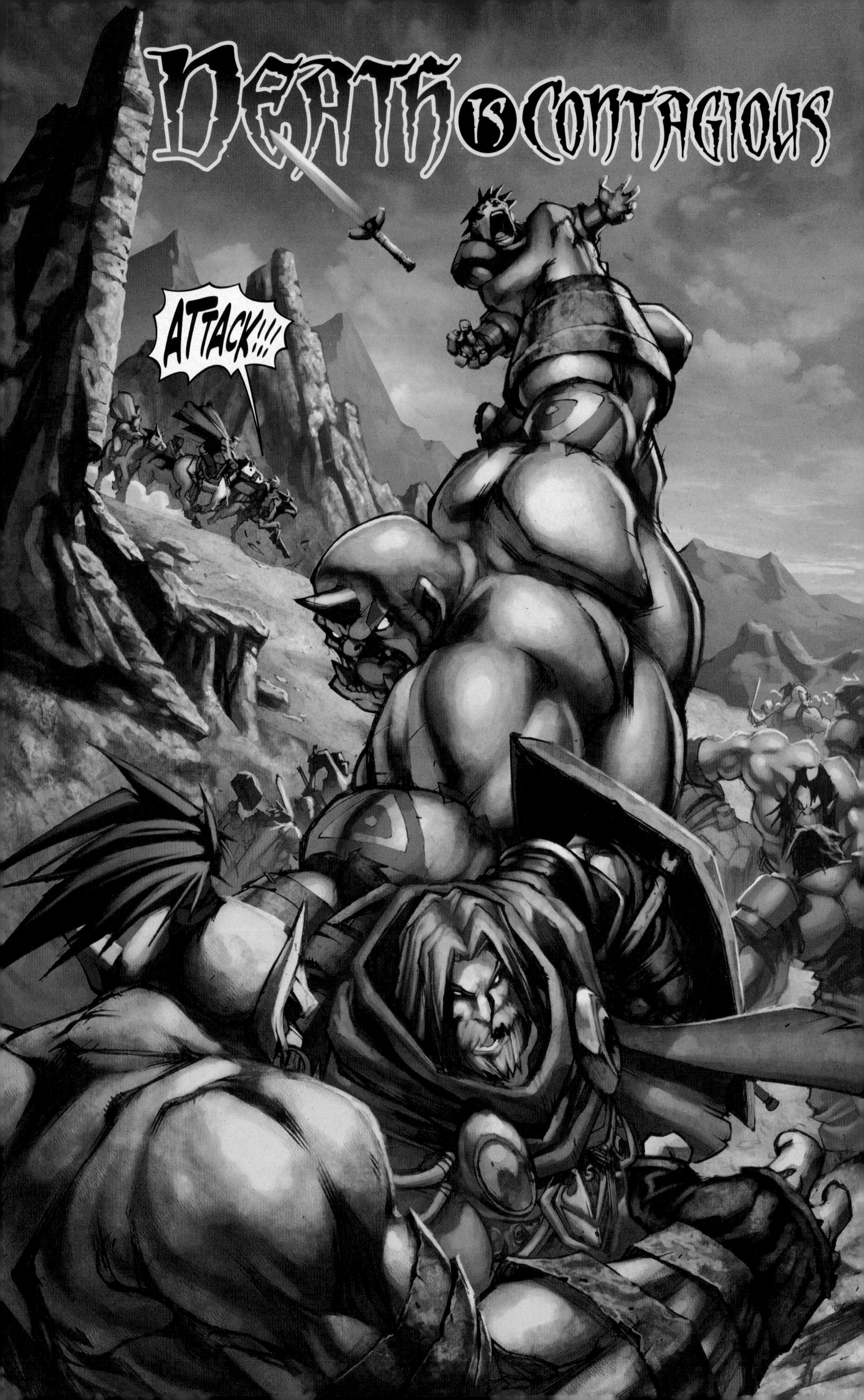
DEATH IS CONTAGIOUS
ATTACK!!!

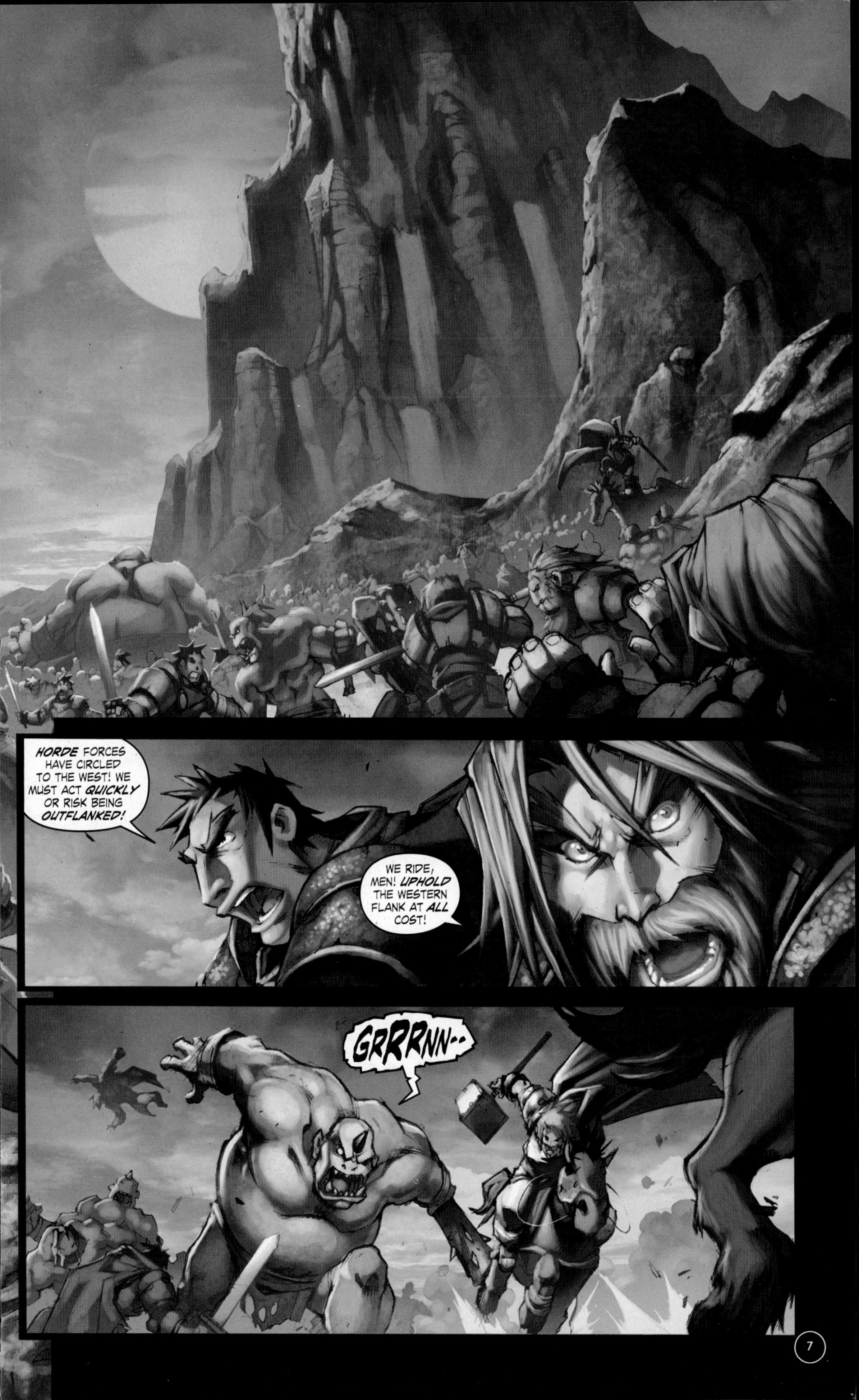
HORDE FORCES HAVE CIRCLED TO THE WEST! WE MUST ACT QUICKLY OR RISK BEING OUTFLANKED!
WE RIDE, MEN! UPHOLD THE WESTERN FLANK AT ALL COST!
GRRRNN--

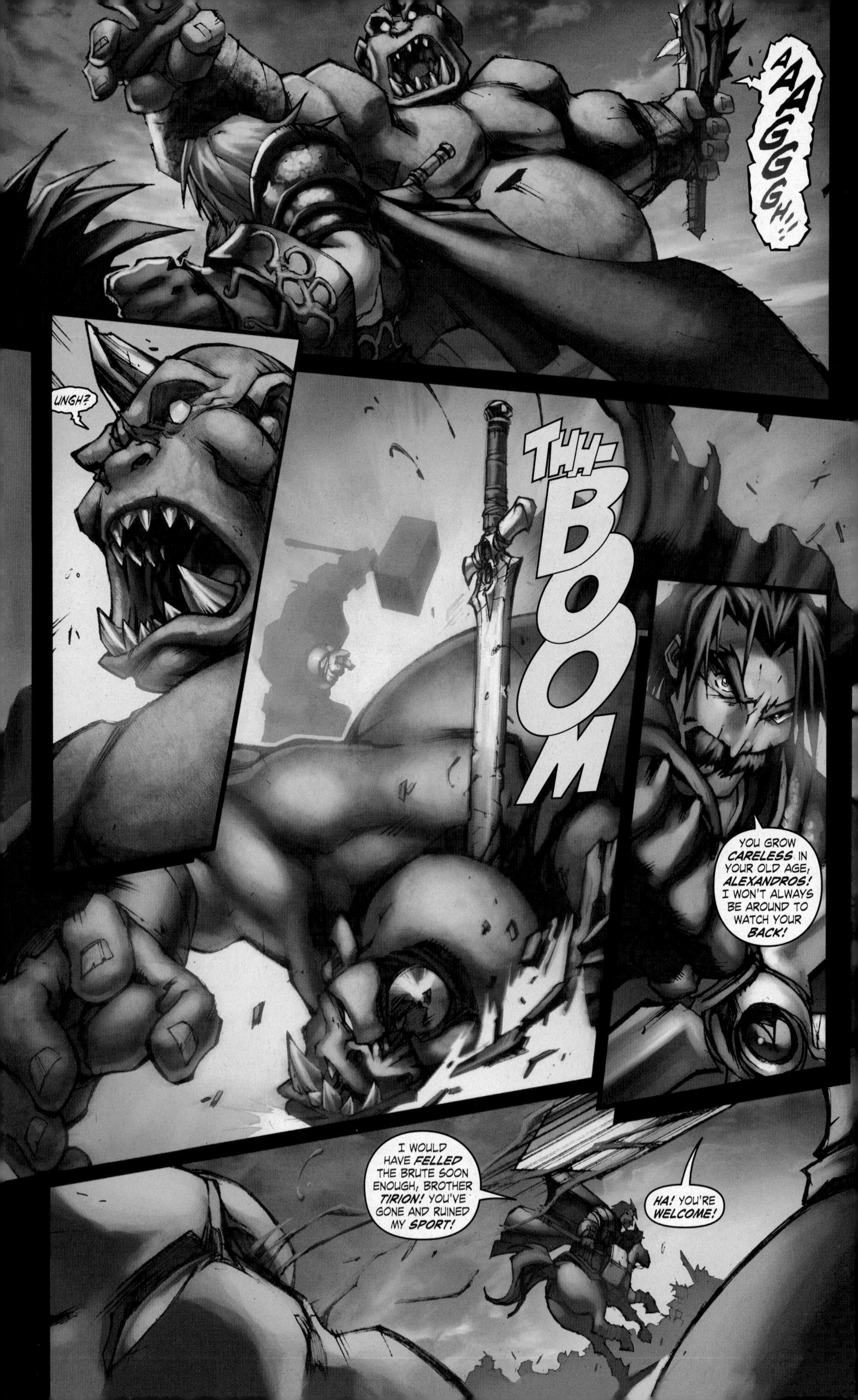
AAAGGGH!!
UNGH?
THH-BOOM
YOU GROW CARELESS IN YOUR OLD AGE, ALEXANDROS! I WON'T ALWAYS BE AROUND TO WATCH YOUR BACK!
I WOULD HAVE FELLED THE BRUTE SOON ENOUGH, BROTHER TIRION! YOU'VE GONE AND RUINED MY SPORT!
HA! YOU'RE WELCOME!

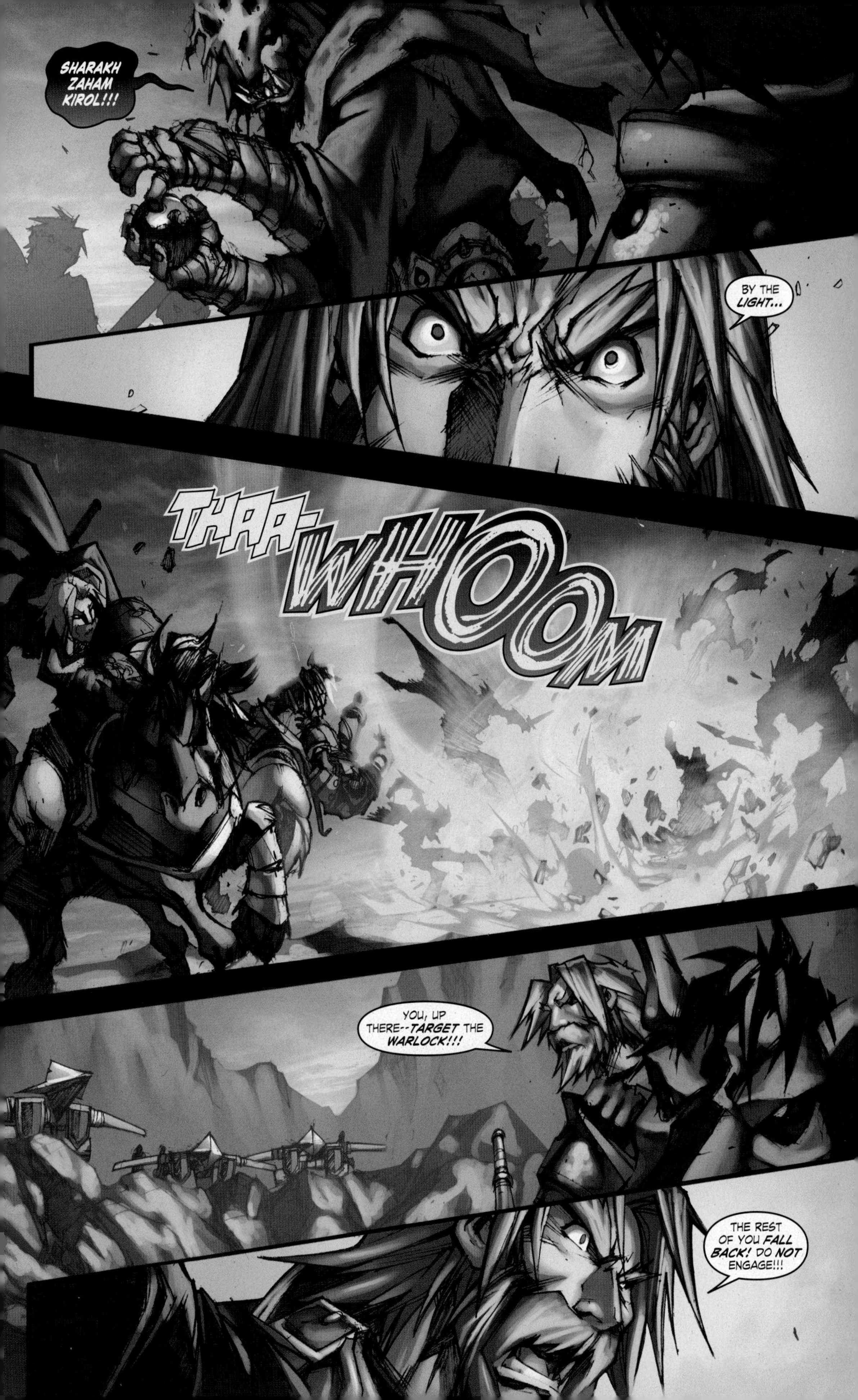
SHARAKH ZAHAM KIROL!!!
BY THE LIGHT...
THAA-WHOOM
YOU, UP THERE--TARGET THE WARLOCK!!!
THE REST OF YOU FALL BACK! DO NOT ENGAGE!!!

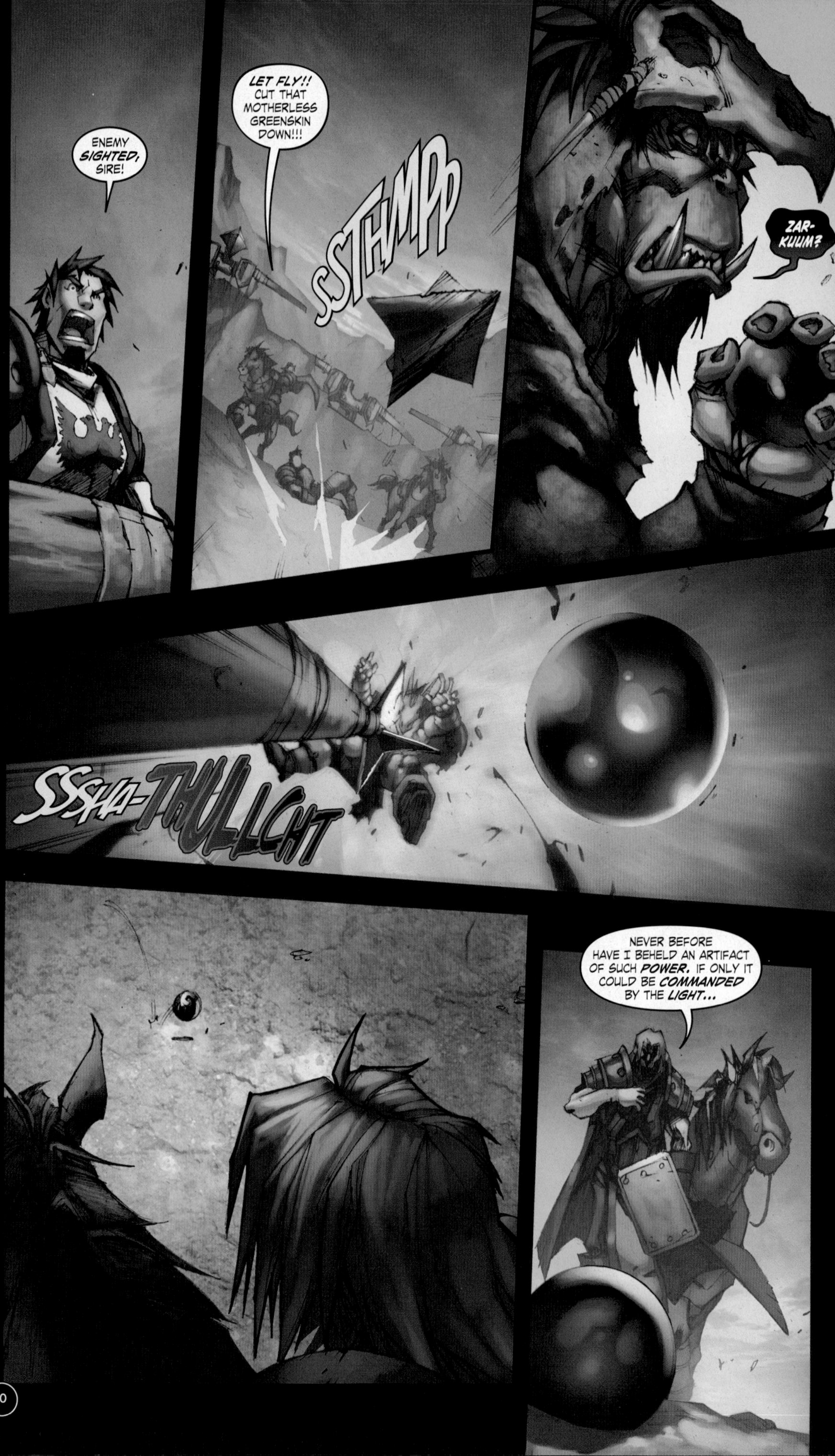
ENEMY SIGHTED, SIRE!
LET FLY!! CUT THAT MOTHERLESS GREENSKIN DOWN!!!
SSTHMPP
ZAR-KUUM?
SSSHA-THULLCHT
NEVER BEFORE HAVE I BEHELD AN ARTIFACT OF SUCH POWER. IF ONLY IT COULD BE COMMANDED BY THE LIGHT...

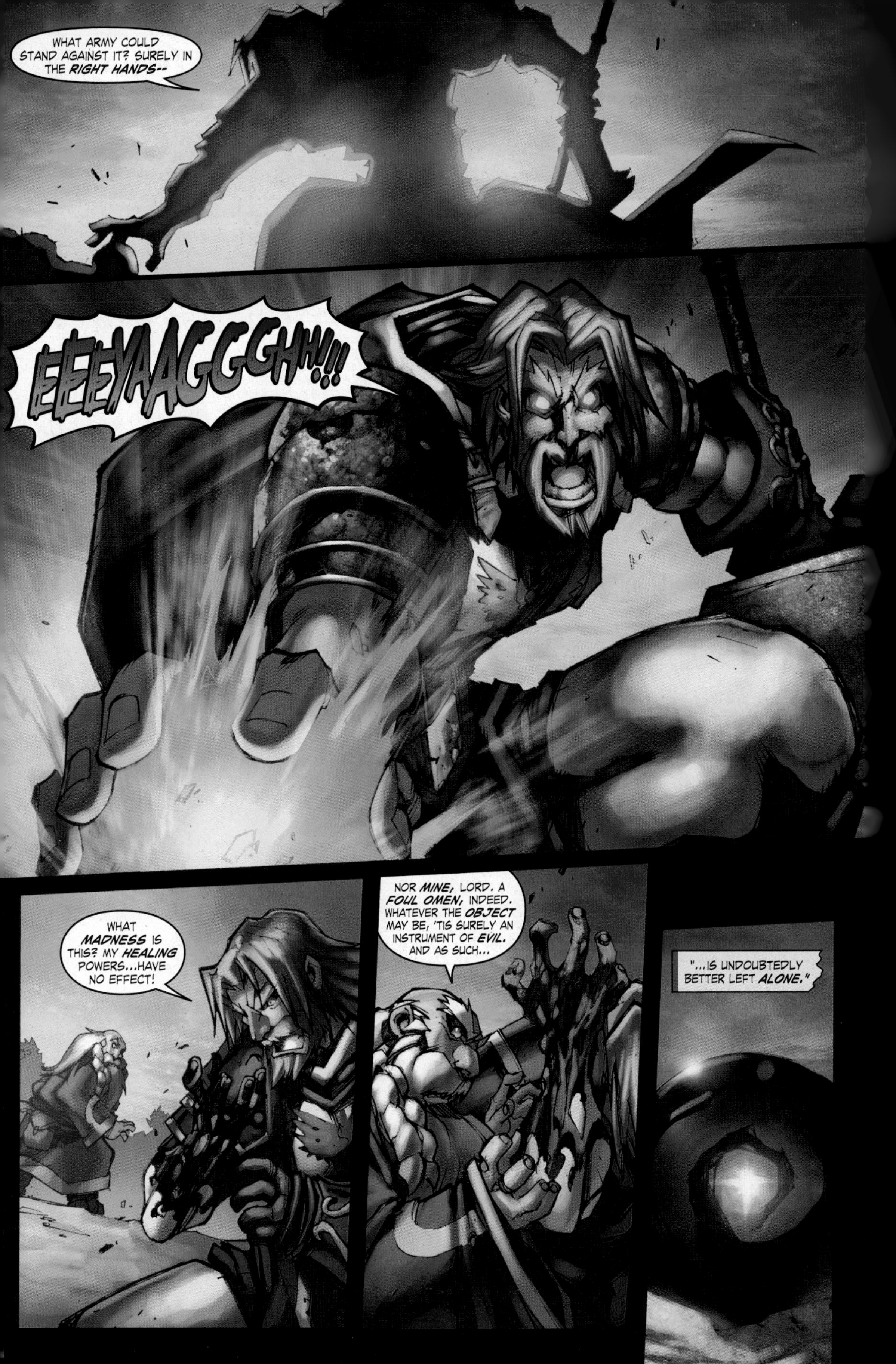
WHAT ARMY COULD STAND AGAINST IT? SURELY IN THE RIGHT HANDS--
EEEYAAGGGHH!!!
WHAT MADNESS IS THIS? MY HEALING POWERS...HAVE NO EFFECT!
NOR MINE, LORD. A FOUL OMEN, INDEED. WHATEVER THE OBJECT MAY BE, 'TIS SURELY AN INSTRUMENT OF EVIL. AND AS SUCH...
"...IS UNDOUBTEDLY BETTER LEFT ALONE."

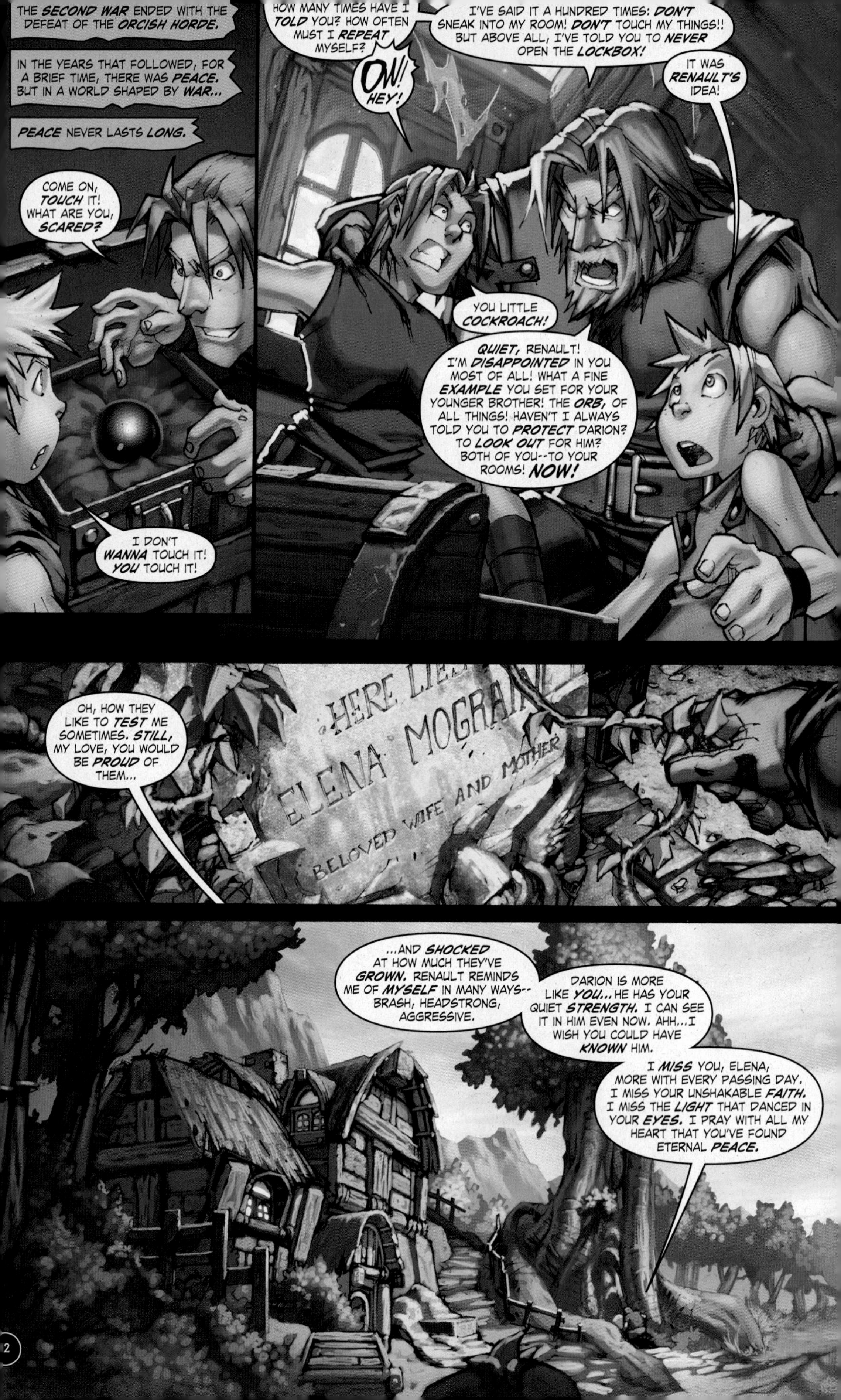
THE SECOND WAR ENDED WITH THE DEFEAT OF THE ORCISH HORDE.
IN THE YEARS THAT FOLLOWED, FOR A BRIEF TIME, THERE WAS PEACE. BUT IN A WORLD SHAPED BY WAR...
PEACE NEVER LASTS LONG.
COME ON, TOUCH IT! WHAT ARE YOU, SCARED?
I DON'T WANNA TOUCH IT! YOU TOUCH IT!
HOW MANY TIMES HAVE I TOLD YOU? HOW OFTEN MUST I REPEAT MYSELF?
OW! HEY!
I'VE SAID IT A HUNDRED TIMES: DON'T SNEAK INTO MY ROOM! DON'T TOUCH MY THINGS!! BUT ABOVE ALL, I'VE TOLD YOU TO NEVER OPEN THE LOCKBOX!
IT WAS RENAULT'S IDEA!
YOU LITTLE COCKROACH!
QUIET, RENAULT! I'M DISAPPOINTED IN YOU MOST OF ALL! WHAT A FINE EXAMPLE YOU SET FOR YOUR YOUNGER BROTHER! THE ORB, OF ALL THINGS! HAVEN'T I ALWAYS TOLD YOU TO PROTECT DARION? TO LOOK OUT FOR HIM? BOTH OF YOU--TO YOUR ROOMS! NOW!
OH, HOW THEY LIKE TO TEST ME SOMETIMES. STILL, MY LOVE, YOU WOULD BE PROUD OF THEM...
HERE LIES
ELENA MOGRAI
BELOVED WIFE AND MOTHER
...AND SHOCKED AT HOW MUCH THEY'VE GROWN. RENAULT REMINDS ME OF MYSELF IN MANY WAYS--BRASH, HEADSTRONG, AGGRESSIVE.
DARION IS MORE LIKE YOU... HE HAS YOUR QUIET STRENGTH. I CAN SEE IT IN HIM EVEN NOW. AHH...I WISH YOU COULD HAVE KNOWN HIM.
I MISS YOU, ELENA, MORE WITH EVERY PASSING DAY. I MISS YOUR UNSHAKABLE FAITH. I MISS THE LIGHT THAT DANCED IN YOUR EYES. I PRAY WITH ALL MY HEART THAT YOU'VE FOUND ETERNAL PEACE.

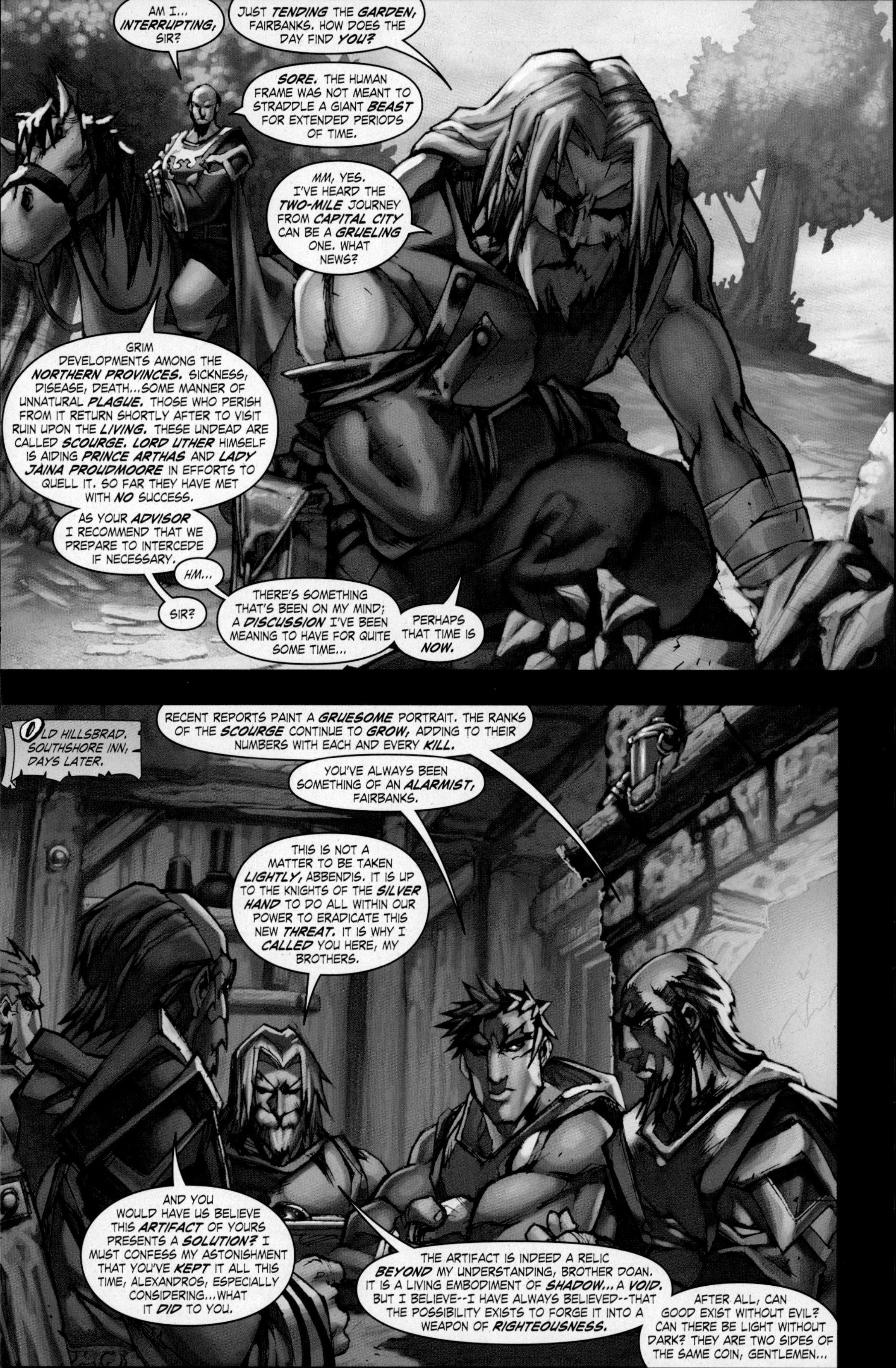
AM I... INTERRUPTING, SIR?
JUST TENDING THE GARDEN, FAIRBANKS. HOW DOES THE DAY FIND YOU?
SORE. THE HUMAN FRAME WAS NOT MEANT TO STRADDLE A GIANT BEAST FOR EXTENDED PERIODS OF TIME.
MM, YES. I'VE HEARD THE TWO-MILE JOURNEY FROM CAPITAL CITY CAN BE A GRUELING ONE. WHAT NEWS?
GRIM DEVELOPMENTS AMONG THE NORTHERN PROVINCES. SICKNESS, DISEASE, DEATH...SOME MANNER OF UNNATURAL PLAGUE. THOSE WHO PERISH FROM IT RETURN SHORTLY AFTER TO VISIT RUIN UPON THE LIVING. THESE UNDEAD ARE CALLED SCOURGE. LORD UTHER HIMSELF IS AIDING PRINCE ARTHAS AND LADY JAINA PROUDMOORE IN EFFORTS TO QUELL IT. SO FAR THEY HAVE MET WITH NO SUCCESS.
AS YOUR ADVISOR I RECOMMEND THAT WE PREPARE TO INTERCEDE IF NECESSARY.
HM...
SIR?
THERE'S SOMETHING THAT'S BEEN ON MY MIND; A DISCUSSION I'VE BEEN MEANING TO HAVE FOR QUITE SOME TIME...
PERHAPS THAT TIME IS NOW.
OLD HILLSBRAD. SOUTHSHORE INN, DAYS LATER.
RECENT REPORTS PAINT A GRUESOME PORTRAIT. THE RANKS OF THE SCOURGE CONTINUE TO GROW, ADDING TO THEIR NUMBERS WITH EACH AND EVERY KILL.
YOU'VE ALWAYS BEEN SOMETHING OF AN ALARMIST, FAIRBANKS.
THIS IS NOT A MATTER TO BE TAKEN LIGHTLY, ABBENDIS. IT IS UP TO THE KNIGHTS OF THE SILVER HAND TO DO ALL WITHIN OUR POWER TO ERADICATE THIS NEW THREAT. IT IS WHY I CALLED YOU HERE, MY BROTHERS.
AND YOU WOULD HAVE US BELIEVE THIS ARTIFACT OF YOURS PRESENTS A SOLUTION? I MUST CONFESS MY ASTONISHMENT THAT YOU'VE KEPT IT ALL THIS TIME, ALEXANDROS, ESPECIALLY CONSIDERING...WHAT IT DID TO YOU.
THE ARTIFACT IS INDEED A RELIC BEYOND MY UNDERSTANDING, BROTHER DOAN. IT IS A LIVING EMBODIMENT OF SHADOW...A VOID. BUT I BELIEVE--I HAVE ALWAYS BELIEVED--THAT THE POSSIBILITY EXISTS TO FORGE IT INTO A WEAPON OF RIGHTEOUSNESS.
AFTER ALL, CAN GOOD EXIST WITHOUT EVIL? CAN THERE BE LIGHT WITHOUT DARK? THEY ARE TWO SIDES OF THE SAME COIN, GENTLEMEN...

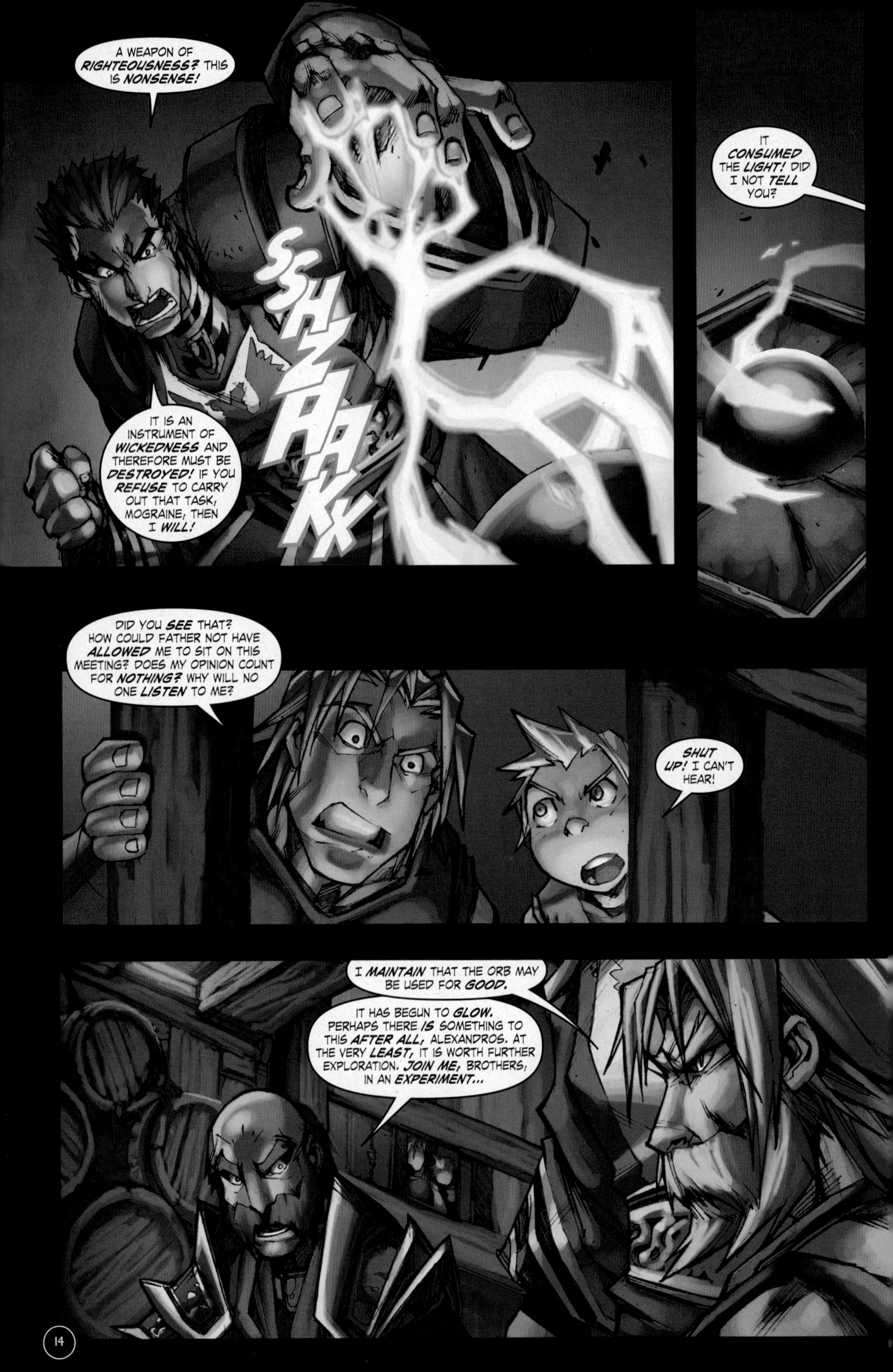

A WEAPON OF RIGHTEOUSNESS? THIS IS NONSENSE!
IT CONSUMED THE LIGHT! DID I NOT TELL YOU?
SSHZAAKX
IT IS AN INSTRUMENT OF WICKEDNESS AND THEREFORE MUST BE DESTROYED! IF YOU REFUSE TO CARRY OUT THAT TASK, MOGRAINE, THEN I WILL!
DID YOU SEE THAT? HOW COULD FATHER NOT HAVE ALLOWED ME TO SIT ON THIS MEETING? DOES MY OPINION COUNT FOR NOTHING? WHY WILL NO ONE LISTEN TO ME?
SHUT UP! I CAN'T HEAR!
I MAINTAIN THAT THE ORB MAY BE USED FOR GOOD.
IT HAS BEGUN TO GLOW. PERHAPS THERE IS SOMETHING TO THIS AFTER ALL, ALEXANDROS. AT THE VERY LEAST, IT IS WORTH FURTHER EXPLORATION. JOIN ME, BROTHERS, IN AN EXPERIMENT...

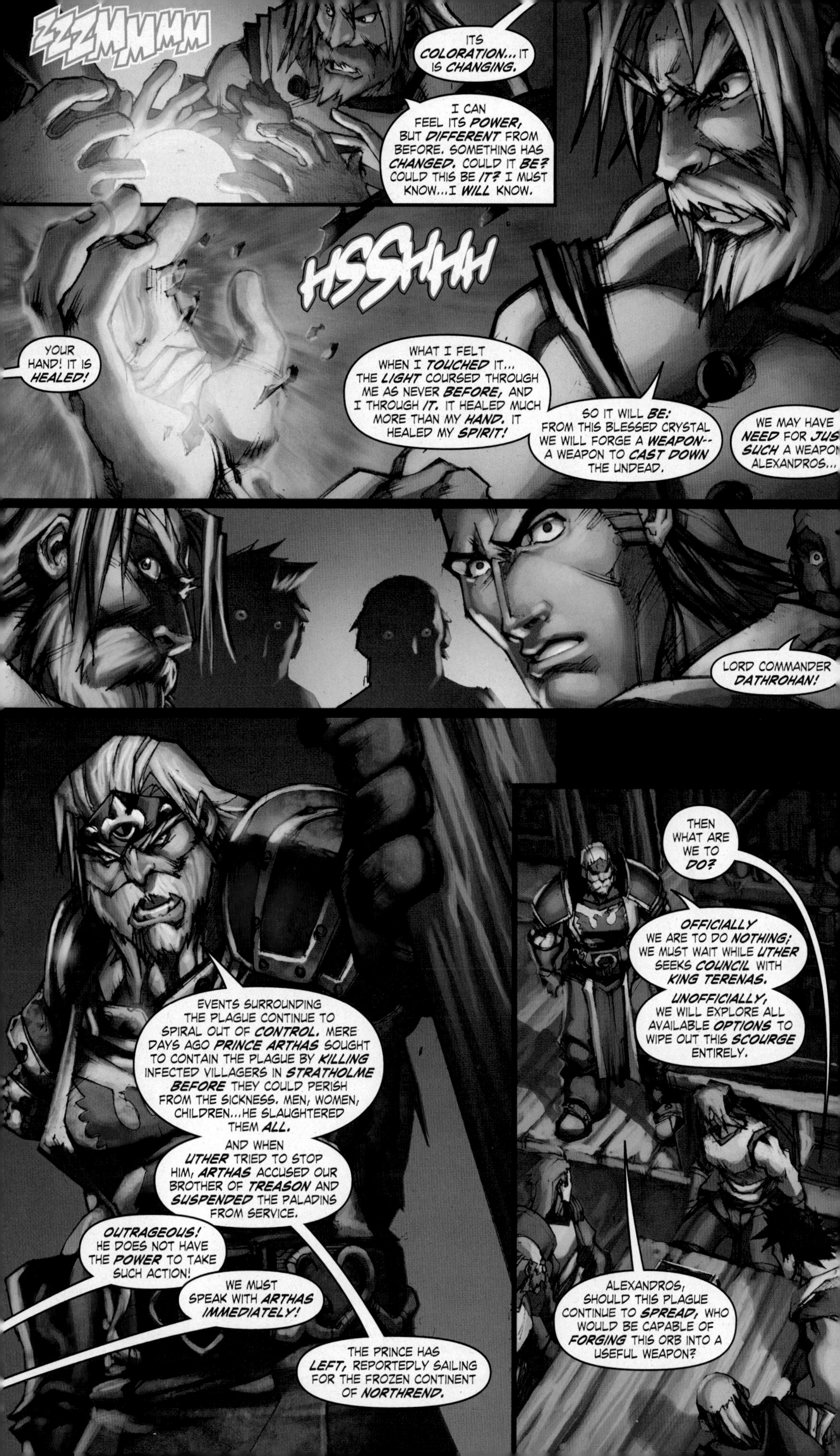
ZZZMMMM
ITS COLORATION... IT IS CHANGING.
I CAN FEEL ITS POWER, BUT DIFFERENT FROM BEFORE. SOMETHING HAS CHANGED. COULD IT BE? COULD THIS BE IT? I MUST KNOW...I WILL KNOW.
HSSHHH
YOUR HAND! IT IS HEALED!
WHAT I FELT WHEN I TOUCHED IT... THE LIGHT COURSED THROUGH ME AS NEVER BEFORE, AND I THROUGH IT. IT HEALED MUCH MORE THAN MY HAND. IT HEALED MY SPIRIT!
SO IT WILL BE: FROM THIS BLESSED CRYSTAL WE WILL FORGE A WEAPON-- A WEAPON TO CAST DOWN THE UNDEAD.
WE MAY HAVE NEED FOR JUS SUCH A WEAPO ALEXANDROS...
LORD COMMANDER DATHROHAN!
EVENTS SURROUNDING THE PLAGUE CONTINUE TO SPIRAL OUT OF CONTROL. MERE DAYS AGO PRINCE ARTHAS SOUGHT TO CONTAIN THE PLAGUE BY KILLING INFECTED VILLAGERS IN STRATHOLME BEFORE THEY COULD PERISH FROM THE SICKNESS. MEN, WOMEN, CHILDREN...HE SLAUGHTERED THEM ALL.
AND WHEN UTHER TRIED TO STOP HIM, ARTHAS ACCUSED OUR BROTHER OF TREASON AND SUSPENDED THE PALADINS FROM SERVICE.
OUTRAGEOUS! HE DOES NOT HAVE THE POWER TO TAKE SUCH ACTION!
WE MUST SPEAK WITH ARTHAS IMMEDIATELY!
THE PRINCE HAS LEFT, REPORTEDLY SAILING FOR THE FROZEN CONTINENT OF NORTHREND.
THEN WHAT ARE WE TO DO?
OFFICIALLY WE ARE TO DO NOTHING; WE MUST WAIT WHILE UTHER SEEKS COUNCIL WITH KING TERENAS.
UNOFFICIALLY, WE WILL EXPLORE ALL AVAILABLE OPTIONS TO WIPE OUT THIS SCOURGE ENTIRELY.
ALEXANDROS, SHOULD THIS PLAGUE CONTINUE TO SPREAD, WHO WOULD BE CAPABLE OF FORGING THIS ORB INTO A USEFUL WEAPON?

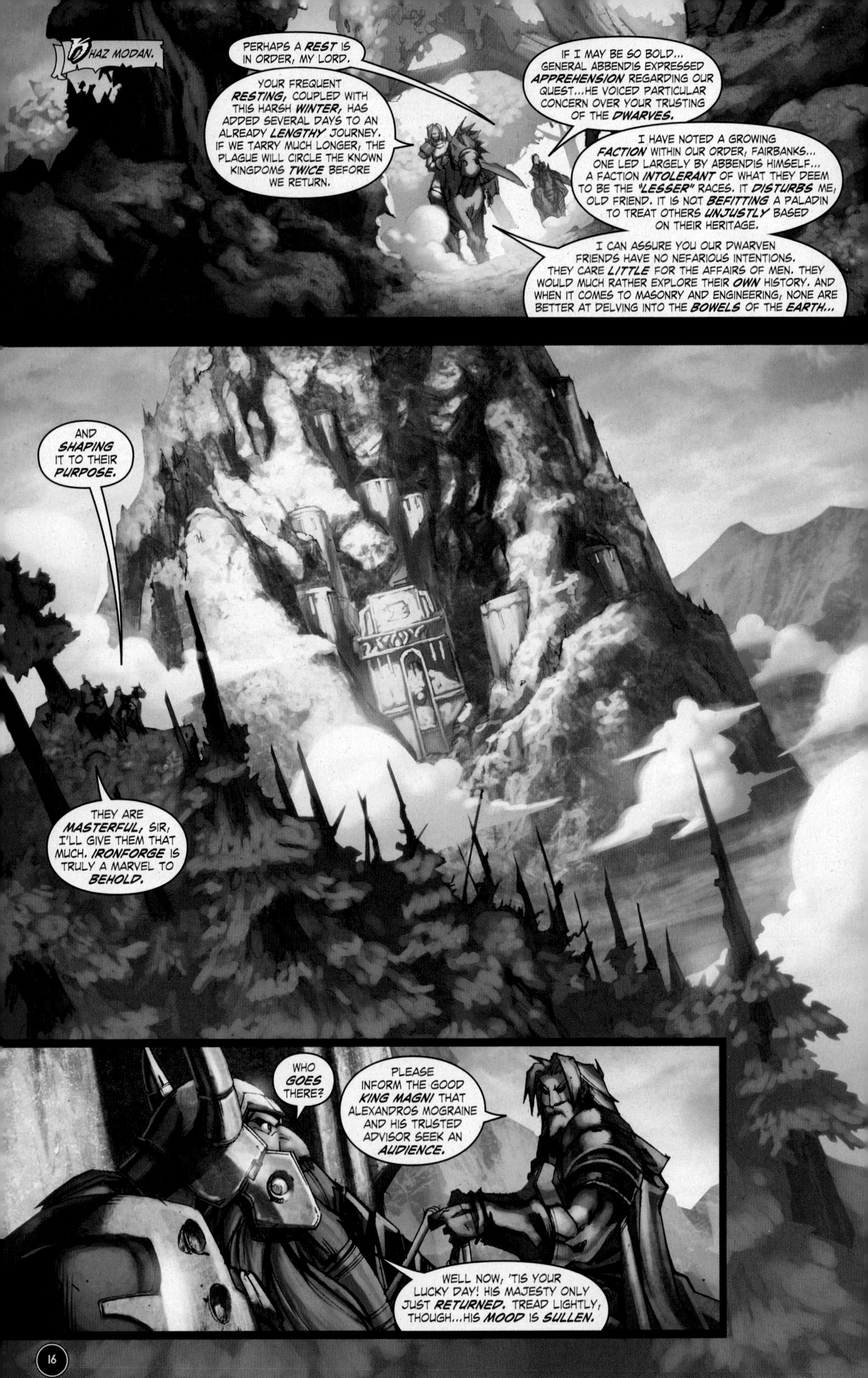
KHAZ MODAN.
PERHAPS A REST IS IN ORDER, MY LORD.
YOUR FREQUENT RESTING, COUPLED WITH THIS HARSH WINTER, HAS ADDED SEVERAL DAYS TO AN ALREADY LENGTHY JOURNEY. IF WE TARRY MUCH LONGER, THE PLAGUE WILL CIRCLE THE KNOWN KINGDOMS TWICE BEFORE WE RETURN.
IF I MAY BE SO BOLD... GENERAL ABBENDIS EXPRESSED APPREHENSION REGARDING OUR QUEST...HE VOICED PARTICULAR CONCERN OVER YOUR TRUSTING OF THE DWARVES.
I HAVE NOTED A GROWING FACTION WITHIN OUR ORDER, FAIRBANKS... ONE LED LARGELY BY ABBENDIS HIMSELF... A FACTION INTOLERANT OF WHAT THEY DEEM TO BE THE "LESSER" RACES. IT DISTURBS ME, OLD FRIEND. IT IS NOT BEFITTING A PALADIN TO TREAT OTHERS UNJUSTLY BASED ON THEIR HERITAGE.
I CAN ASSURE YOU OUR DWARVEN FRIENDS HAVE NO NEFARIOUS INTENTIONS. THEY CARE LITTLE FOR THE AFFAIRS OF MEN. THEY WOULD MUCH RATHER EXPLORE THEIR OWN HISTORY. AND WHEN IT COMES TO MASONRY AND ENGINEERING, NONE ARE BETTER AT DELVING INTO THE BOWELS OF THE EARTH...
AND SHAPING IT TO THEIR PURPOSE.
THEY ARE MASTERFUL, SIR, I'LL GIVE THEM THAT MUCH. IRONFORGE IS TRULY A MARVEL TO BEHOLD.
WHO GOES THERE?
PLEASE INFORM THE GOOD KING MAGNI THAT ALEXANDROS MOGRAINE AND HIS TRUSTED ADVISOR SEEK AN AUDIENCE.
WELL NOW, 'TIS YOUR LUCKY DAY! HIS MAJESTY ONLY JUST RETURNED. TREAD LIGHTLY, THOUGH...HIS MOOD IS SULLEN.

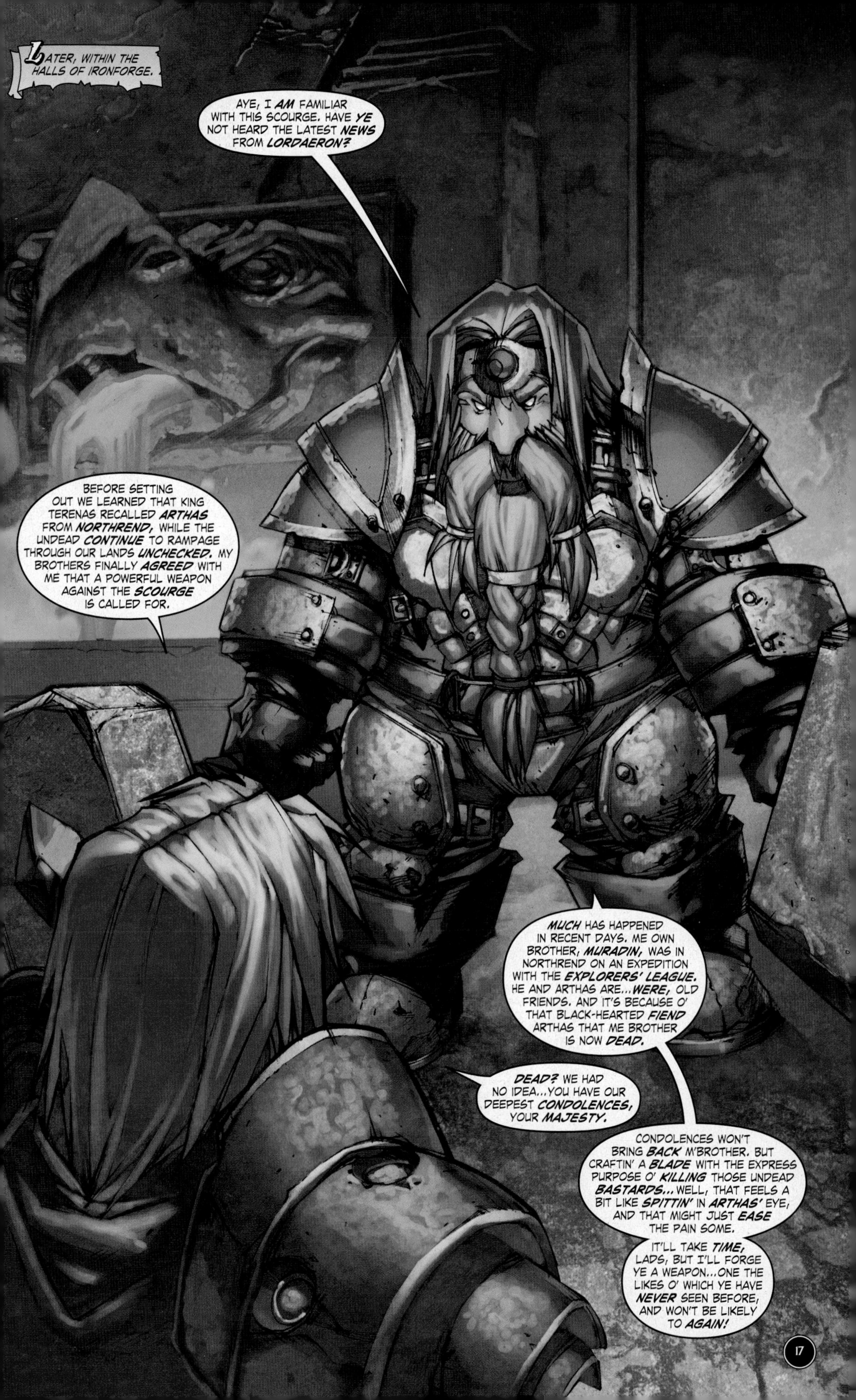
LATER, WITHIN THE HALLS OF IRONFORGE.
AYE, I AM FAMILIAR WITH THIS SCOURGE. HAVE YE NOT HEARD THE LATEST NEWS FROM LORDAERON?
BEFORE SETTING OUT WE LEARNED THAT KING TERENAS RECALLED ARTHAS FROM NORTHREND, WHILE THE UNDEAD CONTINUE TO RAMPAGE THROUGH OUR LANDS UNCHECKED. MY BROTHERS FINALLY AGREED WITH ME THAT A POWERFUL WEAPON AGAINST THE SCOURGE IS CALLED FOR.
MUCH HAS HAPPENED IN RECENT DAYS. ME OWN BROTHER, MURADIN, WAS IN NORTHREND ON AN EXPEDITION WITH THE EXPLORERS' LEAGUE. HE AND ARTHAS ARE...WERE, OLD FRIENDS. AND IT'S BECAUSE O' THAT BLACK-HEARTED FIEND ARTHAS THAT ME BROTHER IS NOW DEAD.
DEAD? WE HAD NO IDEA...YOU HAVE OUR DEEPEST CONDOLENCES, YOUR MAJESTY.
CONDOLENCES WON'T BRING BACK M'BROTHER. BUT CRAFTIN' A BLADE WITH THE EXPRESS PURPOSE O' KILLING THOSE UNDEAD BASTARDS... WELL, THAT FEELS A BIT LIKE SPITTIN' IN ARTHAS' EYE, AND THAT MIGHT JUST EASE THE PAIN SOME.
IT'LL TAKE TIME, LADS, BUT I'LL FORGE YE A WEAPON...ONE THE LIKES O' WHICH YE HAVE NEVER SEEN BEFORE, AND WON'T BE LIKELY TO AGAIN!

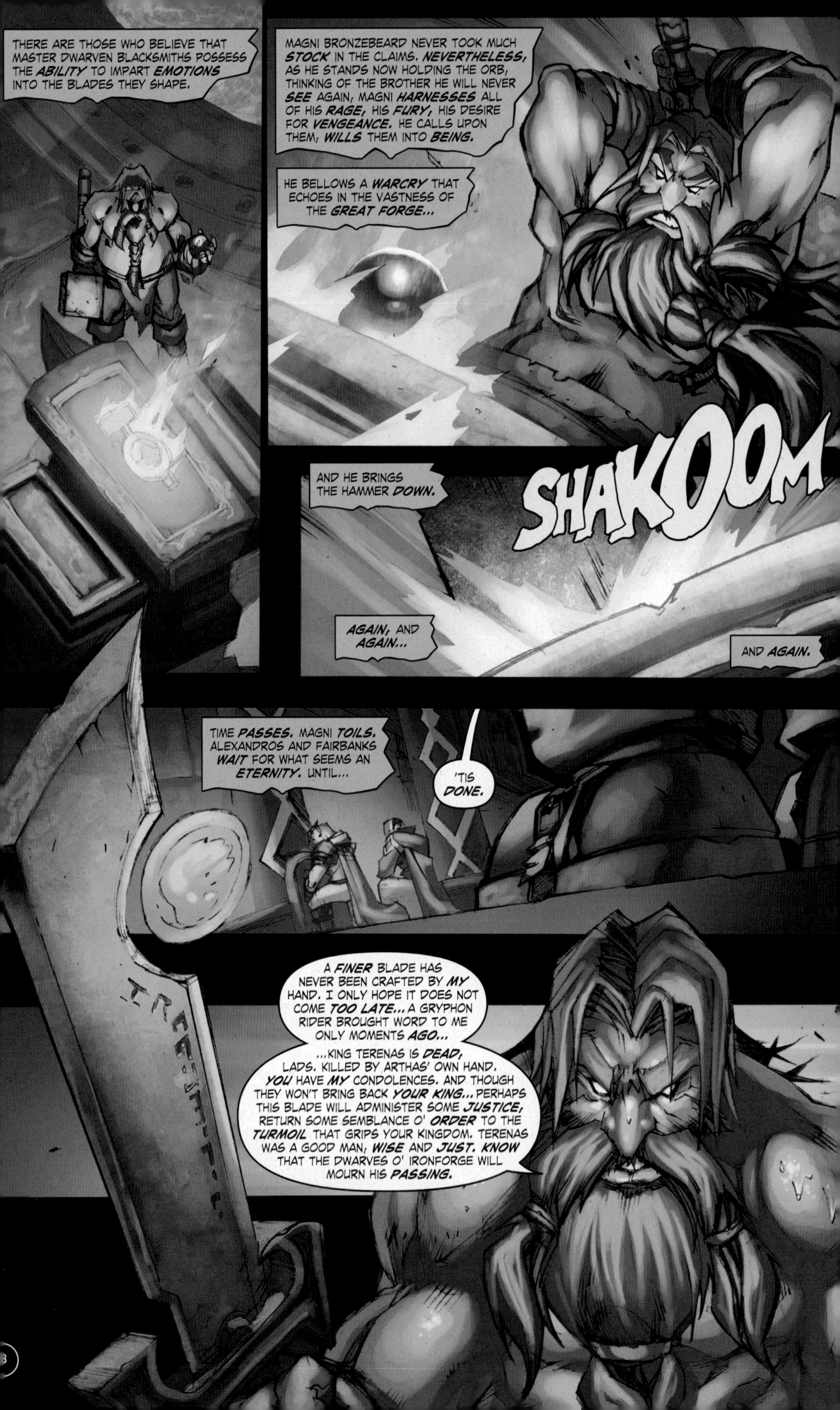
THERE ARE THOSE WHO BELIEVE THAT MASTER DWARVEN BLACKSMITHS POSSESS THE ABILITY TO IMPART EMOTIONS INTO THE BLADES THEY SHAPE.
MAGNI BRONZEBEARD NEVER TOOK MUCH STOCK IN THE CLAIMS. NEVERTHELESS, AS HE STANDS NOW HOLDING THE ORB, THINKING OF THE BROTHER HE WILL NEVER SEE AGAIN, MAGNI HARNESSES ALL OF HIS RAGE, HIS FURY, HIS DESIRE FOR VENGEANCE. HE CALLS UPON THEM, WILLS THEM INTO BEING.
HE BELLOWS A WARCRY THAT ECHOES IN THE VASTNESS OF THE GREAT FORGE...
AND HE BRINGS THE HAMMER DOWN.
SHAKOOM
AGAIN, AND AGAIN...
AND AGAIN.
TIME PASSES. MAGNI TOILS. ALEXANDROS AND FAIRBANKS WAIT FOR WHAT SEEMS AN ETERNITY. UNTIL...
'TIS DONE.
A FINER BLADE HAS NEVER BEEN CRAFTED BY MY HAND. I ONLY HOPE IT DOES NOT COME TOO LATE... A GRYPHON RIDER BROUGHT WORD TO ME ONLY MOMENTS AGO...
...KING TERENAS IS DEAD, LADS. KILLED BY ARTHAS' OWN HAND. YOU HAVE MY CONDOLENCES. AND THOUGH THEY WON'T BRING BACK YOUR KING... PERHAPS THIS BLADE WILL ADMINISTER SOME JUSTICE, RETURN SOME SEMBLANCE O' ORDER TO THE TURMOIL THAT GRIPS YOUR KINGDOM. TERENAS WAS A GOOD MAN, WISE AND JUST. KNOW THAT THE DWARVES O' IRONFORGE WILL MOURN HIS PASSING.

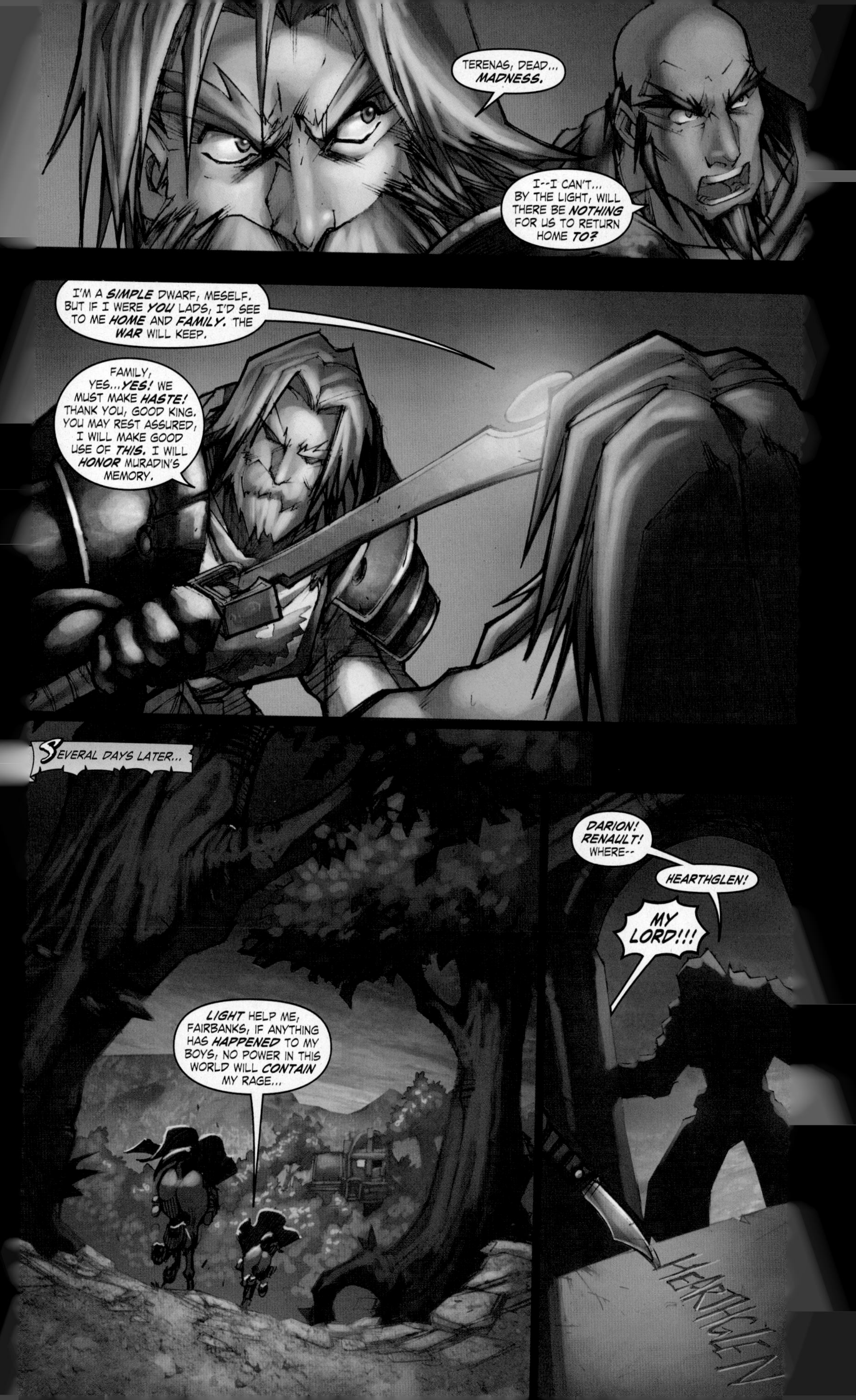

TERENAS, DEAD... MADNESS.
I--I CAN'T... BY THE LIGHT, WILL THERE BE NOTHING FOR US TO RETURN HOME TO?
I'M A SIMPLE DWARF, MESELF. BUT IF I WERE YOU LADS, I'D SEE TO ME HOME AND FAMILY. THE WAR WILL KEEP.
FAMILY, YES...YES! WE MUST MAKE HASTE! THANK YOU, GOOD KING. YOU MAY REST ASSURED, I WILL MAKE GOOD USE OF THIS. I WILL HONOR MURADIN'S MEMORY.
SEVERAL DAYS LATER...
LIGHT HELP ME, FAIRBANKS, IF ANYTHING HAS HAPPENED TO MY BOYS, NO POWER IN THIS WORLD WILL CONTAIN MY RAGE...
DARION! RENAULT! WHERE--
HEARTHGLEN!
MY LORD!!!
HEARTHGLEN

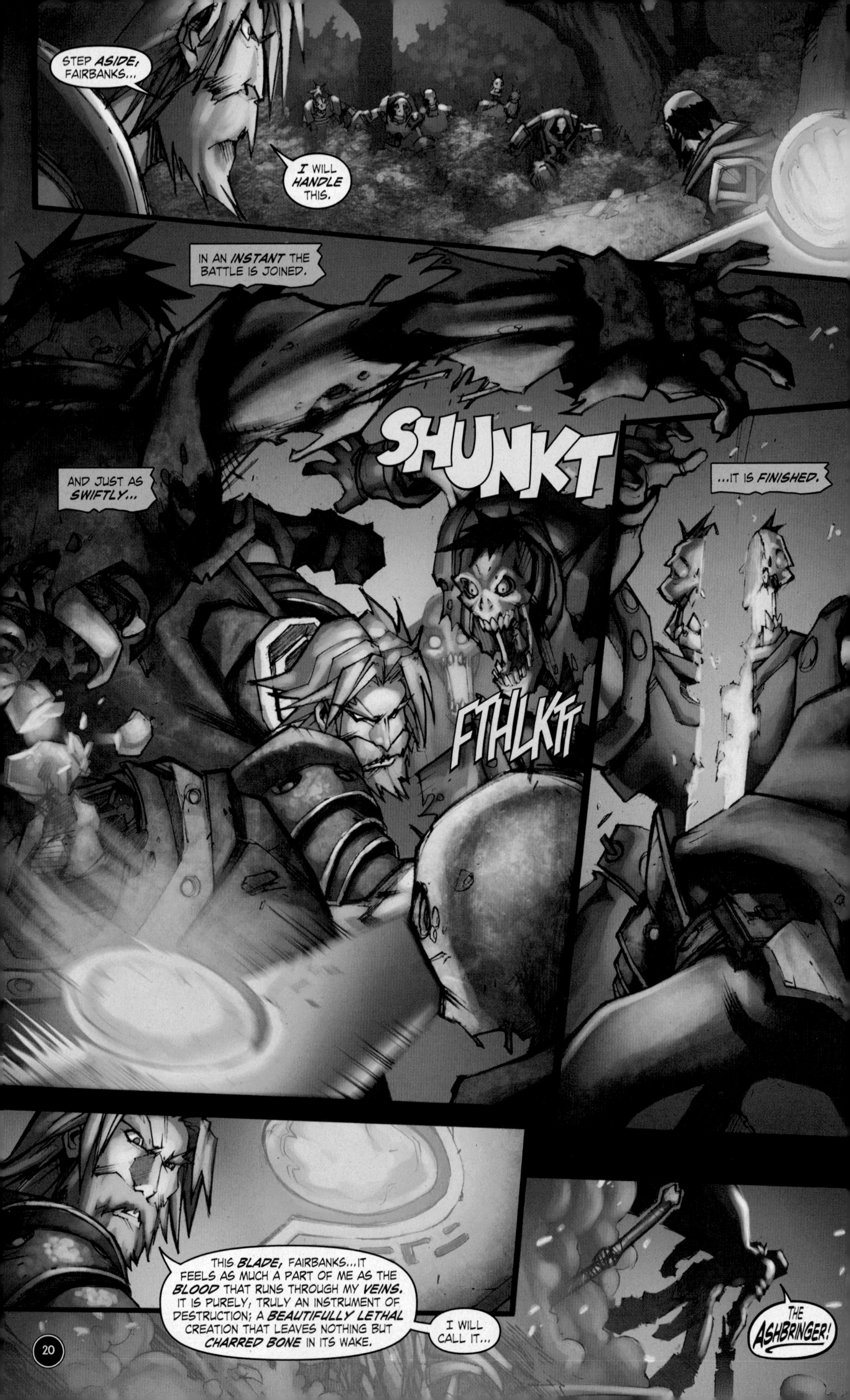
STEP ASIDE, FAIRBANKS...
I WILL HANDLE THIS.
IN AN INSTANT THE BATTLE IS JOINED.
SHUNKT
AND JUST AS SWIFTLY...
FTHLKTT
...IT IS FINISHED.
THIS BLADE, FAIRBANKS...IT FEELS AS MUCH A PART OF ME AS THE BLOOD THAT RUNS THROUGH MY VEINS. IT IS PURELY, TRULY AN INSTRUMENT OF DESTRUCTION; A BEAUTIFULLY LETHAL CREATION THAT LEAVES NOTHING BUT CHARRED BONE IN ITS WAKE.
I WILL CALL IT...
THE ASHBRINGER!

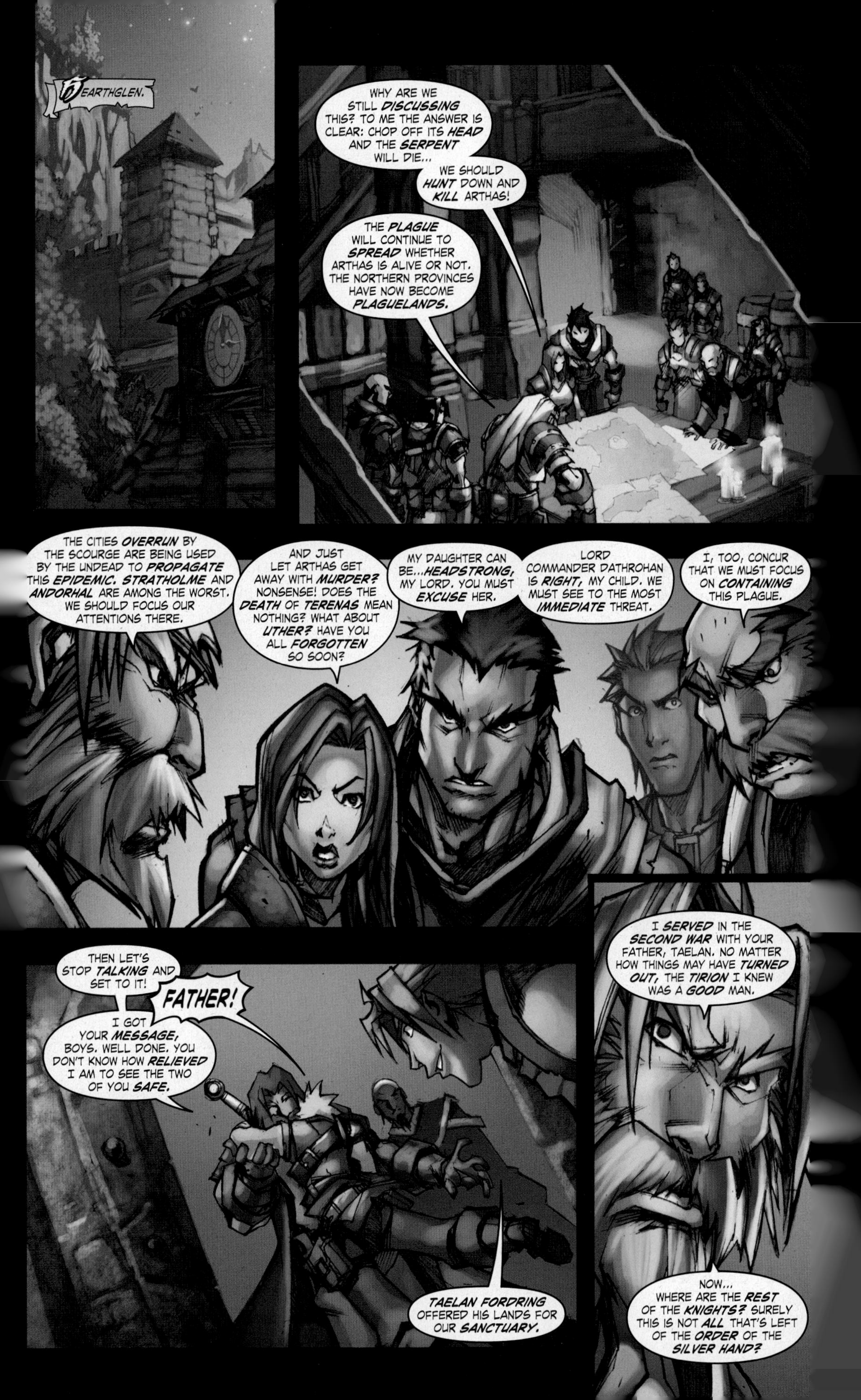
HEARTHGLEN.
WHY ARE WE STILL DISCUSSING THIS? TO ME THE ANSWER IS CLEAR: CHOP OFF ITS HEAD AND THE SERPENT WILL DIE...
WE SHOULD HUNT DOWN AND KILL ARTHAS!
THE PLAGUE WILL CONTINUE TO SPREAD WHETHER ARTHAS IS ALIVE OR NOT. THE NORTHERN PROVINCES HAVE NOW BECOME PLAGUELANDS.
THE CITIES OVERRUN BY THE SCOURGE ARE BEING USED BY THE UNDEAD TO PROPAGATE THIS EPIDEMIC. STRATHOLME AND ANDORHAL ARE AMONG THE WORST. WE SHOULD FOCUS OUR ATTENTIONS THERE.
AND JUST LET ARTHAS GET AWAY WITH MURDER? NONSENSE! DOES THE DEATH OF TERENAS MEAN NOTHING? WHAT ABOUT UTHER? HAVE YOU ALL FORGOTTEN SO SOON?
MY DAUGHTER CAN BE...HEADSTRONG, MY LORD. YOU MUST EXCUSE HER.
LORD COMMANDER DATHROHAN IS RIGHT, MY CHILD. WE MUST SEE TO THE MOST IMMEDIATE THREAT.
I, TOO, CONCUR THAT WE MUST FOCUS ON CONTAINING THIS PLAGUE.
THEN LET'S STOP TALKING AND SET TO IT!
FATHER!
I GOT YOUR MESSAGE, BOYS. WELL DONE. YOU DON'T KNOW HOW RELIEVED I AM TO SEE THE TWO OF YOU SAFE.
TAELAN FORDRING OFFERED HIS LANDS FOR OUR SANCTUARY.
I SERVED IN THE SECOND WAR WITH YOUR FATHER, TAELAN. NO MATTER HOW THINGS MAY HAVE TURNED OUT, THE TIRION I KNEW WAS A GOOD MAN.
NOW... WHERE ARE THE REST OF THE KNIGHTS? SURELY THIS IS NOT ALL THAT'S LEFT OF THE ORDER OF THE SILVER HAND?

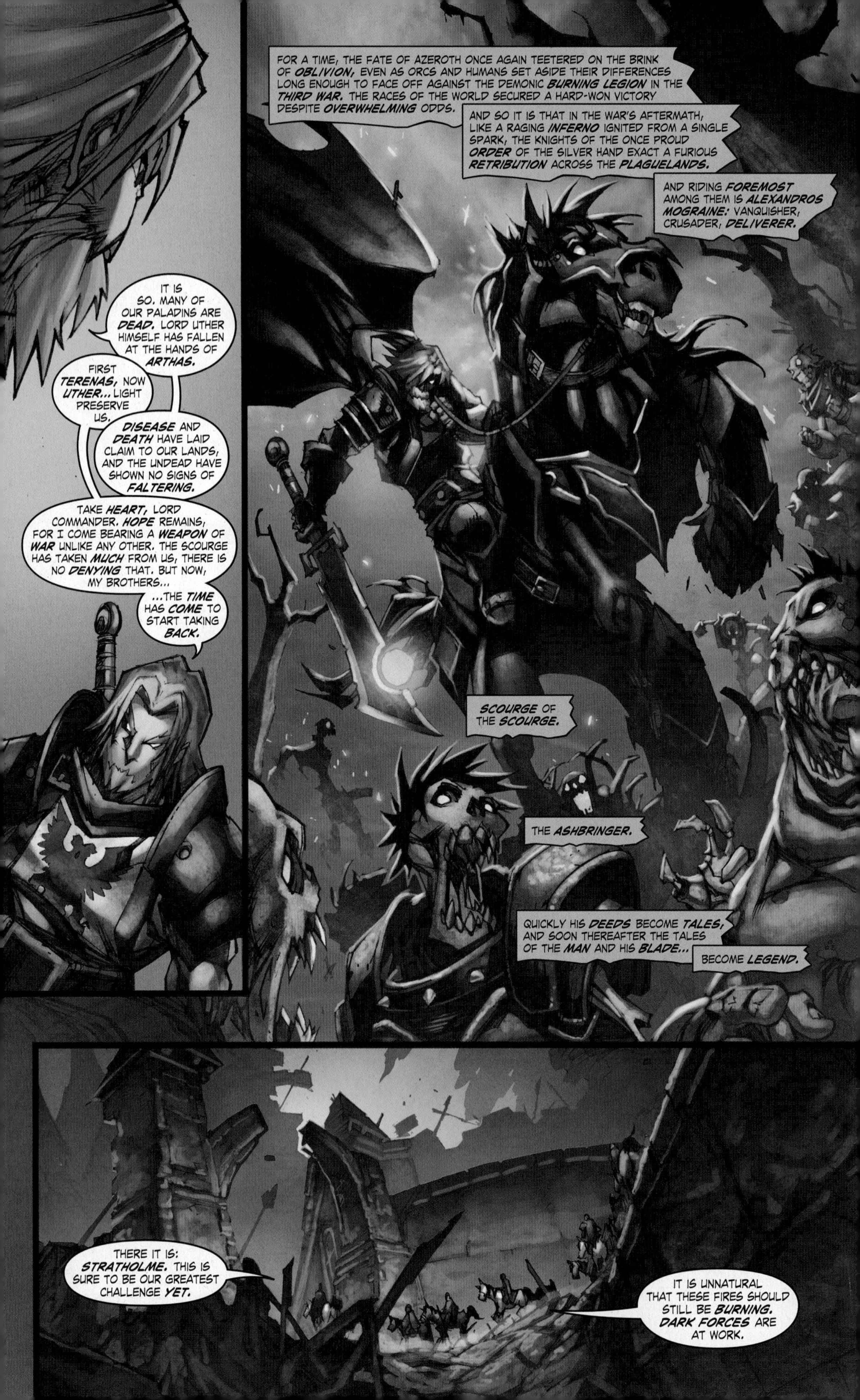

FOR A TIME, THE FATE OF AZEROTH ONCE AGAIN TEETERED ON THE BRINK OF OBLIVION, EVEN AS ORCS AND HUMANS SET ASIDE THEIR DIFFERENCES LONG ENOUGH TO FACE OFF AGAINST THE DEMONIC BURNING LEGION IN THE THIRD WAR. THE RACES OF THE WORLD SECURED A HARD-WON VICTORY DESPITE OVERWHELMING ODDS.
AND SO IT IS THAT IN THE WAR'S AFTERMATH, LIKE A RAGING INFERNO IGNITED FROM A SINGLE SPARK, THE KNIGHTS OF THE ONCE PROUD ORDER OF THE SILVER HAND EXACT A FURIOUS RETRIBUTION ACROSS THE PLAGUELANDS.
AND RIDING FOREMOST AMONG THEM IS ALEXANDROS MOGRAINE: VANQUISHER, CRUSADER, DELIVERER.
SCOURGE OF THE SCOURGE.
THE ASHBRINGER.
QUICKLY HIS DEEDS BECOME TALES, AND SOON THEREAFTER THE TALES OF THE MAN AND HIS BLADE...
BECOME LEGEND.
IT IS SO. MANY OF OUR PALADINS ARE DEAD. LORD UTHER HIMSELF HAS FALLEN AT THE HANDS OF ARTHAS.
FIRST TERENAS, NOW UTHER... LIGHT PRESERVE US.
DISEASE AND DEATH HAVE LAID CLAIM TO OUR LANDS, AND THE UNDEAD HAVE SHOWN NO SIGNS OF FALTERING.
TAKE HEART, LORD COMMANDER. HOPE REMAINS, FOR I COME BEARING A WEAPON OF WAR UNLIKE ANY OTHER. THE SCOURGE HAS TAKEN MUCH FROM US, THERE IS NO DENYING THAT. BUT NOW, MY BROTHERS...
...THE TIME HAS COME TO START TAKING BACK.
THERE IT IS: STRATHOLME. THIS IS SURE TO BE OUR GREATEST CHALLENGE YET.
IT IS UNNATURAL THAT THESE FIRES SHOULD STILL BE BURNING. DARK FORCES ARE AT WORK.

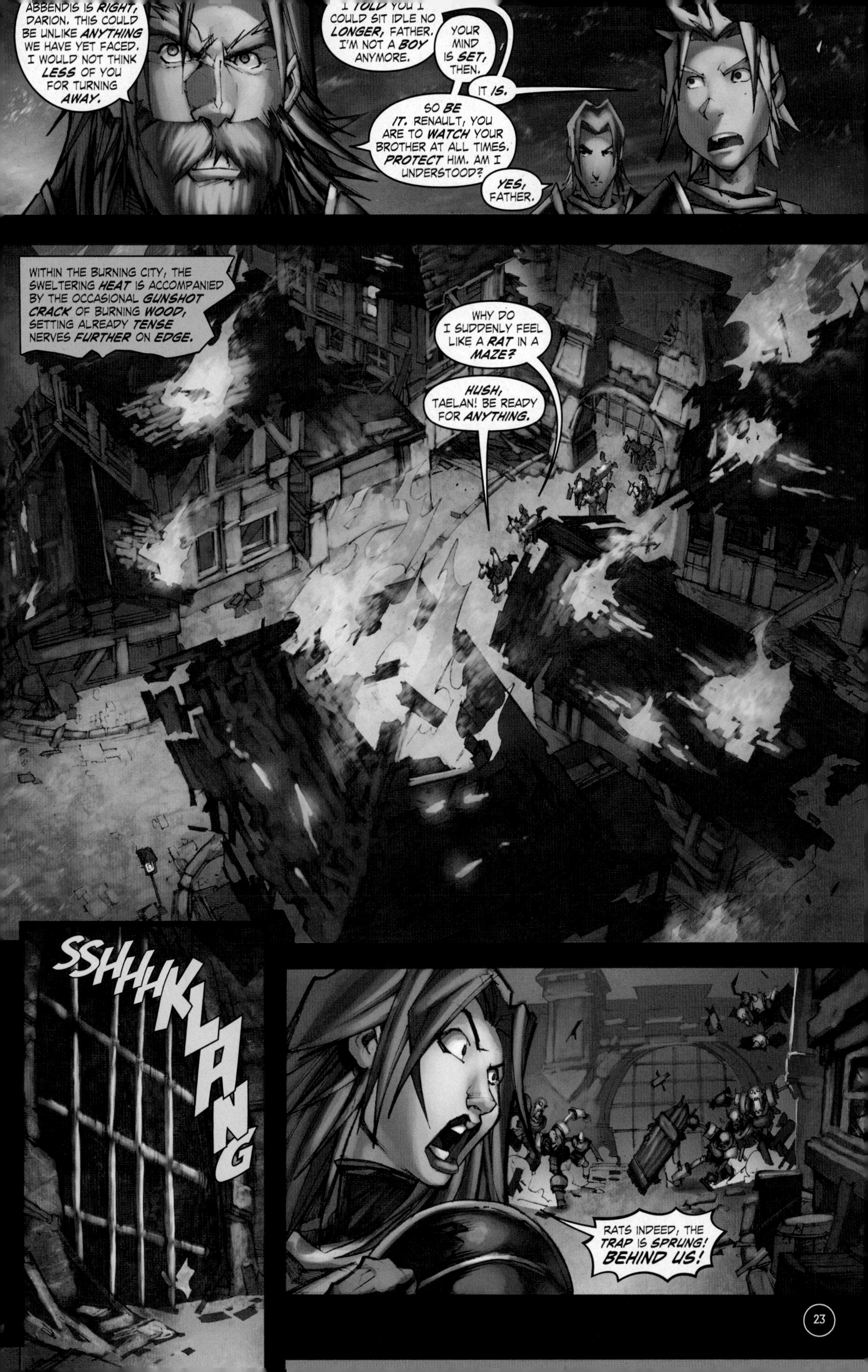
ABBENDIS IS RIGHT, DARION. THIS COULD BE UNLIKE ANYTHING WE HAVE YET FACED. I WOULD NOT THINK LESS OF YOU FOR TURNING AWAY.
I TOLD YOU I COULD SIT IDLE NO LONGER, FATHER. I'M NOT A BOY ANYMORE.
YOUR MIND IS SET, THEN.
IT IS.
SO BE IT. RENAULT, YOU ARE TO WATCH YOUR BROTHER AT ALL TIMES. PROTECT HIM. AM I UNDERSTOOD?
YES, FATHER.
WITHIN THE BURNING CITY, THE SWELTERING HEAT IS ACCOMPANIED BY THE OCCASIONAL GUNSHOT CRACK OF BURNING WOOD, SETTING ALREADY TENSE NERVES FURTHER ON EDGE.
WHY DO I SUDDENLY FEEL LIKE A RAT IN A MAZE?
HUSH, TAELAN! BE READY FOR ANYTHING.
SSHHHKLANG
RATS INDEED, THE TRAP IS SPRUNG! BEHIND US!

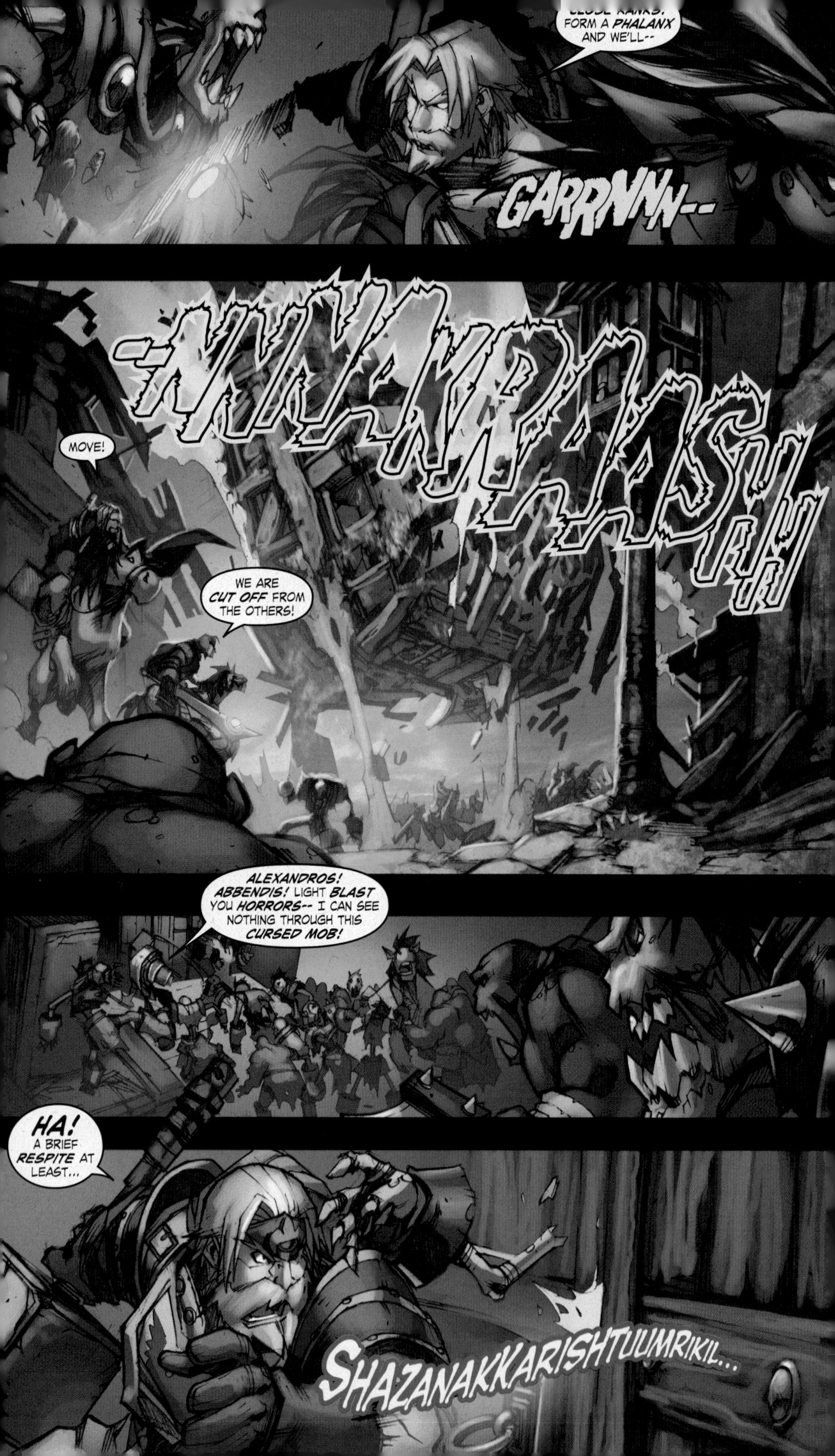
FORM A PHALANX AND WE'LL--
GARRNNN--
MOVE!
WE ARE CUT OFF FROM THE OTHERS!
ALEXANDROS! ABBENDIS! LIGHT BLAST YOU HORRORS-- I CAN SEE NOTHING THROUGH THIS CURSED MOB!
HA! A BRIEF RESPITE AT LEAST...
SHAZANAKKARISHTUUMRIKIL...

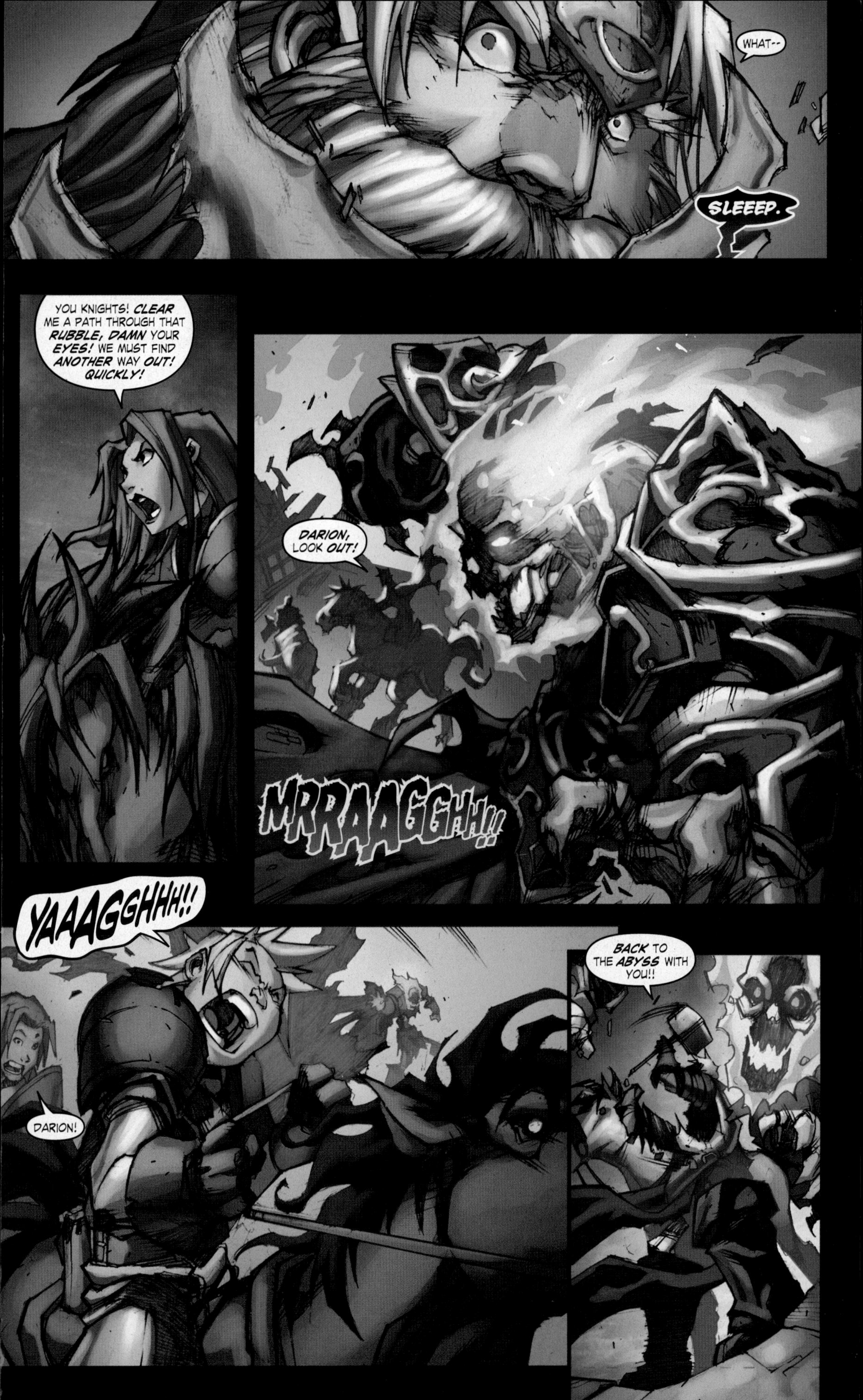
WHAT--
SLEEEP.
YOU KNIGHTS! CLEAR ME A PATH THROUGH THAT RUBBLE, DAMN YOUR EYES! WE MUST FIND ANOTHER WAY OUT! QUICKLY!
DARION, LOOK OUT!
MRRAAGGHH!!
YAAAGGHHH!!
DARION!
BACK TO THE ABYSS WITH YOU!!

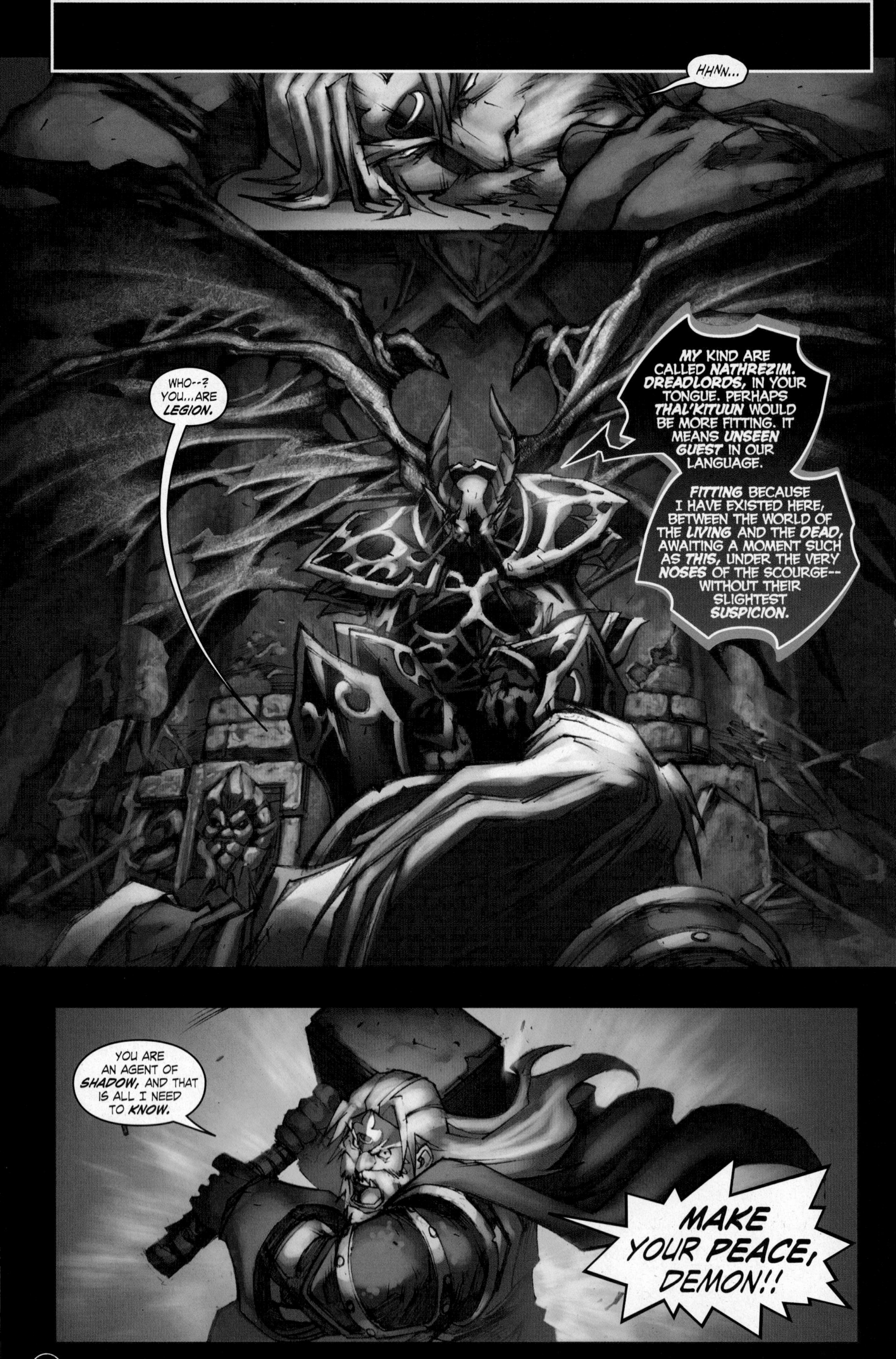

HHNN...
WHO--? YOU...ARE LEGION.
MY KIND ARE CALLED NATHREZIM. DREADLORDS, IN YOUR TONGUE. PERHAPS THAL'KITUUN WOULD BE MORE FITTING. IT MEANS UNSEEN GUEST IN OUR LANGUAGE.
FITTING BECAUSE I HAVE EXISTED HERE, BETWEEN THE WORLD OF THE LIVING AND THE DEAD, AWAITING A MOMENT SUCH AS THIS, UNDER THE VERY NOSES OF THE SCOURGE--WITHOUT THEIR SLIGHTEST SUSPICION.
YOU ARE AN AGENT OF SHADOW, AND THAT IS ALL I NEED TO KNOW.
MAKE YOUR PEACE, DEMON!!

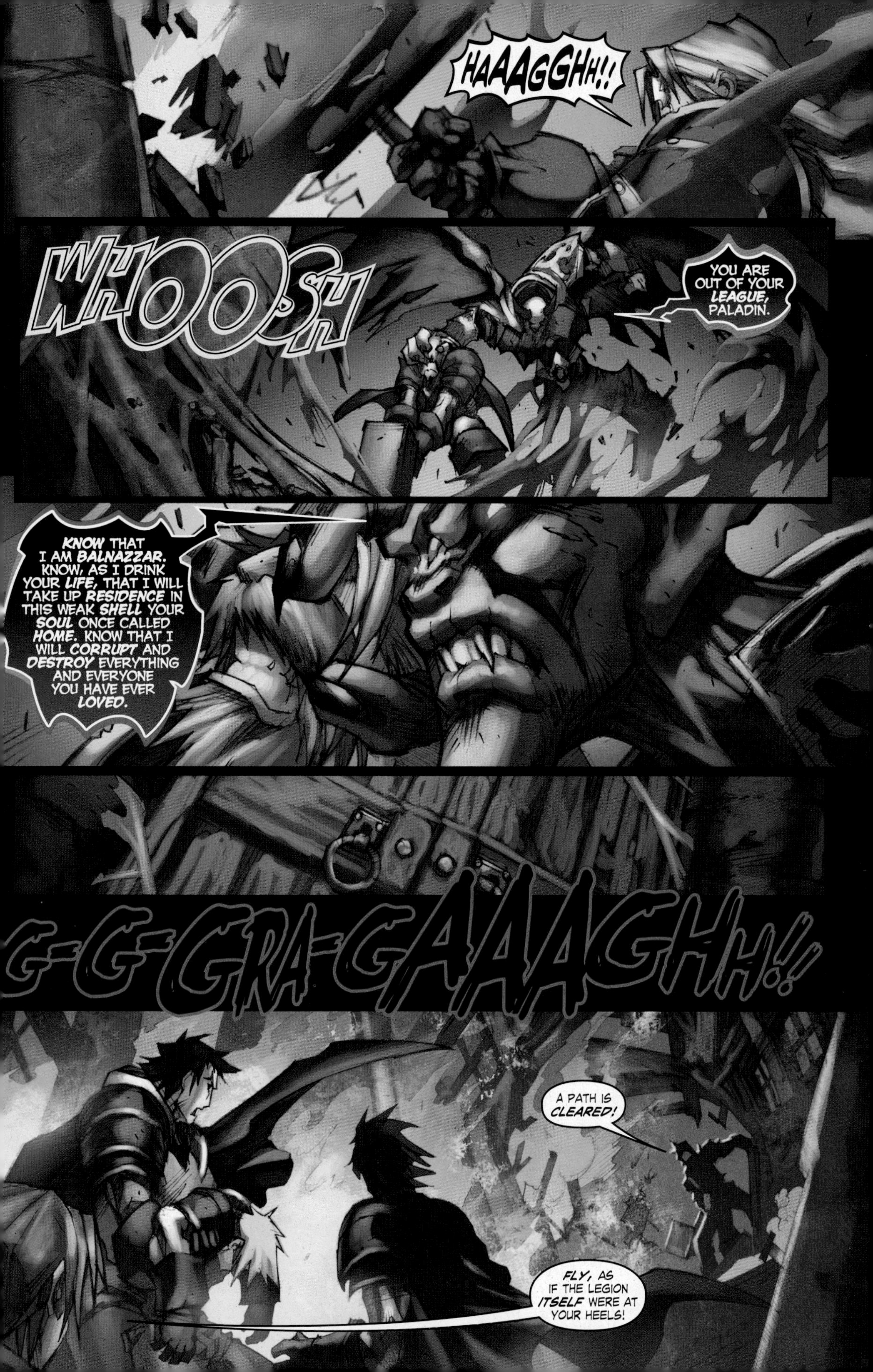
HAAAAGGHH!!
WHOOOSH
YOU ARE OUT OF YOUR LEAGUE, PALADIN.
KNOW THAT I AM BALNAZZAR. KNOW, AS I DRINK YOUR LIFE, THAT I WILL TAKE UP RESIDENCE IN THIS WEAK SHELL YOUR SOUL ONCE CALLED HOME. KNOW THAT I WILL CORRUPT AND DESTROY EVERYTHING AND EVERYONE YOU HAVE EVER LOVED.
G-G-GRA-GAAAGHH!!
A PATH IS CLEARED!
FLY, AS IF THE LEGION ITSELF WERE AT YOUR HEELS!

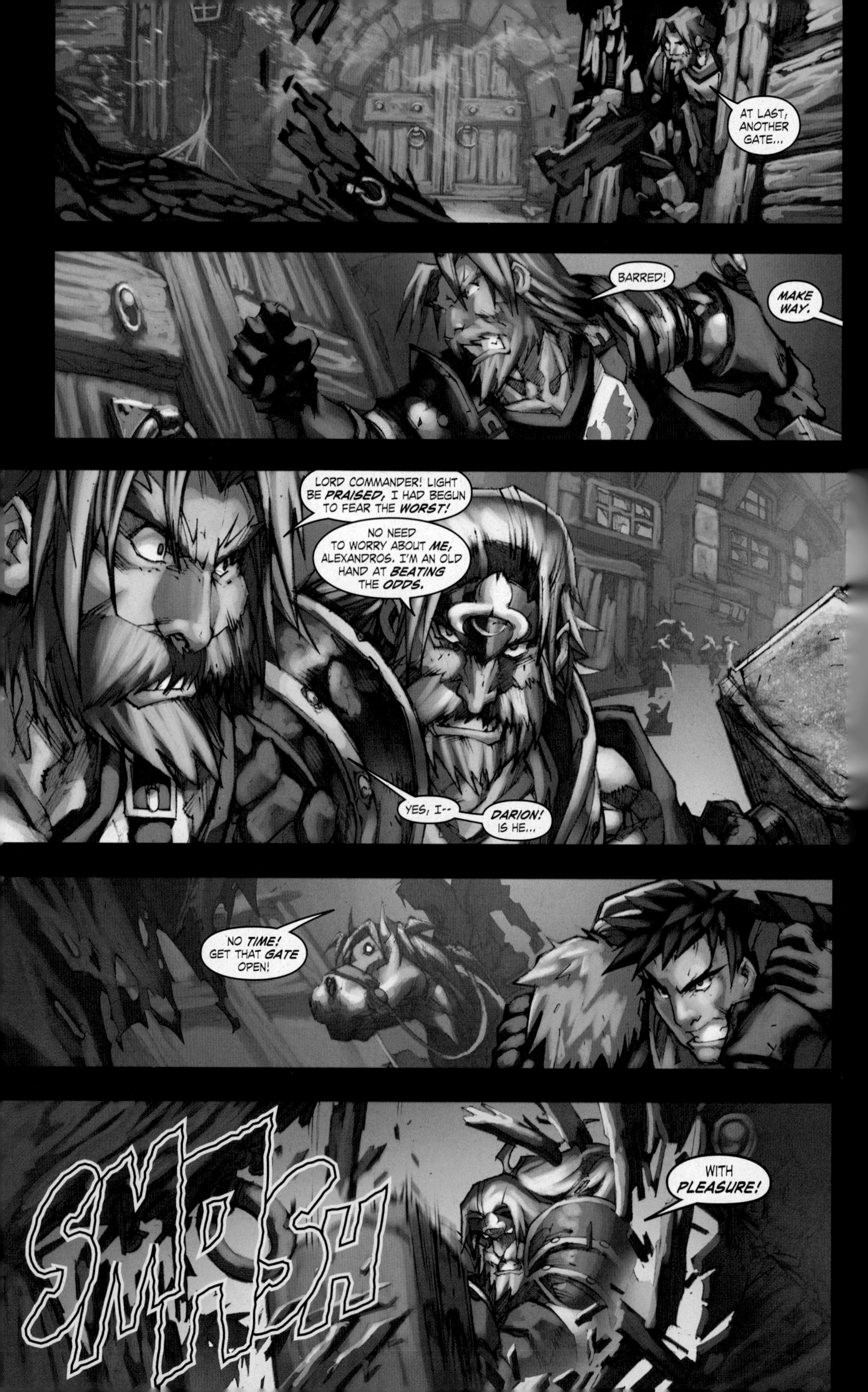
AT LAST, ANOTHER GATE...
BARRED!
MAKE WAY.
LORD COMMANDER! LIGHT BE PRAISED, I HAD BEGUN TO FEAR THE WORST!
NO NEED TO WORRY ABOUT ME, ALEXANDROS. I'M AN OLD HAND AT BEATING THE ODDS.
YES, I--
DARION! IS HE...
NO TIME! GET THAT GATE OPEN!
WITH PLEASURE!
SMASH

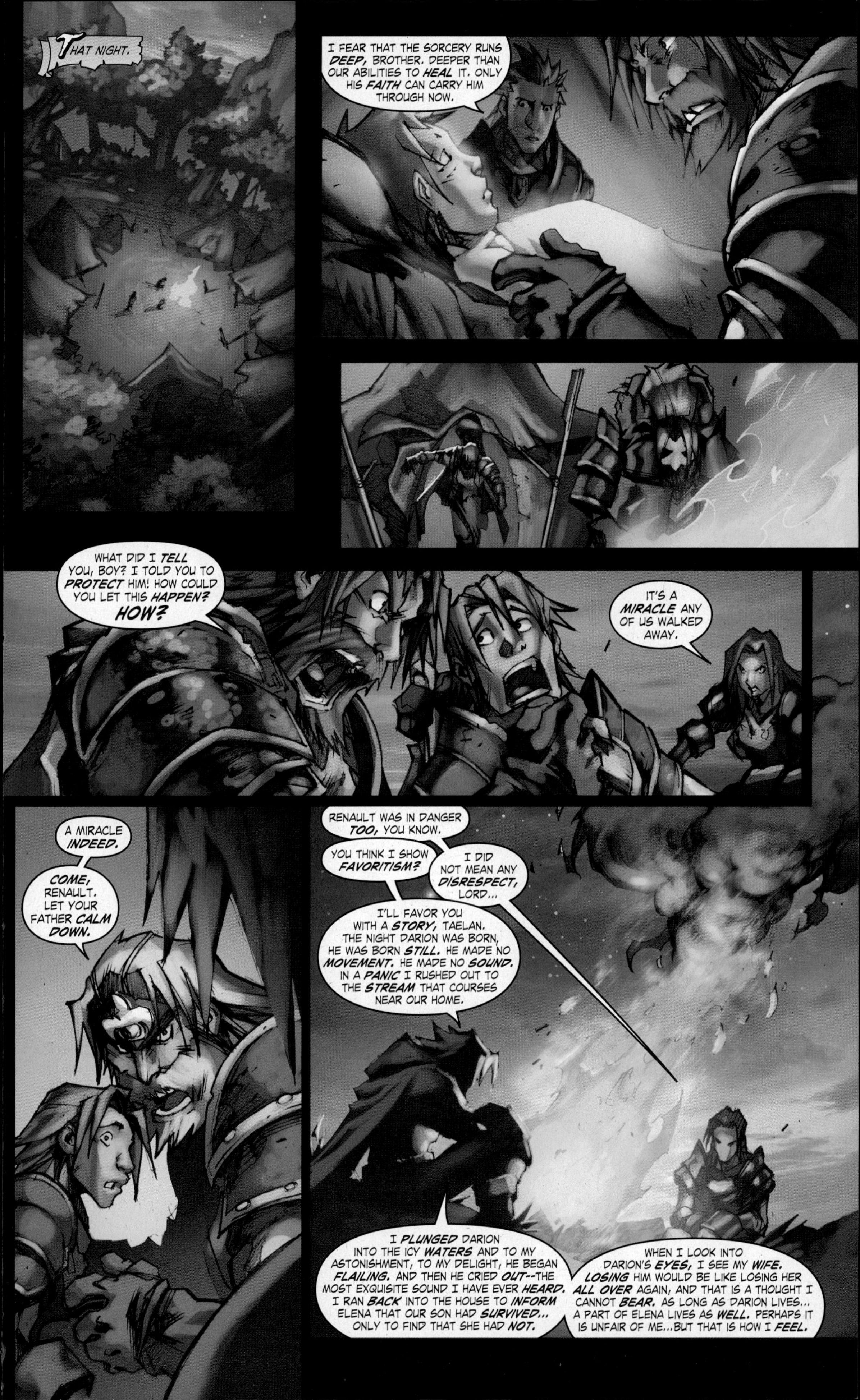
THAT NIGHT.
I FEAR THAT THE SORCERY RUNS DEEP, BROTHER. DEEPER THAN OUR ABILITIES TO HEAL IT. ONLY HIS FAITH CAN CARRY HIM THROUGH NOW.
WHAT DID I TELL YOU, BOY? I TOLD YOU TO PROTECT HIM! HOW COULD YOU LET THIS HAPPEN? HOW?
IT'S A MIRACLE ANY OF US WALKED AWAY.
A MIRACLE INDEED.
COME, RENAULT. LET YOUR FATHER CALM DOWN.
RENAULT WAS IN DANGER TOO, YOU KNOW.
YOU THINK I SHOW FAVORITISM?
I DID NOT MEAN ANY DISRESPECT, LORD...
I'LL FAVOR YOU WITH A STORY, TAELAN. THE NIGHT DARION WAS BORN, HE WAS BORN STILL. HE MADE NO MOVEMENT. HE MADE NO SOUND. IN A PANIC I RUSHED OUT TO THE STREAM THAT COURSES NEAR OUR HOME.
I PLUNGED DARION INTO THE ICY WATERS AND TO MY ASTONISHMENT, TO MY DELIGHT, HE BEGAN FLAILING. AND THEN HE CRIED OUT--THE MOST EXQUISITE SOUND I HAVE EVER HEARD. I RAN BACK INTO THE HOUSE TO INFORM ELENA THAT OUR SON HAD SURVIVED... ONLY TO FIND THAT SHE HAD NOT.
WHEN I LOOK INTO DARION'S EYES, I SEE MY WIFE. LOSING HIM WOULD BE LIKE LOSING HER ALL OVER AGAIN, AND THAT IS A THOUGHT I CANNOT BEAR. AS LONG AS DARION LIVES... A PART OF ELENA LIVES AS WELL. PERHAPS IT IS UNFAIR OF ME...BUT THAT IS HOW I FEEL.

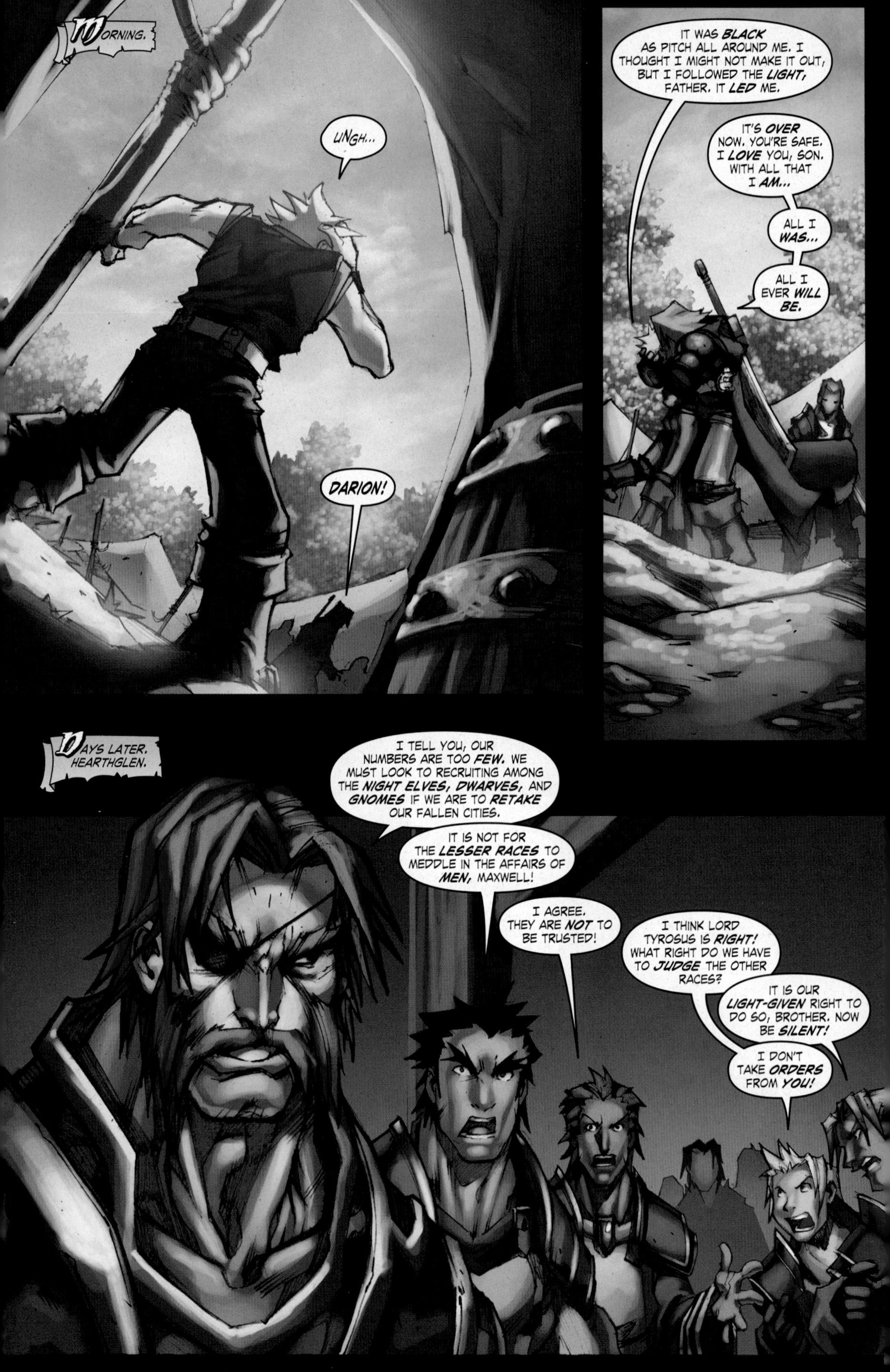
MORNING.
UNGH...
DARION!
IT WAS BLACK AS PITCH ALL AROUND ME. I THOUGHT I MIGHT NOT MAKE IT OUT, BUT I FOLLOWED THE LIGHT, FATHER. IT LED ME.
IT'S OVER NOW. YOU'RE SAFE. I LOVE YOU, SON. WITH ALL THAT I AM...
ALL I WAS...
ALL I EVER WILL BE.
DAYS LATER. HEARTHGLEN.
I TELL YOU, OUR NUMBERS ARE TOO FEW. WE MUST LOOK TO RECRUITING AMONG THE NIGHT ELVES, DWARVES, AND GNOMES IF WE ARE TO RETAKE OUR FALLEN CITIES.
IT IS NOT FOR THE LESSER RACES TO MEDDLE IN THE AFFAIRS OF MEN, MAXWELL!
I AGREE. THEY ARE NOT TO BE TRUSTED!
I THINK LORD TYROSUS IS RIGHT! WHAT RIGHT DO WE HAVE TO JUDGE THE OTHER RACES?
IT IS OUR LIGHT-GIVEN RIGHT TO DO SO, BROTHER. NOW BE SILENT!
I DON'T TAKE ORDERS FROM YOU!

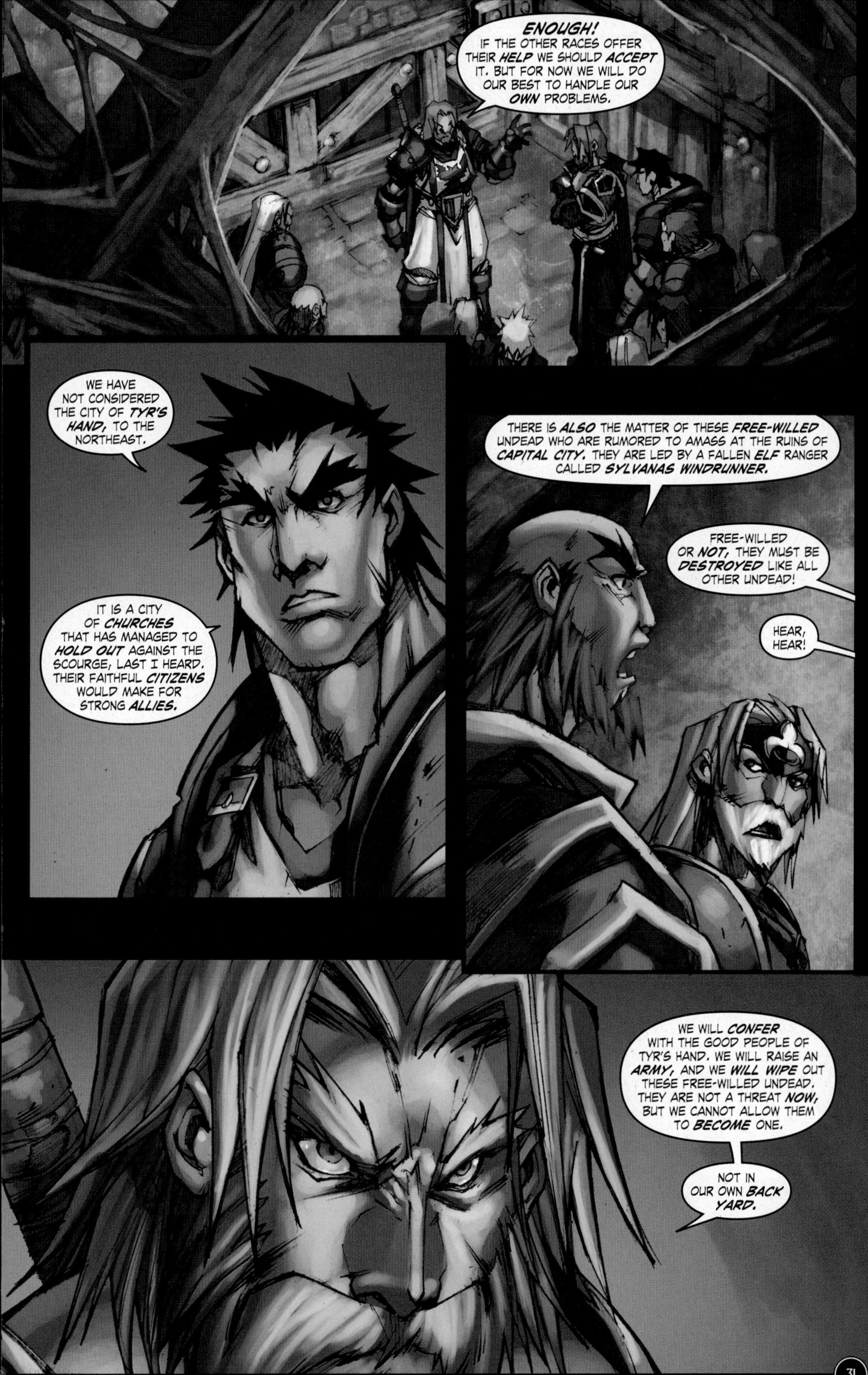
ENOUGH! IF THE OTHER RACES OFFER THEIR HELP WE SHOULD ACCEPT IT. BUT FOR NOW WE WILL DO OUR BEST TO HANDLE OUR OWN PROBLEMS.
WE HAVE NOT CONSIDERED THE CITY OF TYR'S HAND, TO THE NORTHEAST.
IT IS A CITY OF CHURCHES THAT HAS MANAGED TO HOLD OUT AGAINST THE SCOURGE, LAST I HEARD. THEIR FAITHFUL CITIZENS WOULD MAKE FOR STRONG ALLIES.
THERE IS ALSO THE MATTER OF THESE FREE-WILLED UNDEAD WHO ARE RUMORED TO AMASS AT THE RUINS OF CAPITAL CITY. THEY ARE LED BY A FALLEN ELF RANGER CALLED SYLVANAS WINDRUNNER.
FREE-WILLED OR NOT, THEY MUST BE DESTROYED LIKE ALL OTHER UNDEAD!
HEAR, HEAR!
WE WILL CONFER WITH THE GOOD PEOPLE OF TYR'S HAND. WE WILL RAISE AN ARMY, AND WE WILL WIPE OUT THESE FREE-WILLED UNDEAD. THEY ARE NOT A THREAT NOW, BUT WE CANNOT ALLOW THEM TO BECOME ONE.
NOT IN OUR OWN BACK YARD.

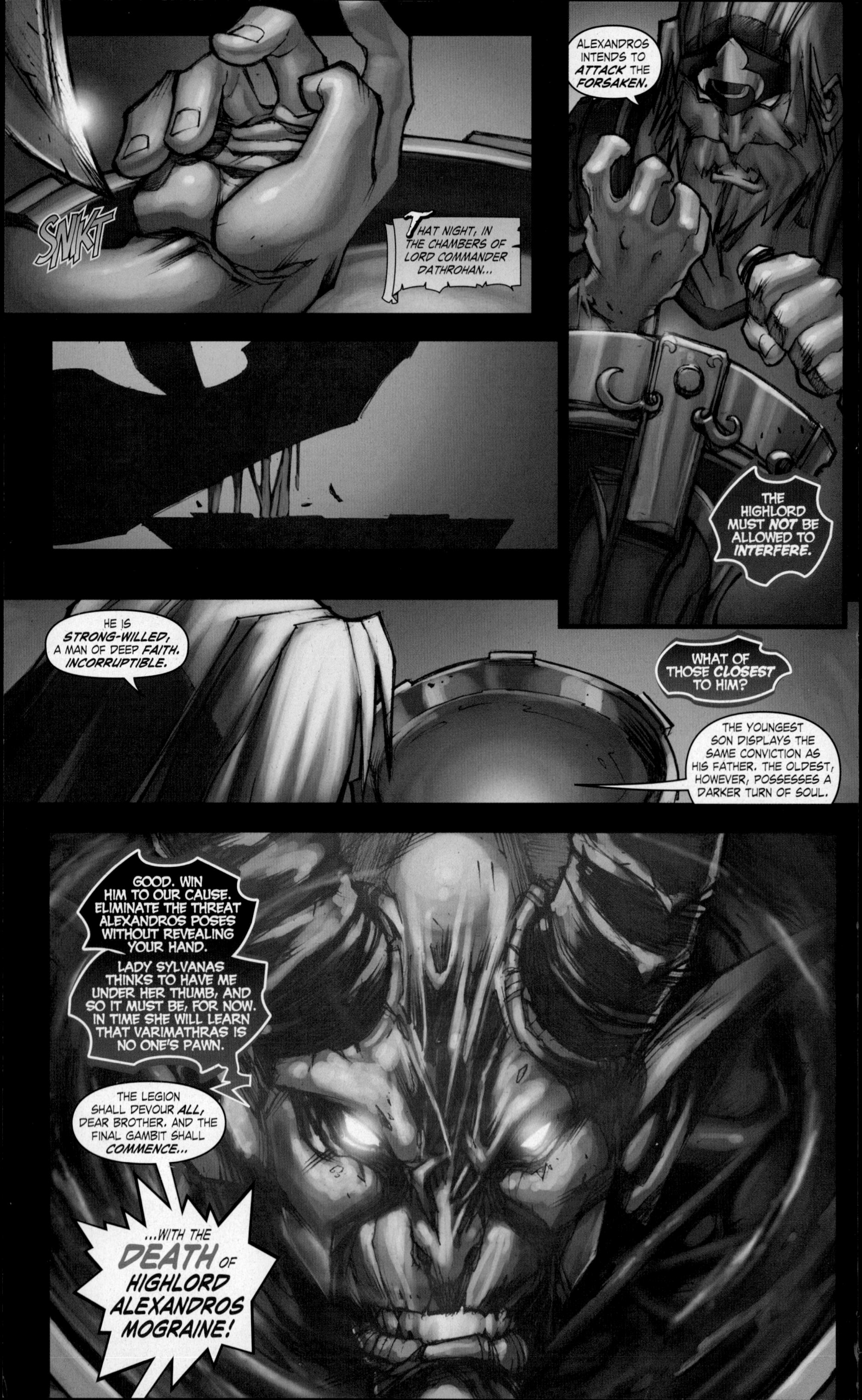
SNIKT
THAT NIGHT, IN THE CHAMBERS OF LORD COMMANDER DATHROHAN...
ALEXANDROS INTENDS TO ATTACK THE FORSAKEN.
THE HIGHLORD MUST NOT BE ALLOWED TO INTERFERE.
HE IS STRONG-WILLED, A MAN OF DEEP FAITH. INCORRUPTIBLE.
WHAT OF THOSE CLOSEST TO HIM?
THE YOUNGEST SON DISPLAYS THE SAME CONVICTION AS HIS FATHER. THE OLDEST, HOWEVER, POSSESSES A DARKER TURN OF SOUL.
GOOD. WIN HIM TO OUR CAUSE. ELIMINATE THE THREAT ALEXANDROS POSES WITHOUT REVEALING YOUR HAND.
LADY SYLVANAS THINKS TO HAVE ME UNDER HER THUMB, AND SO IT MUST BE, FOR NOW. IN TIME SHE WILL LEARN THAT VARIMATHRAS IS NO ONE'S PAWN.
THE LEGION SHALL DEVOUR ALL, DEAR BROTHER. AND THE FINAL GAMBIT SHALL COMMENCE...
...WITH THE DEATH OF HIGHLORD ALEXANDROS MOGRAINE!

CHAPTER 2

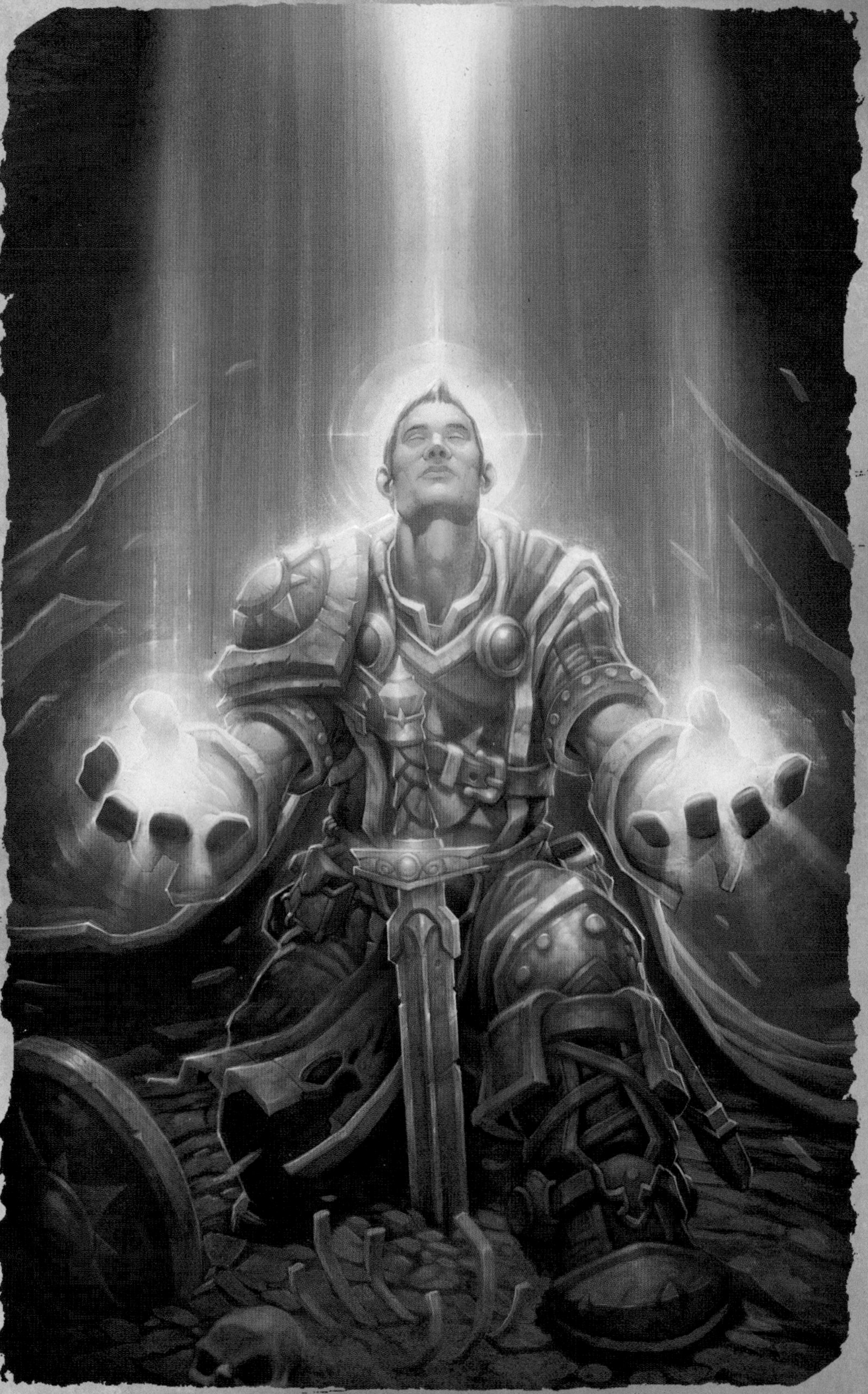

Cover by Chris Robinson

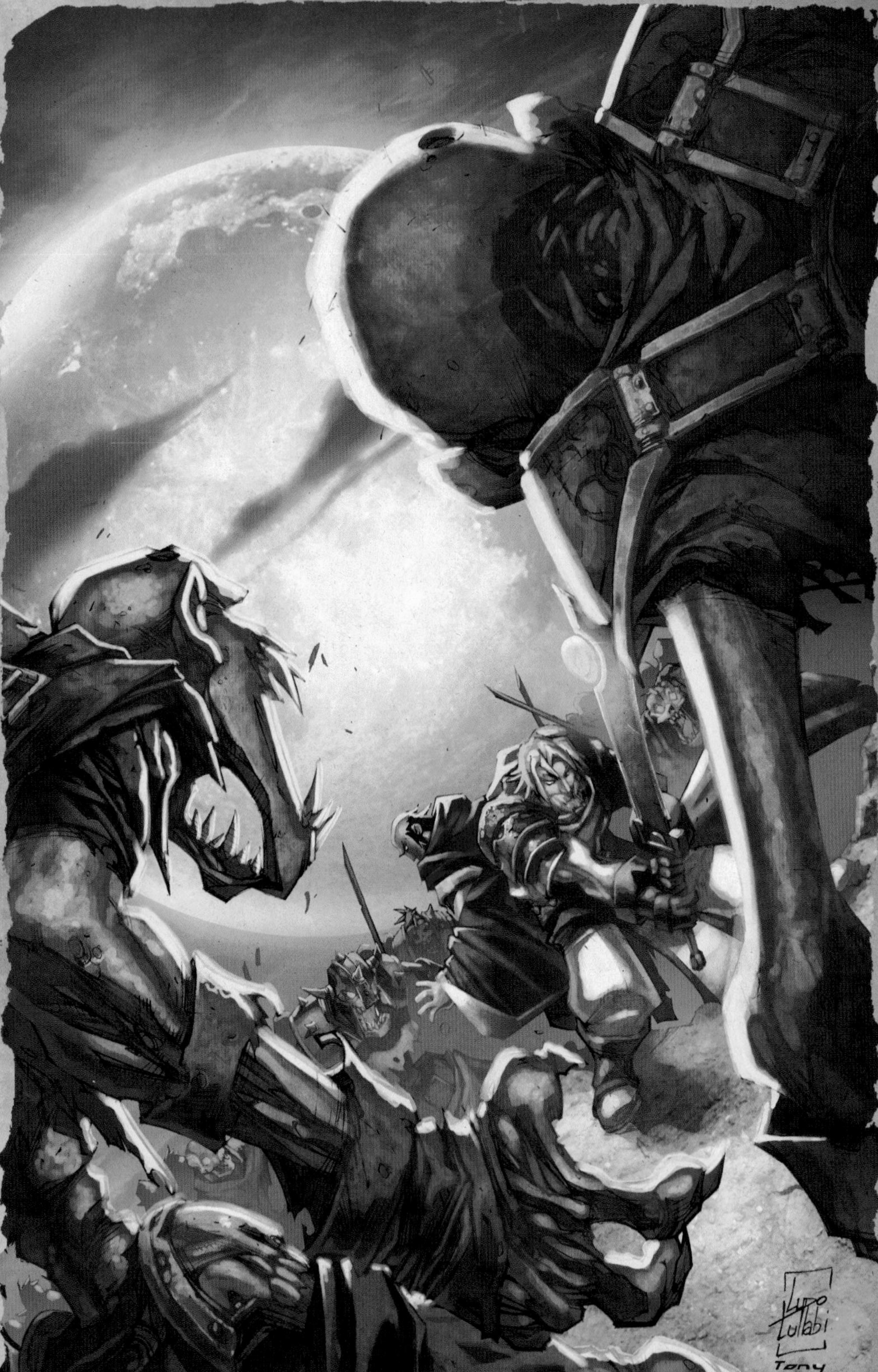
Ludo Lullabi
Tony

Cover by Ludo Lullabi and Tony Washington

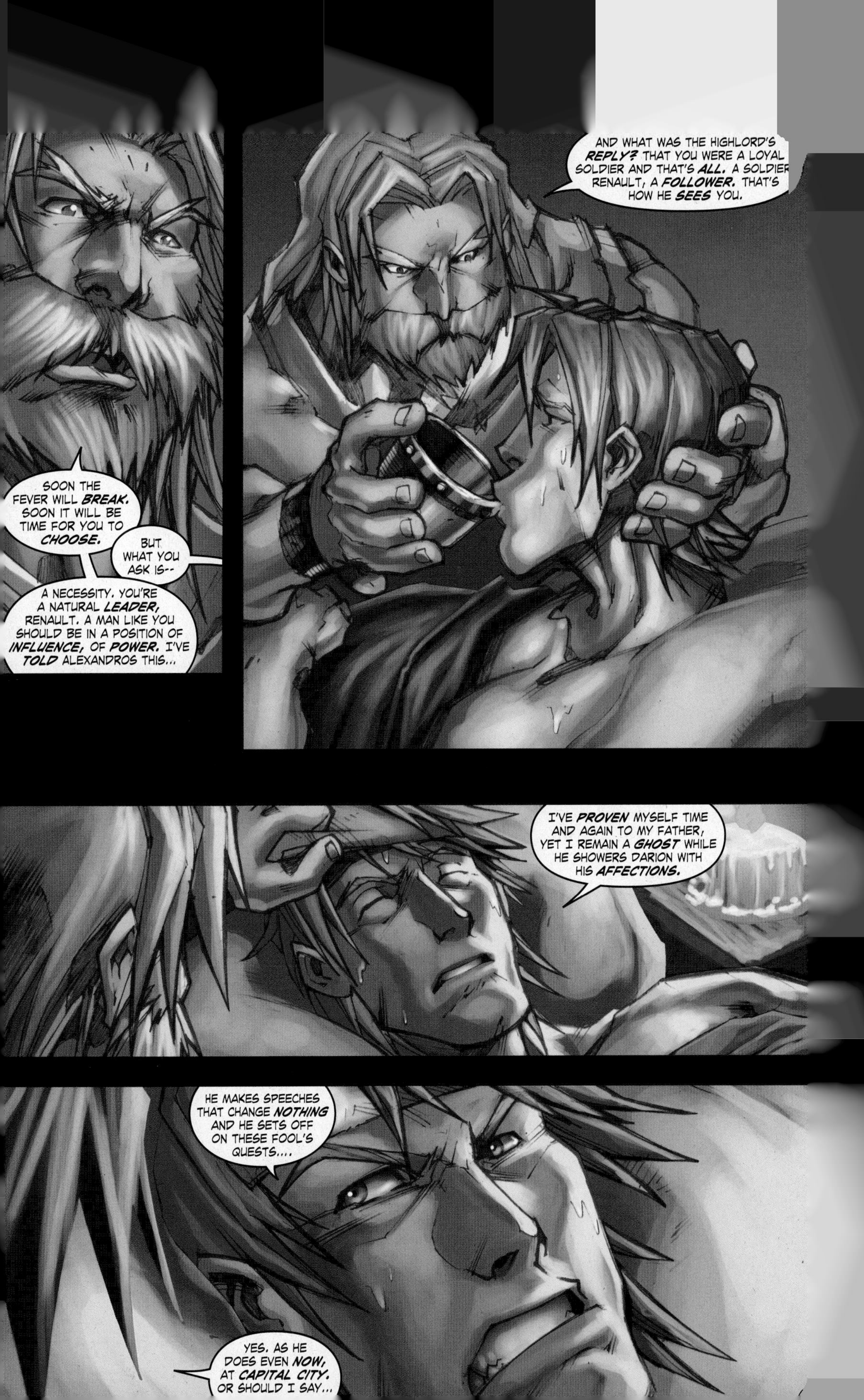
AND WHAT WAS THE HIGHLORD'S REPLY? THAT YOU WERE A LOYAL SOLDIER AND THAT'S ALL. A SOLDIER RENAULT, A FOLLOWER. THAT'S HOW HE SEES YOU.
SOON THE FEVER WILL BREAK. SOON IT WILL BE TIME FOR YOU TO CHOOSE.
BUT WHAT YOU ASK IS--
A NECESSITY. YOU'RE A NATURAL LEADER, RENAULT. A MAN LIKE YOU SHOULD BE IN A POSITION OF INFLUENCE, OF POWER. I'VE TOLD ALEXANDROS THIS...
I'VE PROVEN MYSELF TIME AND AGAIN TO MY FATHER, YET I REMAIN A GHOST WHILE HE SHOWERS DARION WITH HIS AFFECTIONS.
HE MAKES SPEECHES THAT CHANGE NOTHING AND HE SETS OFF ON THESE FOOL'S QUESTS....
YES. AS HE DOES EVEN NOW, AT CAPITAL CITY. OR SHOULD I SAY...

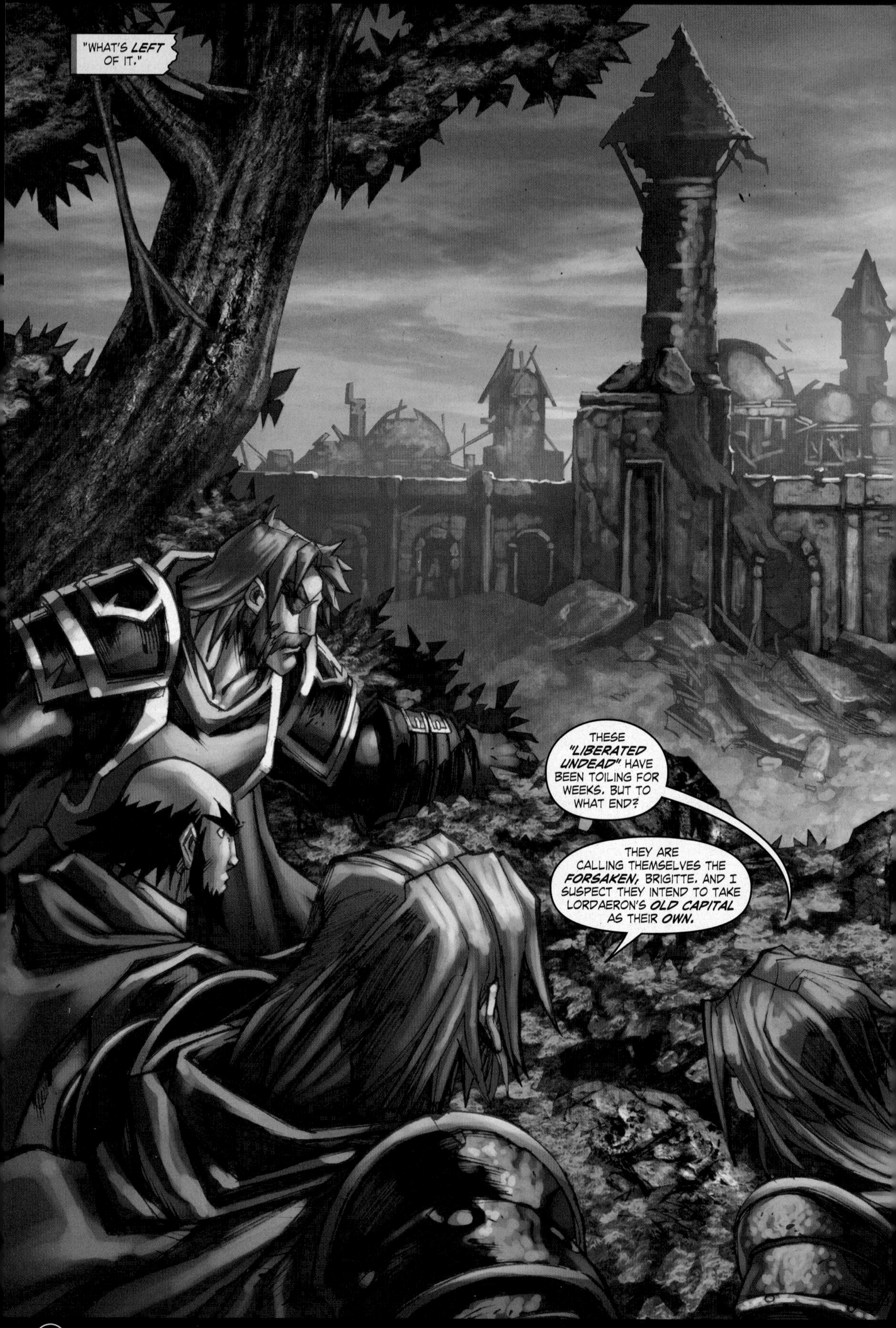
"WHAT'S *LEFT* OF IT."
THESE *"LIBERATED UNDEAD"* HAVE BEEN TOILING FOR WEEKS. BUT TO WHAT END?
THEY ARE CALLING THEMSELVES THE ***FORSAKEN,*** BRIGITTE. AND I SUSPECT THEY INTEND TO TAKE LORDAERON'S ***OLD CAPITAL*** AS THEIR ***OWN.***

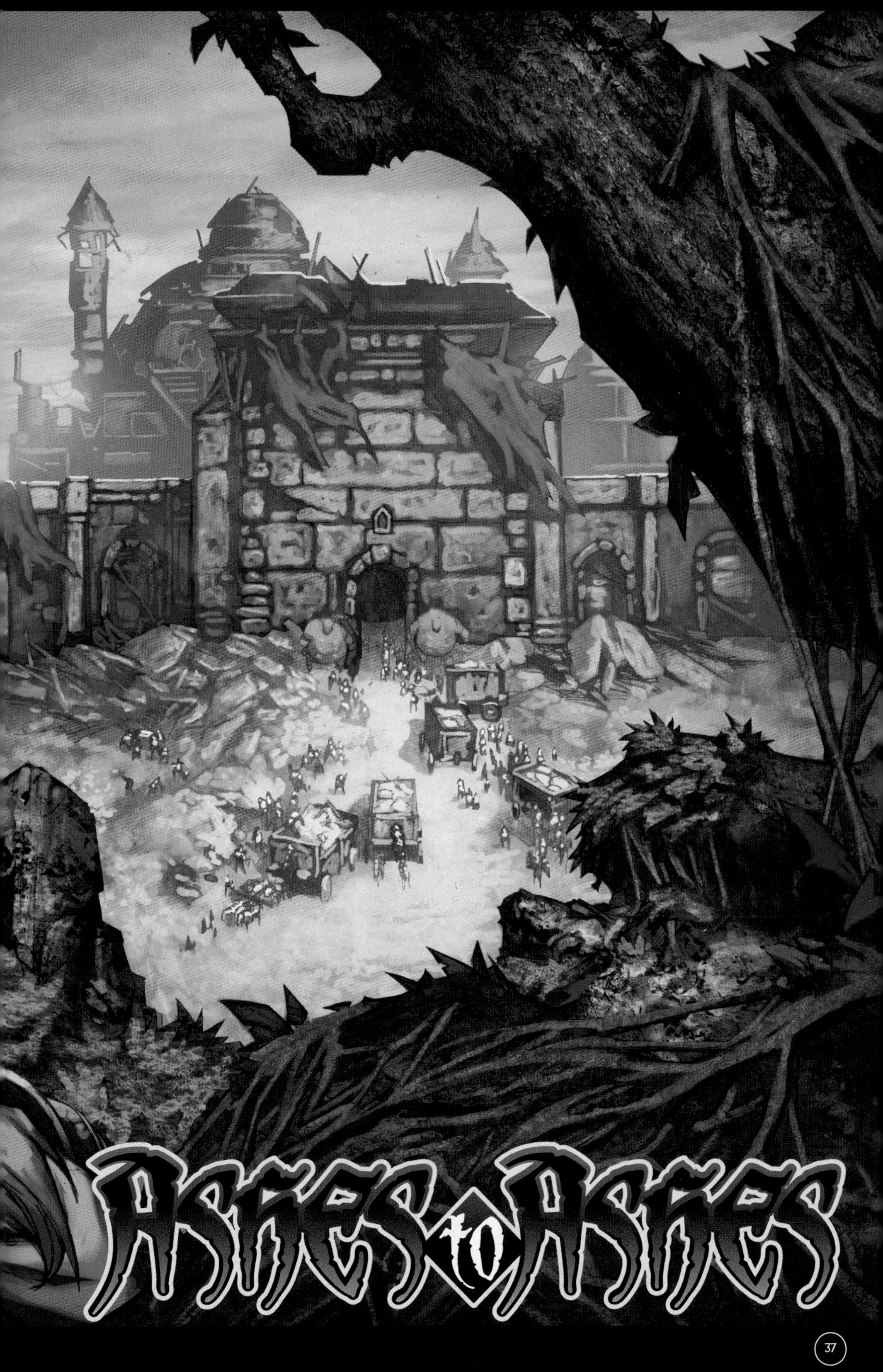
ASHES to ASHES

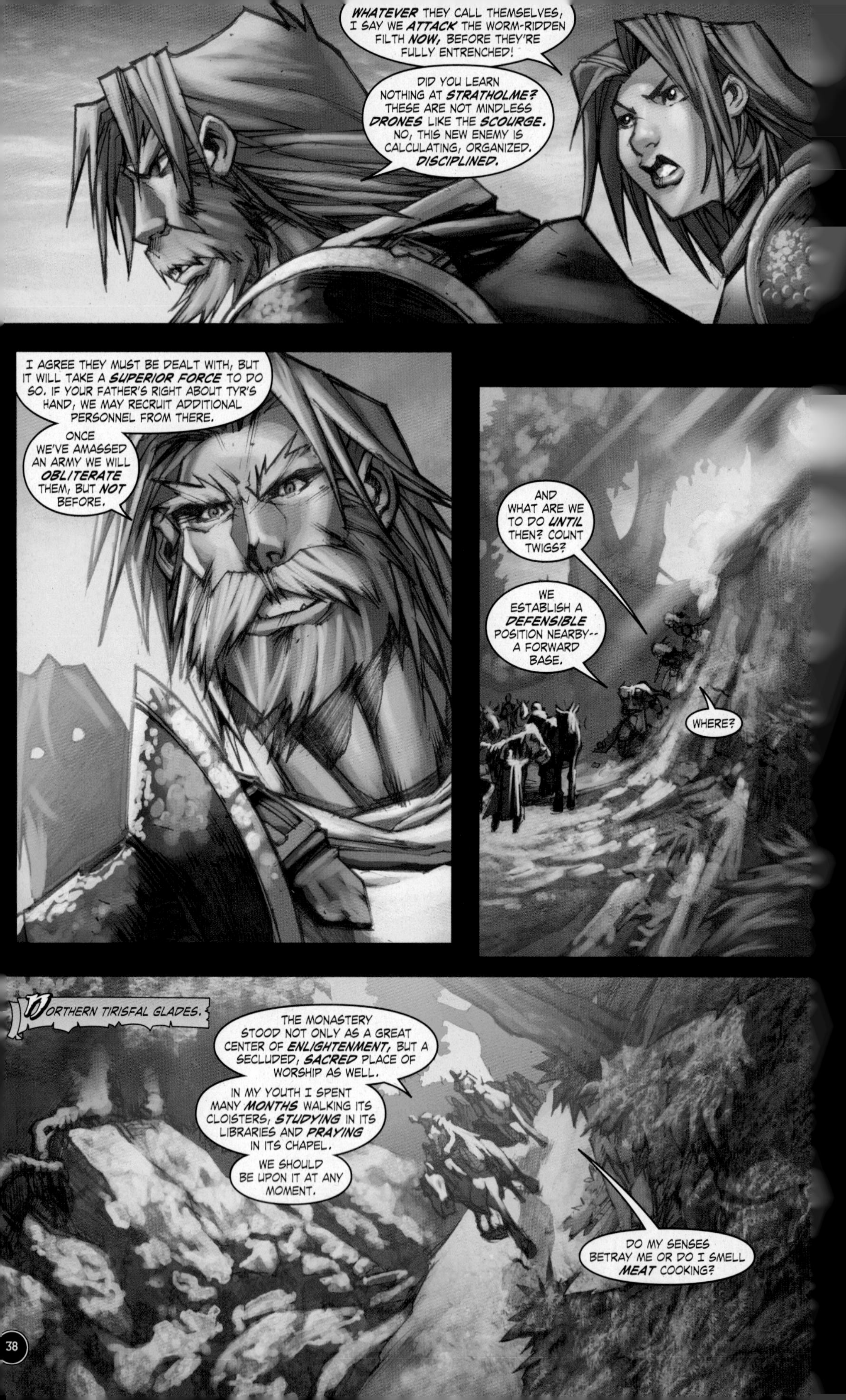
WHATEVER THEY CALL THEMSELVES, I SAY WE ATTACK THE WORM-RIDDEN FILTH NOW, BEFORE THEY'RE FULLY ENTRENCHED!
DID YOU LEARN NOTHING AT STRATHOLME? THESE ARE NOT MINDLESS DRONES LIKE THE SCOURGE. NO, THIS NEW ENEMY IS CALCULATING, ORGANIZED. DISCIPLINED.
I AGREE THEY MUST BE DEALT WITH, BUT IT WILL TAKE A SUPERIOR FORCE TO DO SO. IF YOUR FATHER'S RIGHT ABOUT TYR'S HAND, WE MAY RECRUIT ADDITIONAL PERSONNEL FROM THERE.
ONCE WE'VE AMASSED AN ARMY WE WILL OBLITERATE THEM, BUT NOT BEFORE.
AND WHAT ARE WE TO DO UNTIL THEN? COUNT TWIGS?
WE ESTABLISH A DEFENSIBLE POSITION NEARBY-- A FORWARD BASE.
WHERE?
NORTHERN TIRISFAL GLADES.
THE MONASTERY STOOD NOT ONLY AS A GREAT CENTER OF ENLIGHTENMENT, BUT A SECLUDED, SACRED PLACE OF WORSHIP AS WELL.
IN MY YOUTH I SPENT MANY MONTHS WALKING ITS CLOISTERS, STUDYING IN ITS LIBRARIES AND PRAYING IN ITS CHAPEL.
WE SHOULD BE UPON IT AT ANY MOMENT.
DO MY SENSES BETRAY ME OR DO I SMELL MEAT COOKING?

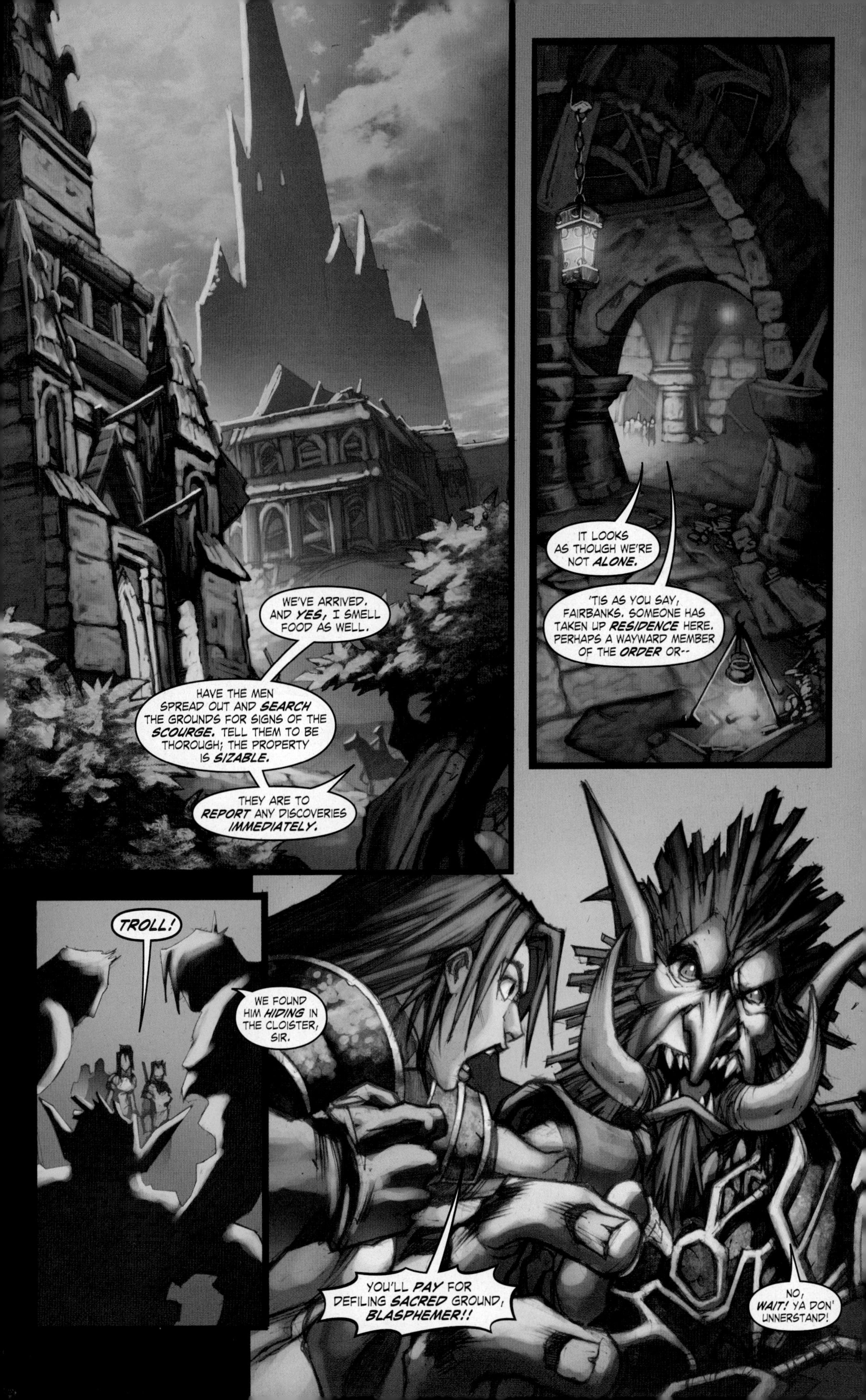
WE'VE ARRIVED. AND YES, I SMELL FOOD AS WELL.
HAVE THE MEN SPREAD OUT AND SEARCH THE GROUNDS FOR SIGNS OF THE SCOURGE. TELL THEM TO BE THOROUGH; THE PROPERTY IS SIZABLE.
THEY ARE TO REPORT ANY DISCOVERIES IMMEDIATELY.
IT LOOKS AS THOUGH WE'RE NOT ALONE.
'TIS AS YOU SAY, FAIRBANKS. SOMEONE HAS TAKEN UP RESIDENCE HERE. PERHAPS A WAYWARD MEMBER OF THE ORDER OR--
TROLL!
WE FOUND HIM HIDING IN THE CLOISTER, SIR.
YOU'LL PAY FOR DEFILING SACRED GROUND, BLASPHEMER!!
NO, WAIT! YA DON' UNNERSTAND!

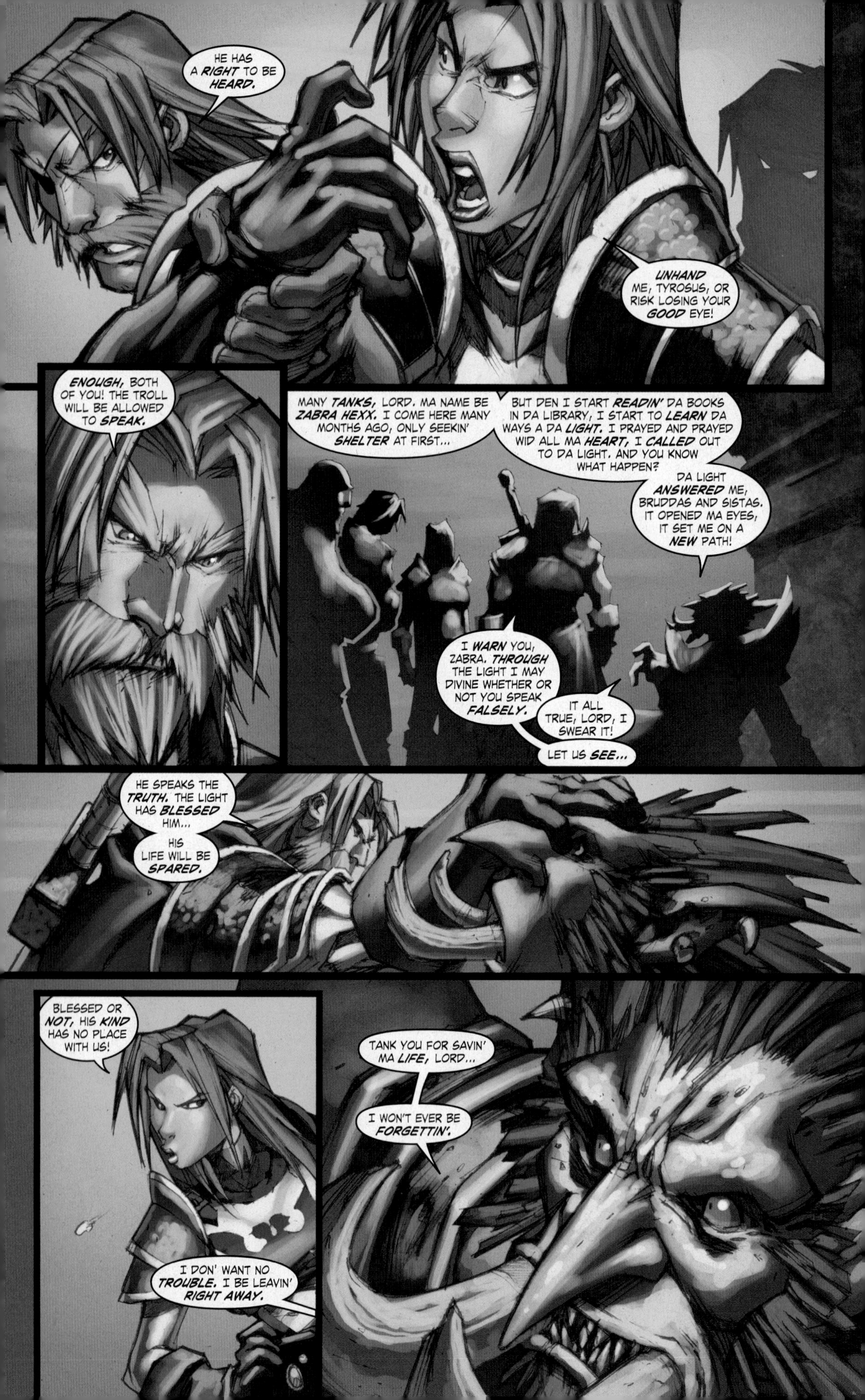
HE HAS A RIGHT TO BE HEARD.
UNHAND ME, TYROSUS, OR RISK LOSING YOUR GOOD EYE!
ENOUGH, BOTH OF YOU! THE TROLL WILL BE ALLOWED TO SPEAK.
MANY TANKS, LORD. MA NAME BE ZABRA HEXX. I COME HERE MANY MONTHS AGO, ONLY SEEKIN' SHELTER AT FIRST...
BUT DEN I START READIN' DA BOOKS IN DA LIBRARY, I START TO LEARN DA WAYS A DA LIGHT. I PRAYED AND PRAYED WID ALL MA HEART, I CALLED OUT TO DA LIGHT. AND YOU KNOW WHAT HAPPEN?
DA LIGHT ANSWERED ME, BRUDDAS AND SISTAS. IT OPENED MA EYES, IT SET ME ON A NEW PATH!
I WARN YOU, ZABRA. THROUGH THE LIGHT I MAY DIVINE WHETHER OR NOT YOU SPEAK FALSELY.
IT ALL TRUE, LORD, I SWEAR IT!
LET US SEE...
HE SPEAKS THE TRUTH. THE LIGHT HAS BLESSED HIM...
HIS LIFE WILL BE SPARED.
BLESSED OR NOT, HIS KIND HAS NO PLACE WITH US!
TANK YOU FOR SAVIN' MA LIFE, LORD...
I WON'T EVER BE FORGETTIN'.
I DON' WANT NO TROUBLE. I BE LEAVIN' RIGHT AWAY.

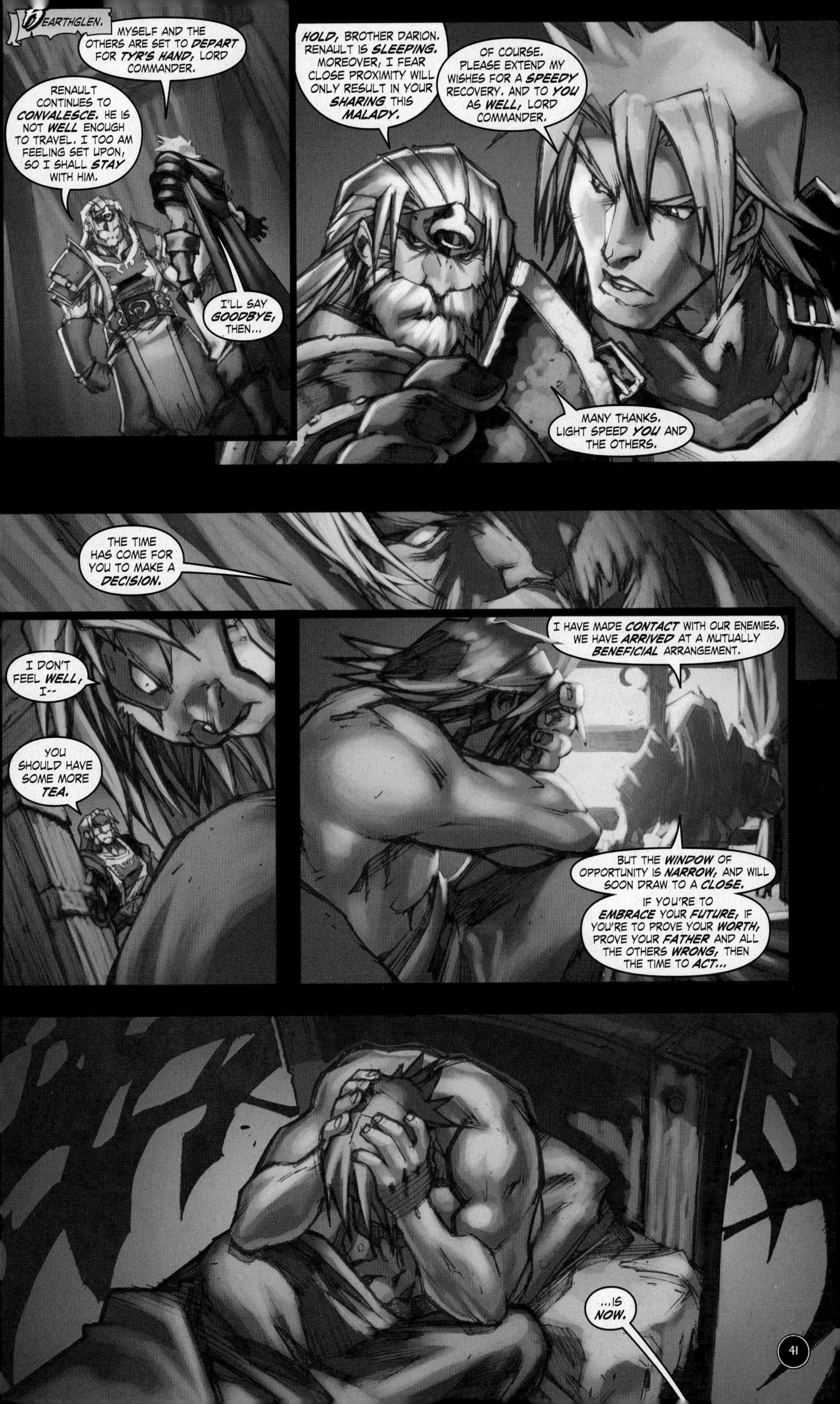
HEARTHGLEN.
MYSELF AND THE OTHERS ARE SET TO DEPART FOR TYR'S HAND, LORD COMMANDER.
RENAULT CONTINUES TO CONVALESCE. HE IS NOT WELL ENOUGH TO TRAVEL. I TOO AM FEELING SET UPON, SO I SHALL STAY WITH HIM.
I'LL SAY GOODBYE, THEN...
HOLD, BROTHER DARION. RENAULT IS SLEEPING. MOREOVER, I FEAR CLOSE PROXIMITY WILL ONLY RESULT IN YOUR SHARING THIS MALADY.
OF COURSE. PLEASE EXTEND MY WISHES FOR A SPEEDY RECOVERY. AND TO YOU AS WELL, LORD COMMANDER.
MANY THANKS. LIGHT SPEED YOU AND THE OTHERS.
THE TIME HAS COME FOR YOU TO MAKE A DECISION.
I DON'T FEEL WELL, I--
YOU SHOULD HAVE SOME MORE TEA.
I HAVE MADE CONTACT WITH OUR ENEMIES. WE HAVE ARRIVED AT A MUTUALLY BENEFICIAL ARRANGEMENT.
BUT THE WINDOW OF OPPORTUNITY IS NARROW, AND WILL SOON DRAW TO A CLOSE.
IF YOU'RE TO EMBRACE YOUR FUTURE, IF YOU'RE TO PROVE YOUR WORTH, PROVE YOUR FATHER AND ALL THE OTHERS WRONG, THEN THE TIME TO ACT...
...IS NOW.

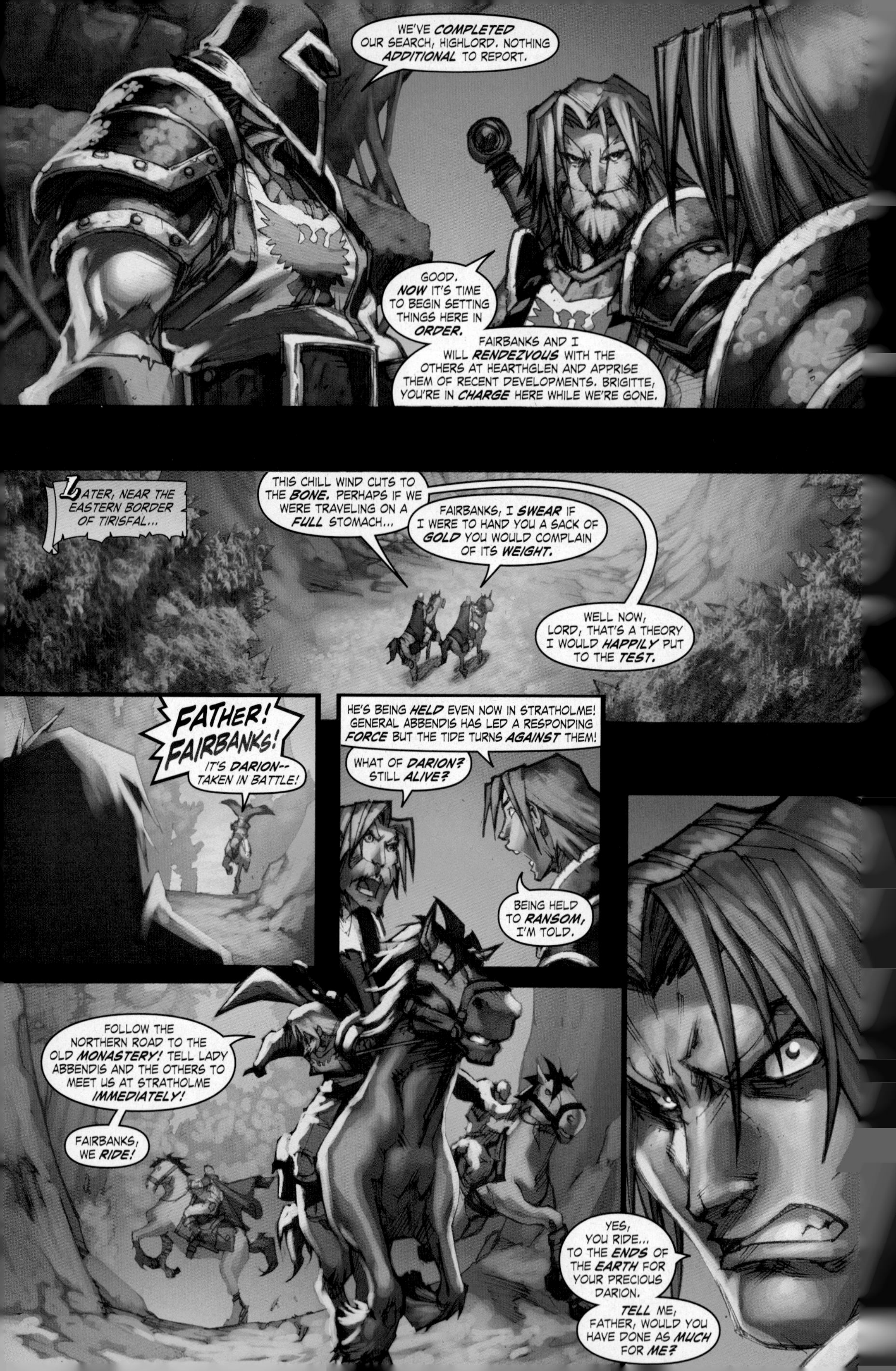

WE'VE COMPLETED OUR SEARCH, HIGHLORD. NOTHING ADDITIONAL TO REPORT.
GOOD. NOW IT'S TIME TO BEGIN SETTING THINGS HERE IN ORDER.
FAIRBANKS AND I WILL RENDEZVOUS WITH THE OTHERS AT HEARTHGLEN AND APPRISE THEM OF RECENT DEVELOPMENTS. BRIGITTE, YOU'RE IN CHARGE HERE WHILE WE'RE GONE.
LATER, NEAR THE EASTERN BORDER OF TIRISFAL...
THIS CHILL WIND CUTS TO THE BONE. PERHAPS IF WE WERE TRAVELING ON A FULL STOMACH...
FAIRBANKS, I SWEAR IF I WERE TO HAND YOU A SACK OF GOLD YOU WOULD COMPLAIN OF ITS WEIGHT.
WELL NOW, LORD, THAT'S A THEORY I WOULD HAPPILY PUT TO THE TEST.
FATHER! FAIRBANKS!
IT'S DARION-- TAKEN IN BATTLE!
HE'S BEING HELD EVEN NOW IN STRATHOLME! GENERAL ABBENDIS HAS LED A RESPONDING FORCE BUT THE TIDE TURNS AGAINST THEM!
WHAT OF DARION? STILL ALIVE?
BEING HELD TO RANSOM, I'M TOLD.
FOLLOW THE NORTHERN ROAD TO THE OLD MONASTERY! TELL LADY ABBENDIS AND THE OTHERS TO MEET US AT STRATHOLME IMMEDIATELY!
FAIRBANKS, WE RIDE!
YES, YOU RIDE... TO THE ENDS OF THE EARTH FOR YOUR PRECIOUS DARION.
TELL ME, FATHER, WOULD YOU HAVE DONE AS MUCH FOR ME?

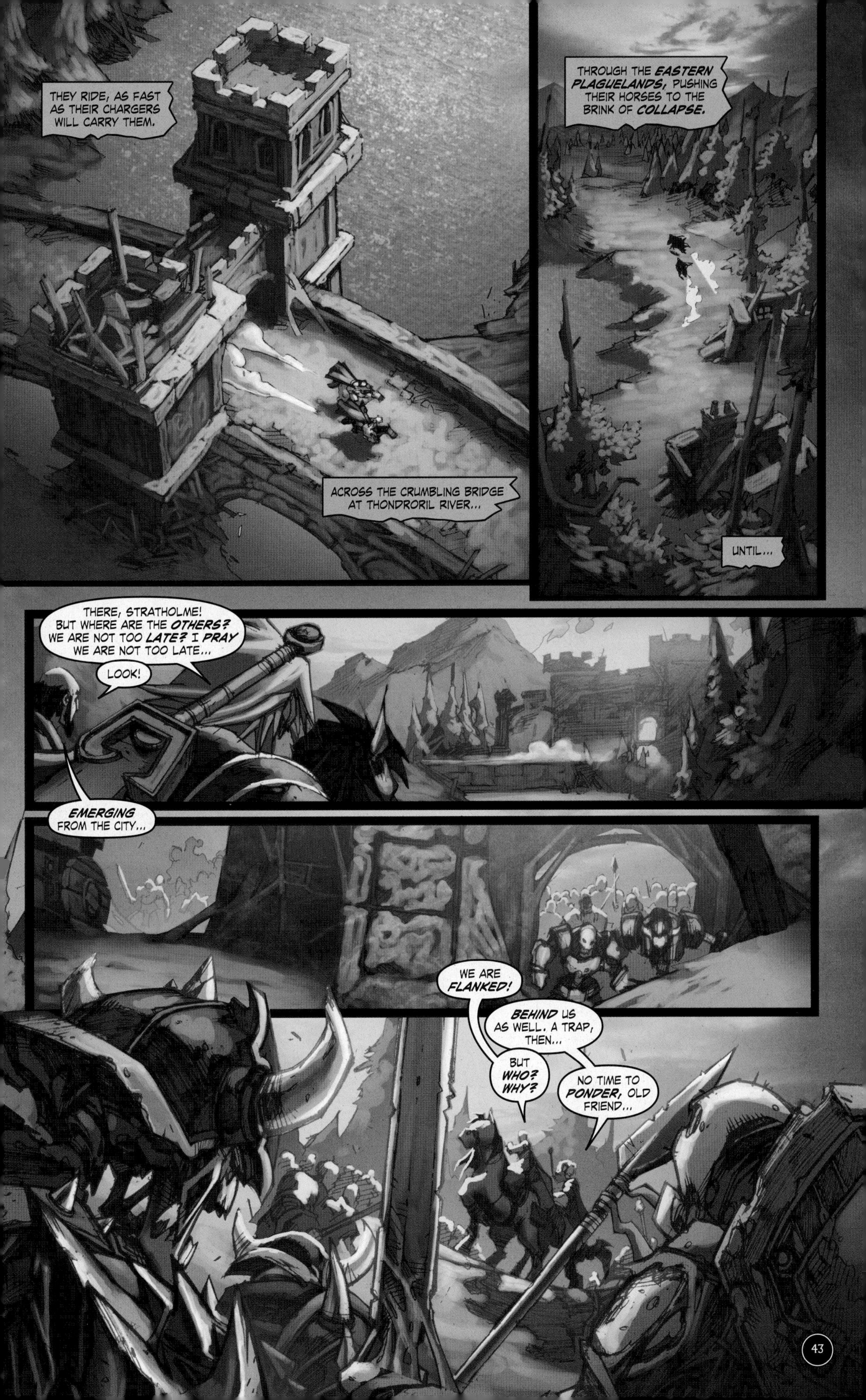
THEY RIDE, AS FAST AS THEIR CHARGERS WILL CARRY THEM.
ACROSS THE CRUMBLING BRIDGE AT THONDRORIL RIVER...
THROUGH THE EASTERN PLAGUELANDS, PUSHING THEIR HORSES TO THE BRINK OF COLLAPSE.
UNTIL...
THERE, STRATHOLME! BUT WHERE ARE THE OTHERS? WE ARE NOT TOO LATE? I PRAY WE ARE NOT TOO LATE...
LOOK!
EMERGING FROM THE CITY...
WE ARE FLANKED!
BEHIND US AS WELL. A TRAP, THEN...
BUT WHO? WHY?
NO TIME TO PONDER, OLD FRIEND...

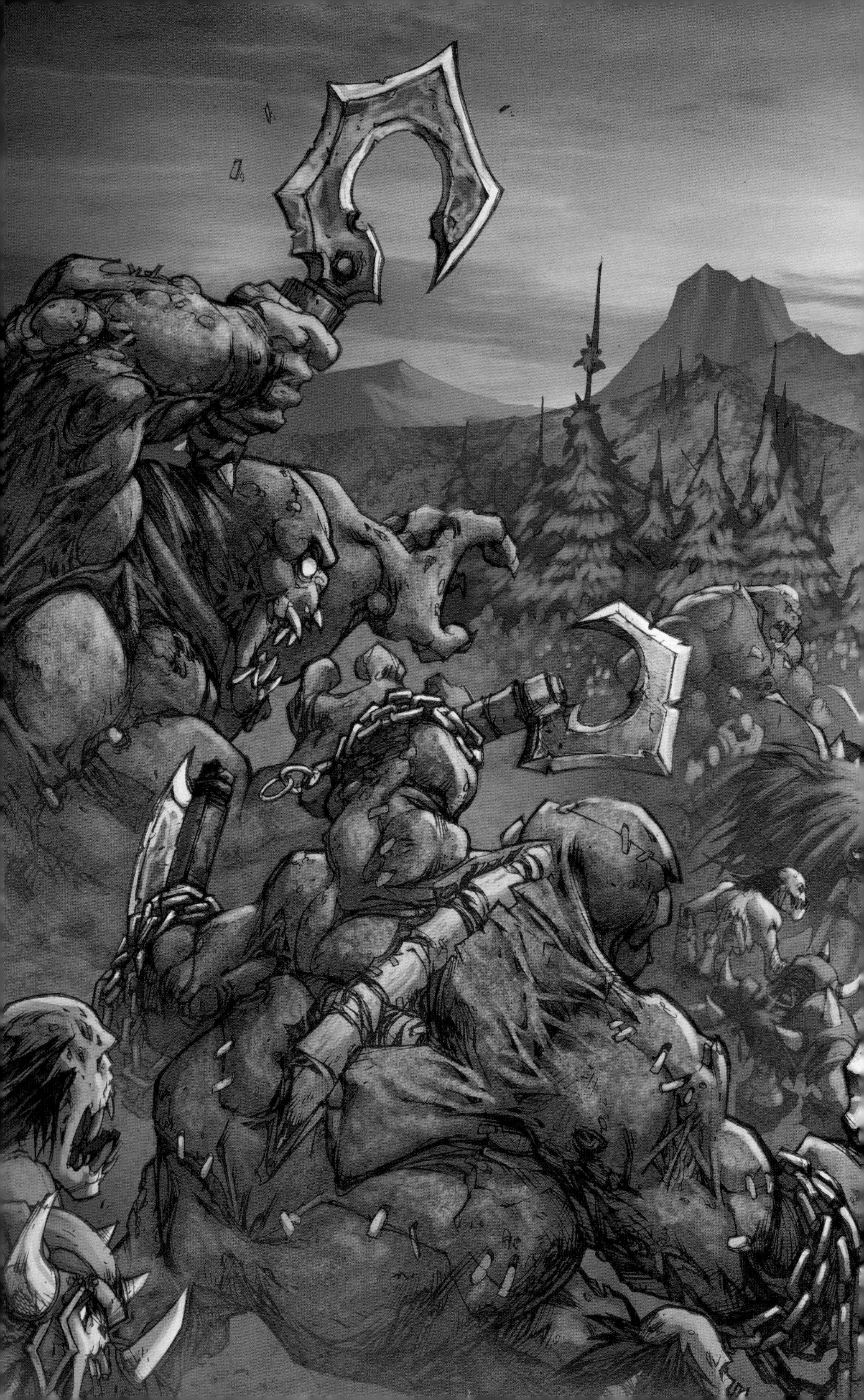

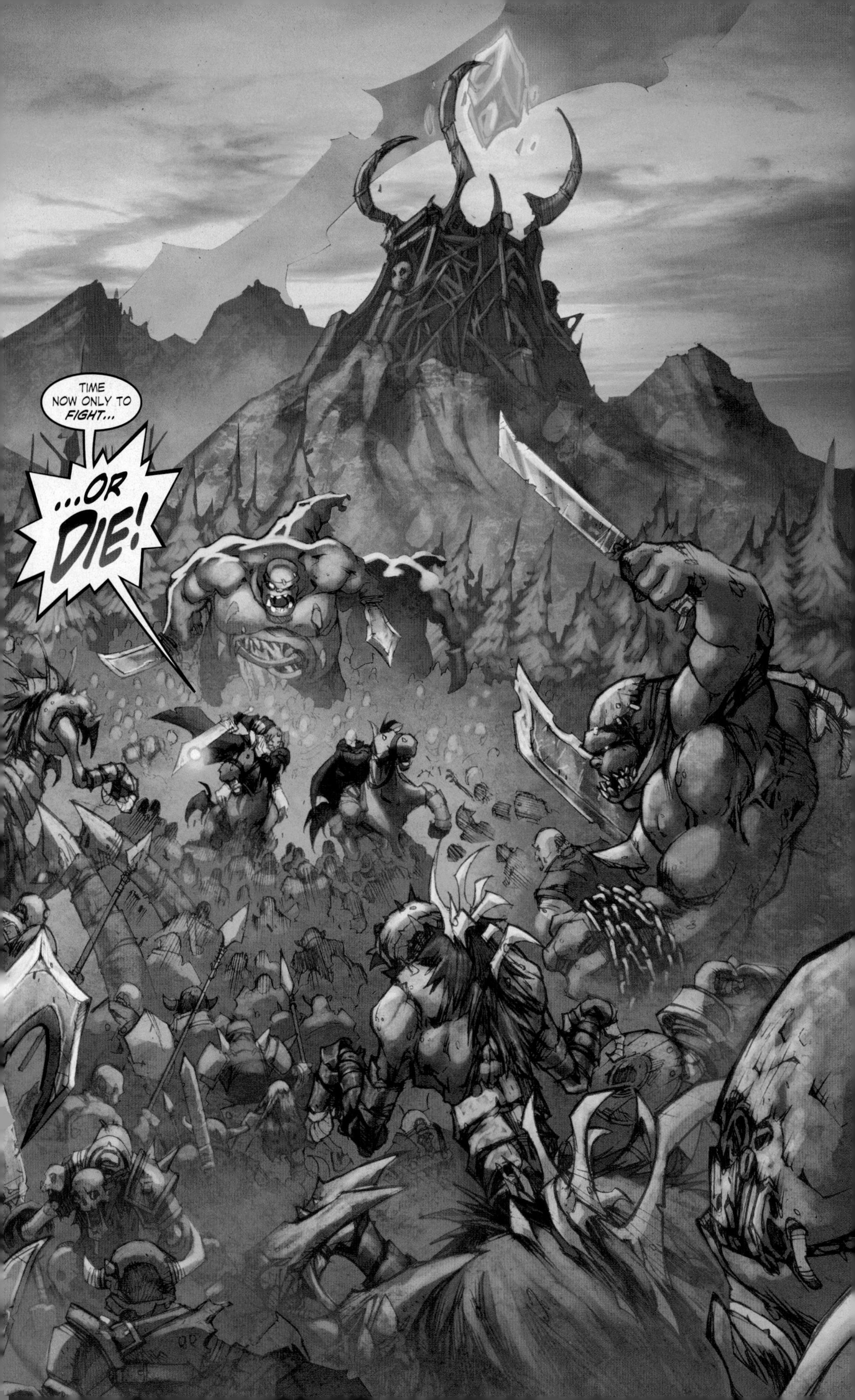
TIME NOW ONLY TO FIGHT...
...OR DIE!

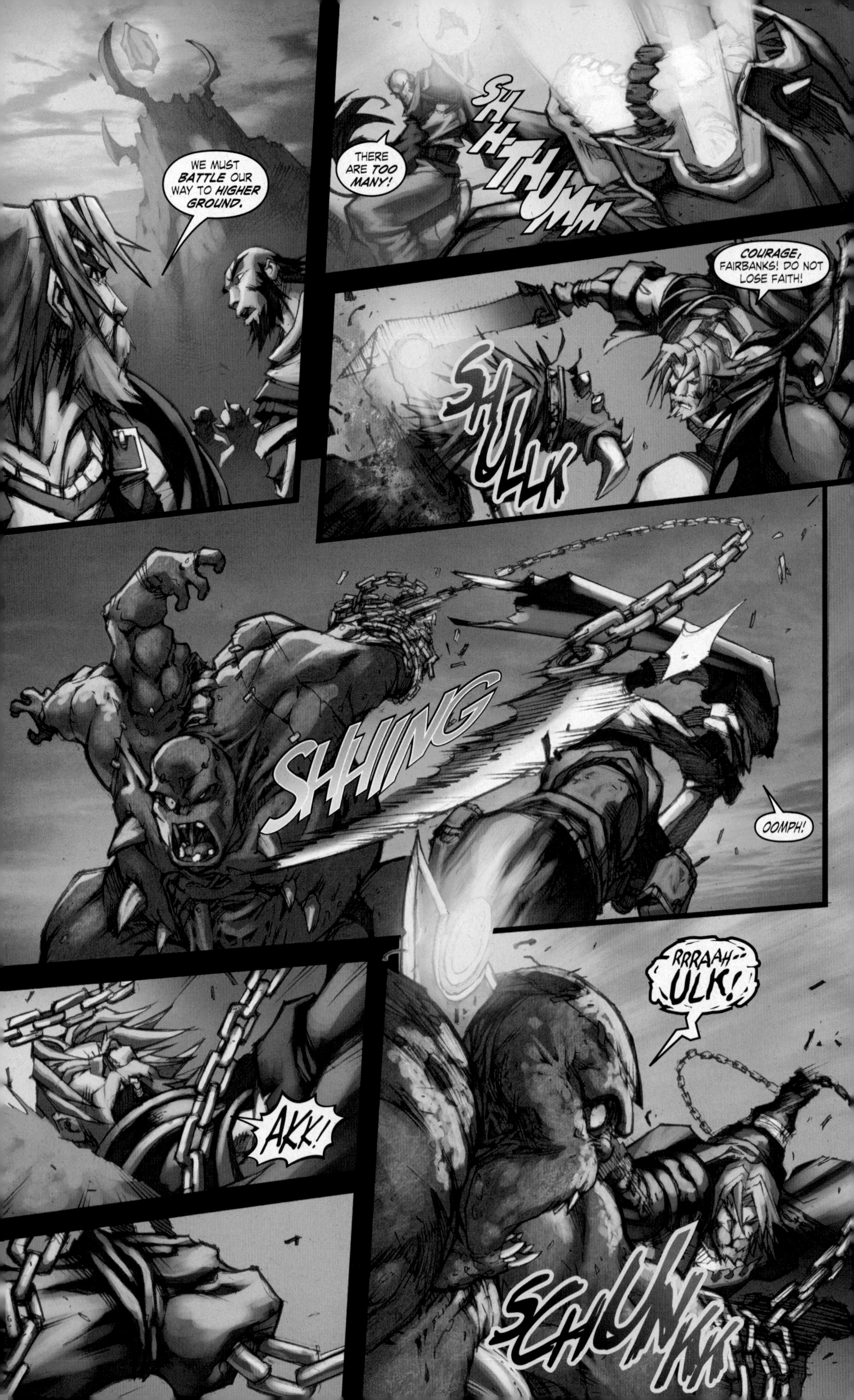
WE MUST BATTLE OUR WAY TO HIGHER GROUND.
THERE ARE TOO MANY!
SH-THUMM
COURAGE, FAIRBANKS! DO NOT LOSE FAITH!
SHULLK
SHING
OOMPH!
RRRAAH-ULK!
AKK!
SCHUNK

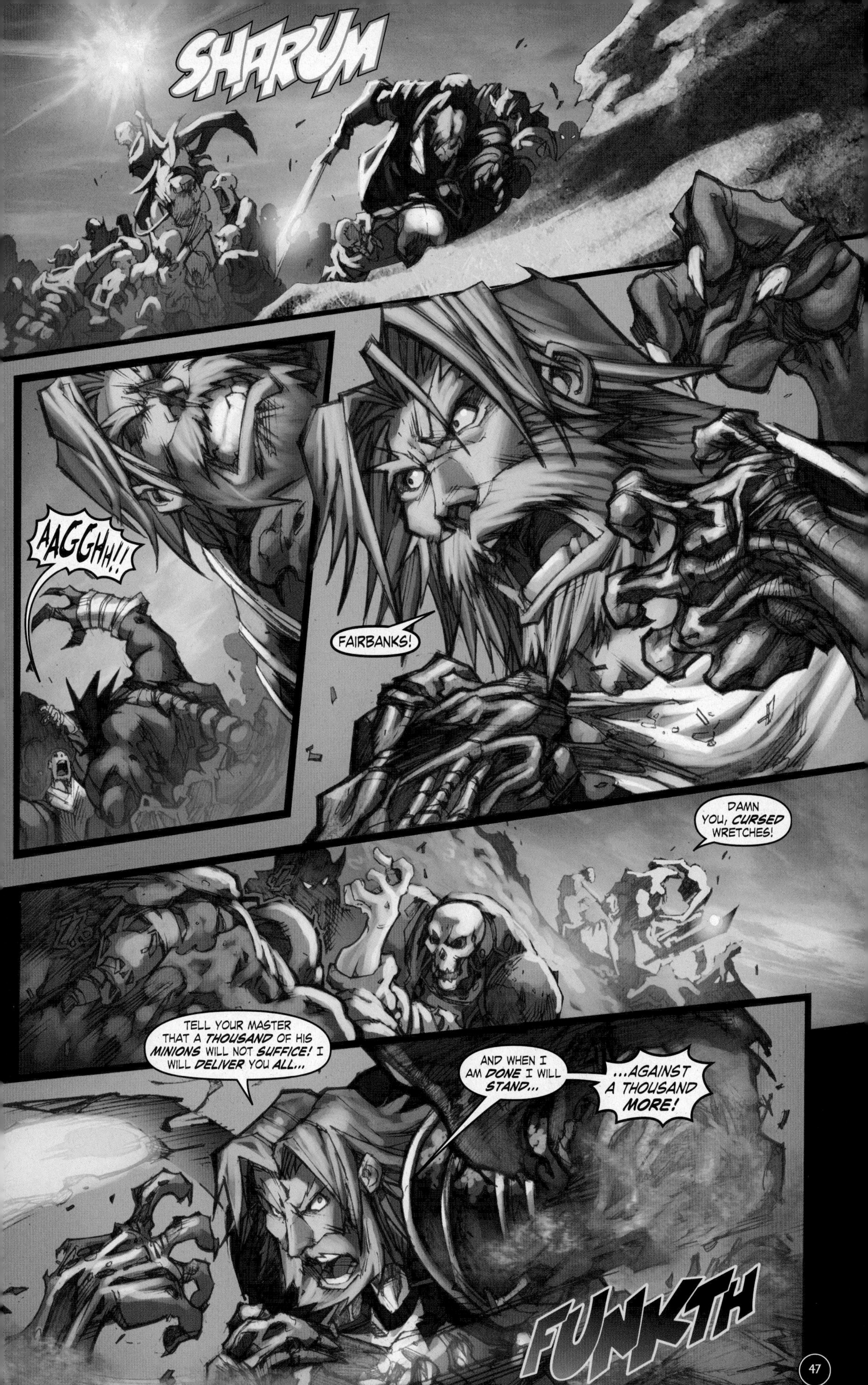
SHARUM
AAGGHH!!
FAIRBANKS!
DAMN YOU, CURSED WRETCHES!
TELL YOUR MASTER THAT A THOUSAND OF HIS MINIONS WILL NOT SUFFICE! I WILL DELIVER YOU ALL...
AND WHEN I AM DONE I WILL STAND...
...AGAINST A THOUSAND MORE!
FUNKTH

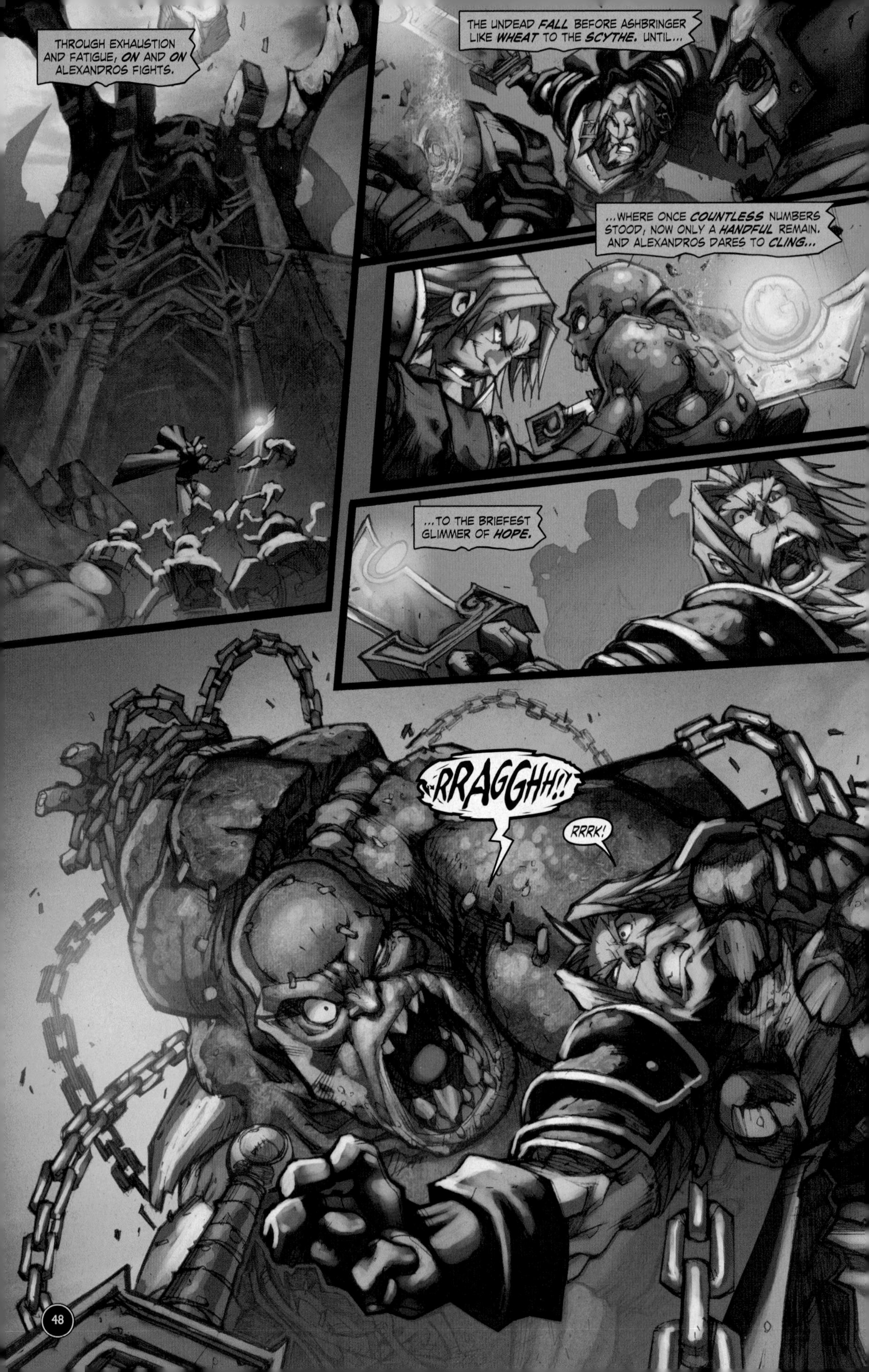
THROUGH EXHAUSTION AND FATIGUE, ON AND ON ALEXANDROS FIGHTS.
THE UNDEAD FALL BEFORE ASHBRINGER LIKE WHEAT TO THE SCYTHE. UNTIL...
...WHERE ONCE COUNTLESS NUMBERS STOOD, NOW ONLY A HANDFUL REMAIN. AND ALEXANDROS DARES TO CLING...
...TO THE BRIEFEST GLIMMER OF HOPE.
RRAGGHH!!
RRRK!

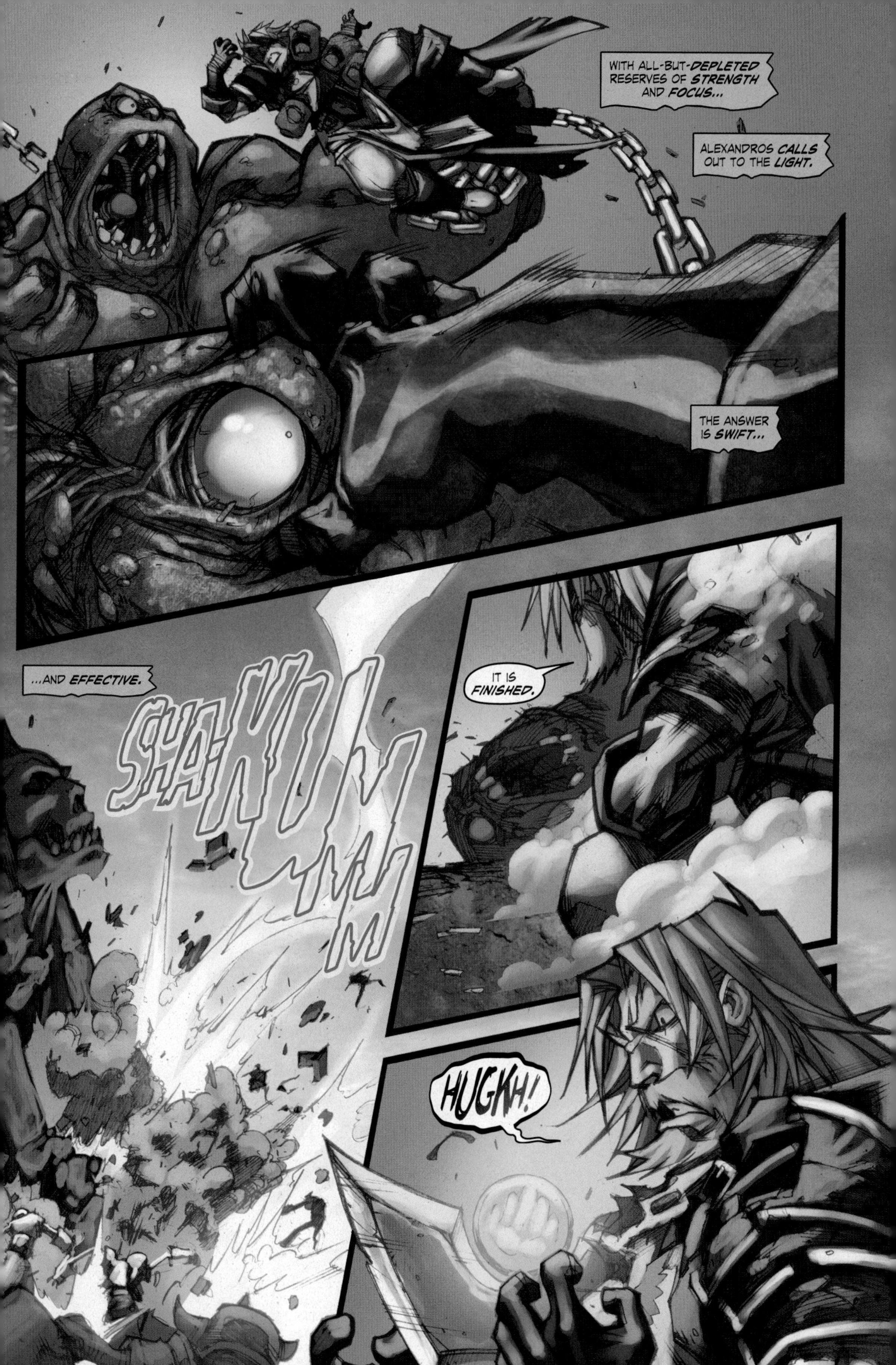

WITH ALL-BUT-DEPLETED RESERVES OF STRENGTH AND FOCUS...
ALEXANDROS CALLS OUT TO THE LIGHT.
THE ANSWER IS SWIFT...
...AND EFFECTIVE.
SHA-KOOMMM
IT IS FINISHED.
HUGKH!

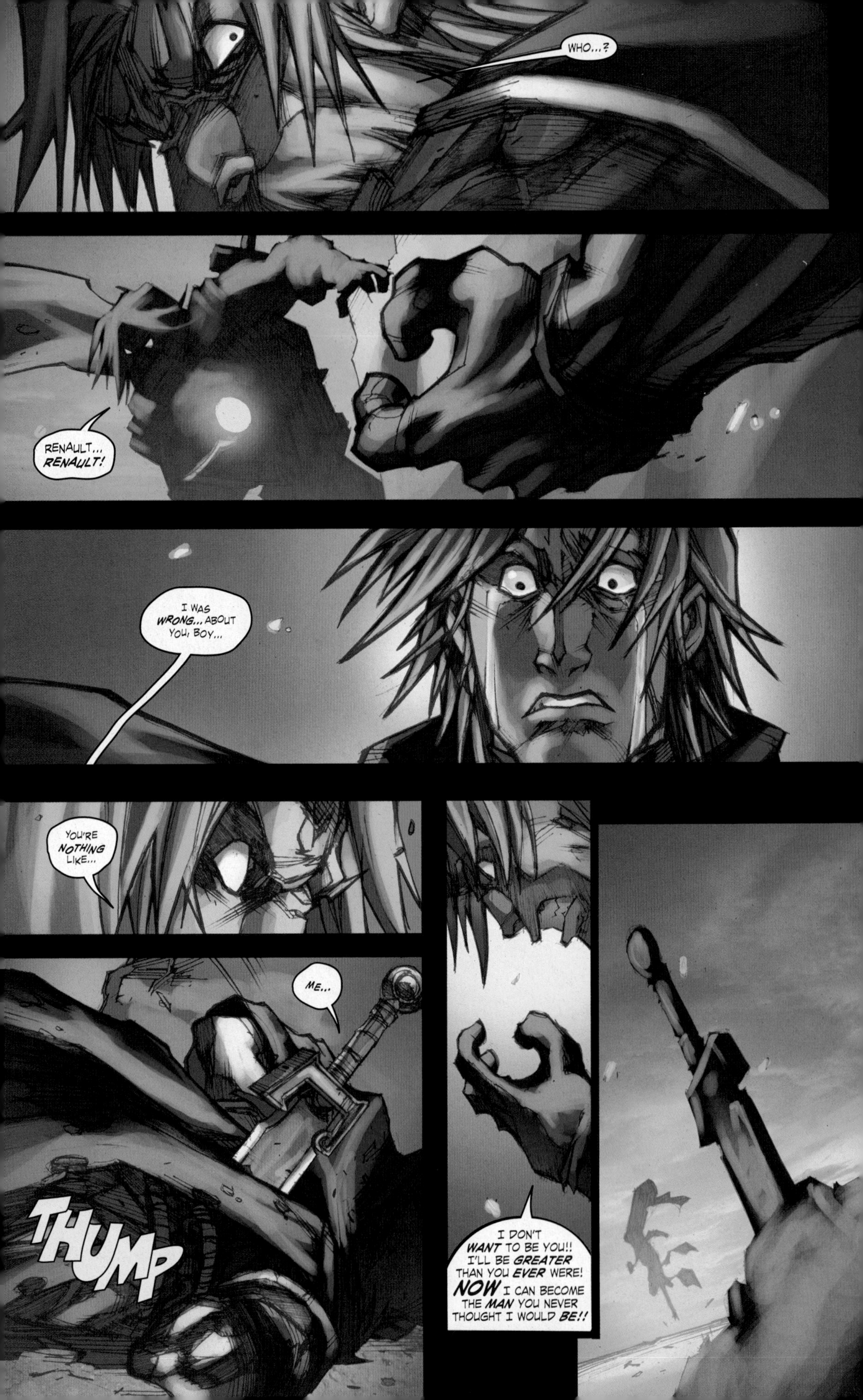
WHO...?
RENAULT... RENAULT!
I WAS WRONG... ABOUT YOU, BOY...
YOU'RE NOTHING LIKE...
ME...
THUMP
I DON'T WANT TO BE YOU!! I'LL BE GREATER THAN YOU EVER WERE! NOW I CAN BECOME THE MAN YOU NEVER THOUGHT I WOULD BE!!

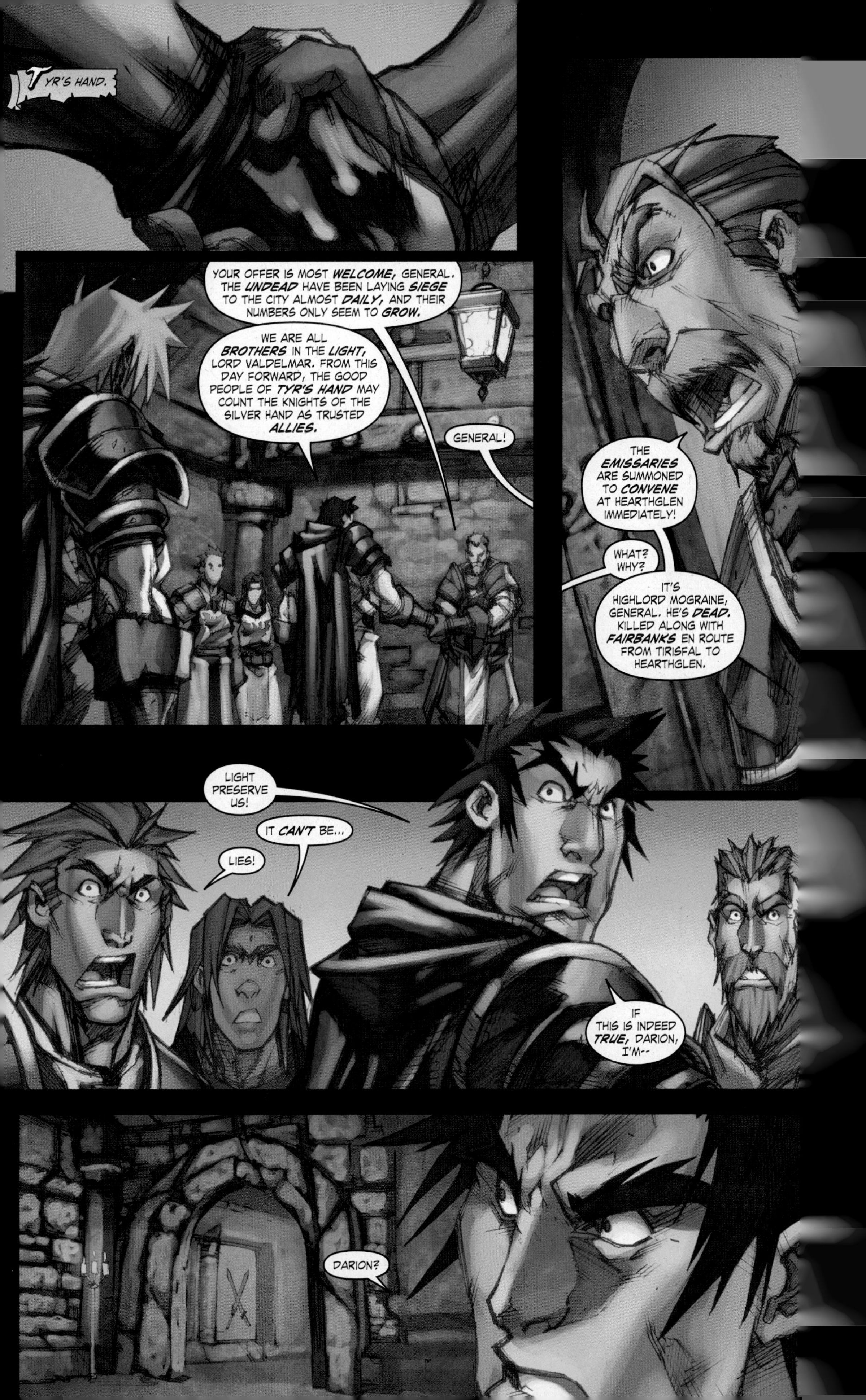
TYR'S HAND.
YOUR OFFER IS MOST WELCOME, GENERAL. THE UNDEAD HAVE BEEN LAYING SIEGE TO THE CITY ALMOST DAILY, AND THEIR NUMBERS ONLY SEEM TO GROW.
WE ARE ALL BROTHERS IN THE LIGHT, LORD VALDELMAR. FROM THIS DAY FORWARD, THE GOOD PEOPLE OF TYR'S HAND MAY COUNT THE KNIGHTS OF THE SILVER HAND AS TRUSTED ALLIES.
GENERAL!
THE EMISSARIES ARE SUMMONED TO CONVENE AT HEARTHGLEN IMMEDIATELY!
WHAT? WHY?
IT'S HIGHLORD MOGRAINE, GENERAL. HE'S DEAD. KILLED ALONG WITH FAIRBANKS EN ROUTE FROM TIRISFAL TO HEARTHGLEN.
LIGHT PRESERVE US!
IT CAN'T BE...
LIES!
IF THIS IS INDEED TRUE, DARION, I'M--
DARION?

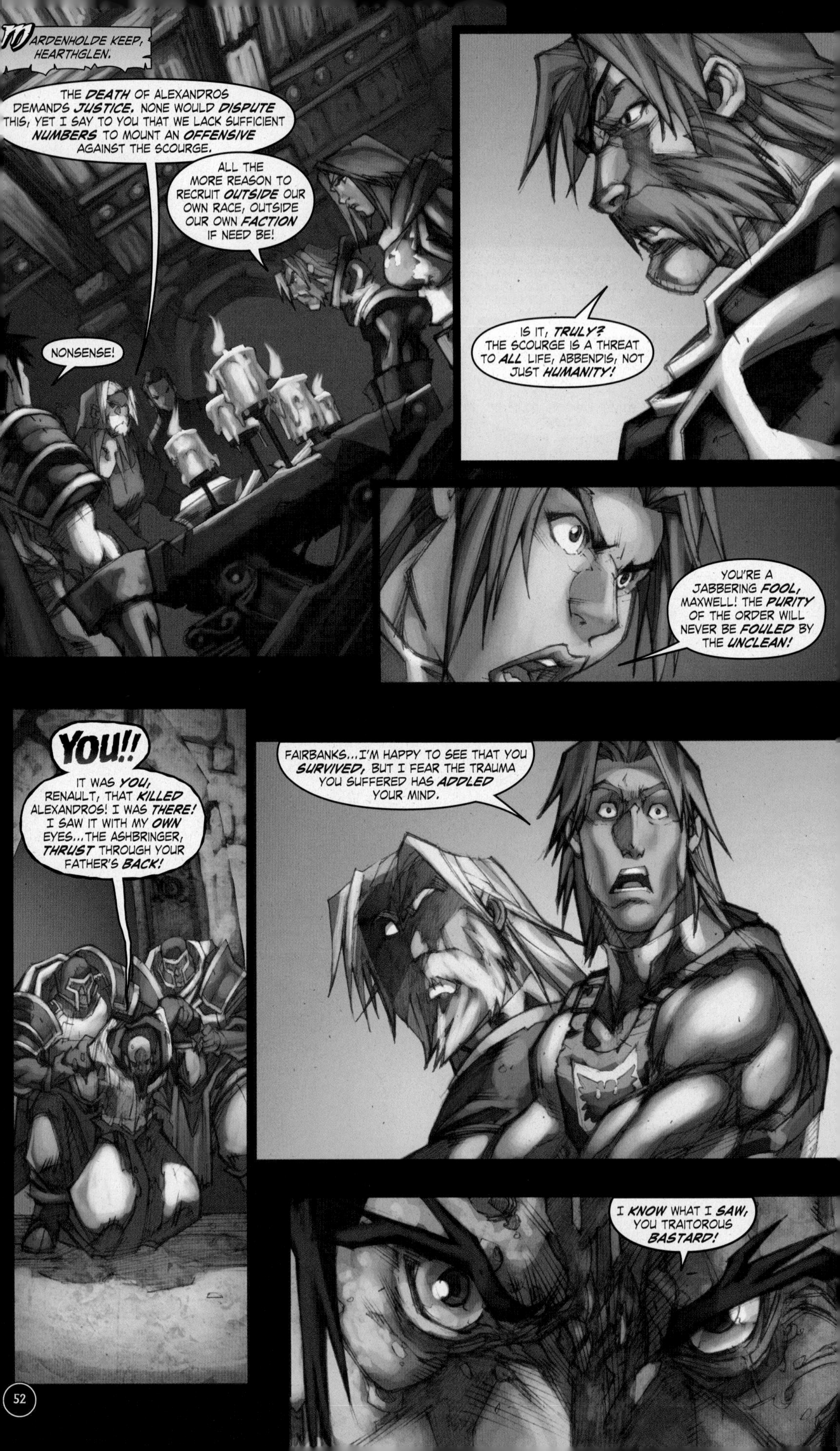
WARDENHOLDE KEEP, HEARTHGLEN.
THE DEATH OF ALEXANDROS DEMANDS JUSTICE. NONE WOULD DISPUTE THIS, YET I SAY TO YOU THAT WE LACK SUFFICIENT NUMBERS TO MOUNT AN OFFENSIVE AGAINST THE SCOURGE.
ALL THE MORE REASON TO RECRUIT OUTSIDE OUR OWN RACE, OUTSIDE OUR OWN FACTION IF NEED BE!
NONSENSE!
IS IT, TRULY? THE SCOURGE IS A THREAT TO ALL LIFE, ABBENDIS, NOT JUST HUMANITY!
YOU'RE A JABBERING FOOL, MAXWELL! THE PURITY OF THE ORDER WILL NEVER BE FOULED BY THE UNCLEAN!
YOU!!
IT WAS YOU, RENAULT, THAT KILLED ALEXANDROS! I WAS THERE! I SAW IT WITH MY OWN EYES...THE ASHBRINGER, THRUST THROUGH YOUR FATHER'S BACK!
FAIRBANKS...I'M HAPPY TO SEE THAT YOU SURVIVED, BUT I FEAR THE TRAUMA YOU SUFFERED HAS ADDLED YOUR MIND.
I KNOW WHAT I SAW, YOU TRAITOROUS BASTARD!

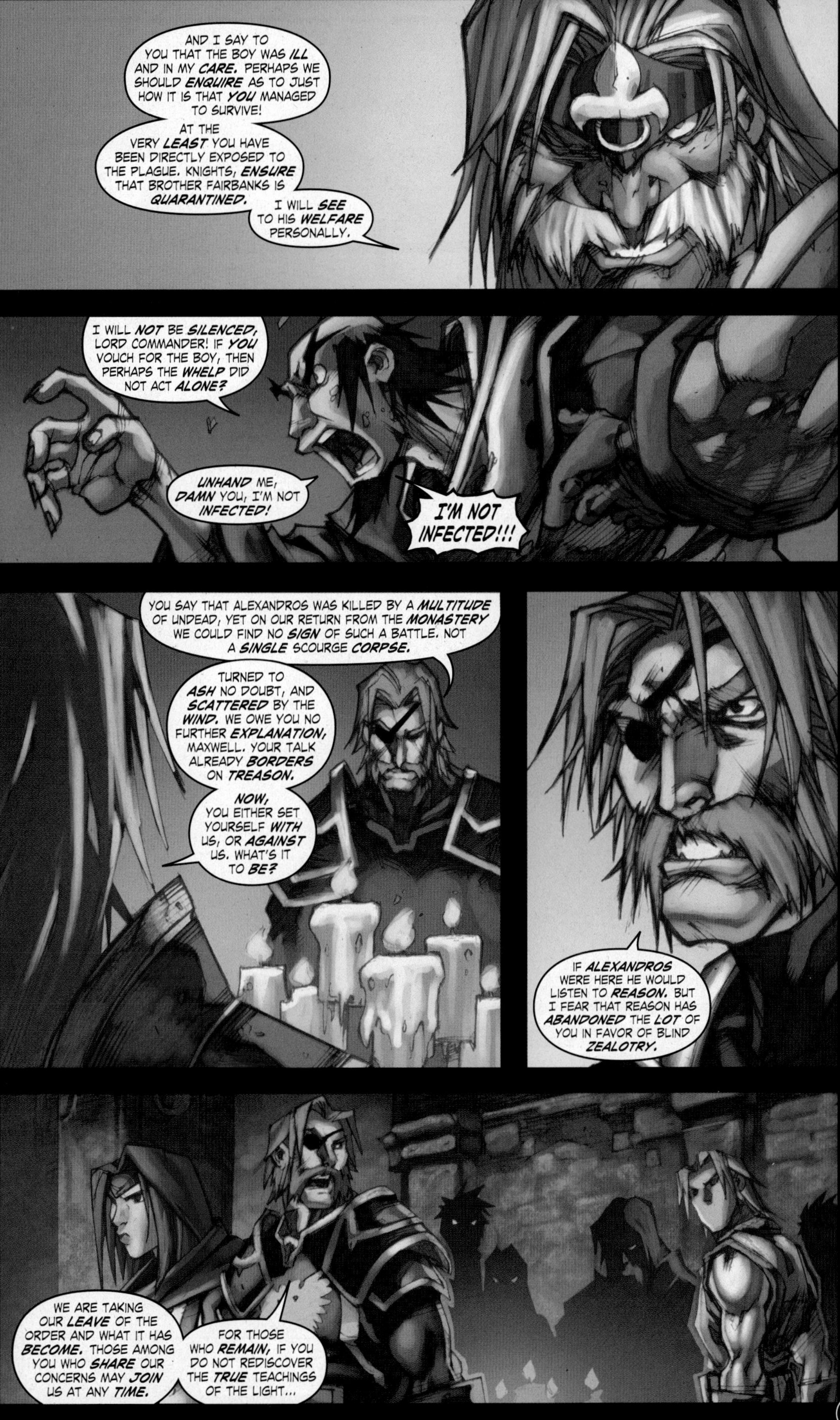

AND I SAY TO YOU THAT THE BOY WAS ILL AND IN MY CARE. PERHAPS WE SHOULD ENQUIRE AS TO JUST HOW IT IS THAT YOU MANAGED TO SURVIVE!
AT THE VERY LEAST YOU HAVE BEEN DIRECTLY EXPOSED TO THE PLAGUE. KNIGHTS, ENSURE THAT BROTHER FAIRBANKS IS QUARANTINED.
I WILL SEE TO HIS WELFARE PERSONALLY.
I WILL NOT BE SILENCED, LORD COMMANDER! IF YOU VOUCH FOR THE BOY, THEN PERHAPS THE WHELP DID NOT ACT ALONE?
UNHAND ME, DAMN YOU, I'M NOT INFECTED!
I'M NOT INFECTED!!!
YOU SAY THAT ALEXANDROS WAS KILLED BY A MULTITUDE OF UNDEAD, YET ON OUR RETURN FROM THE MONASTERY WE COULD FIND NO SIGN OF SUCH A BATTLE. NOT A SINGLE SCOURGE CORPSE.
TURNED TO ASH NO DOUBT, AND SCATTERED BY THE WIND. WE OWE YOU NO FURTHER EXPLANATION, MAXWELL. YOUR TALK ALREADY BORDERS ON TREASON.
NOW, YOU EITHER SET YOURSELF WITH US, OR AGAINST US. WHAT'S IT TO BE?
IF ALEXANDROS WERE HERE HE WOULD LISTEN TO REASON. BUT I FEAR THAT REASON HAS ABANDONED THE LOT OF YOU IN FAVOR OF BLIND ZEALOTRY.
WE ARE TAKING OUR LEAVE OF THE ORDER AND WHAT IT HAS BECOME. THOSE AMONG YOU WHO SHARE OUR CONCERNS MAY JOIN US AT ANY TIME.
FOR THOSE WHO REMAIN, IF YOU DO NOT REDISCOVER THE TRUE TEACHINGS OF THE LIGHT...

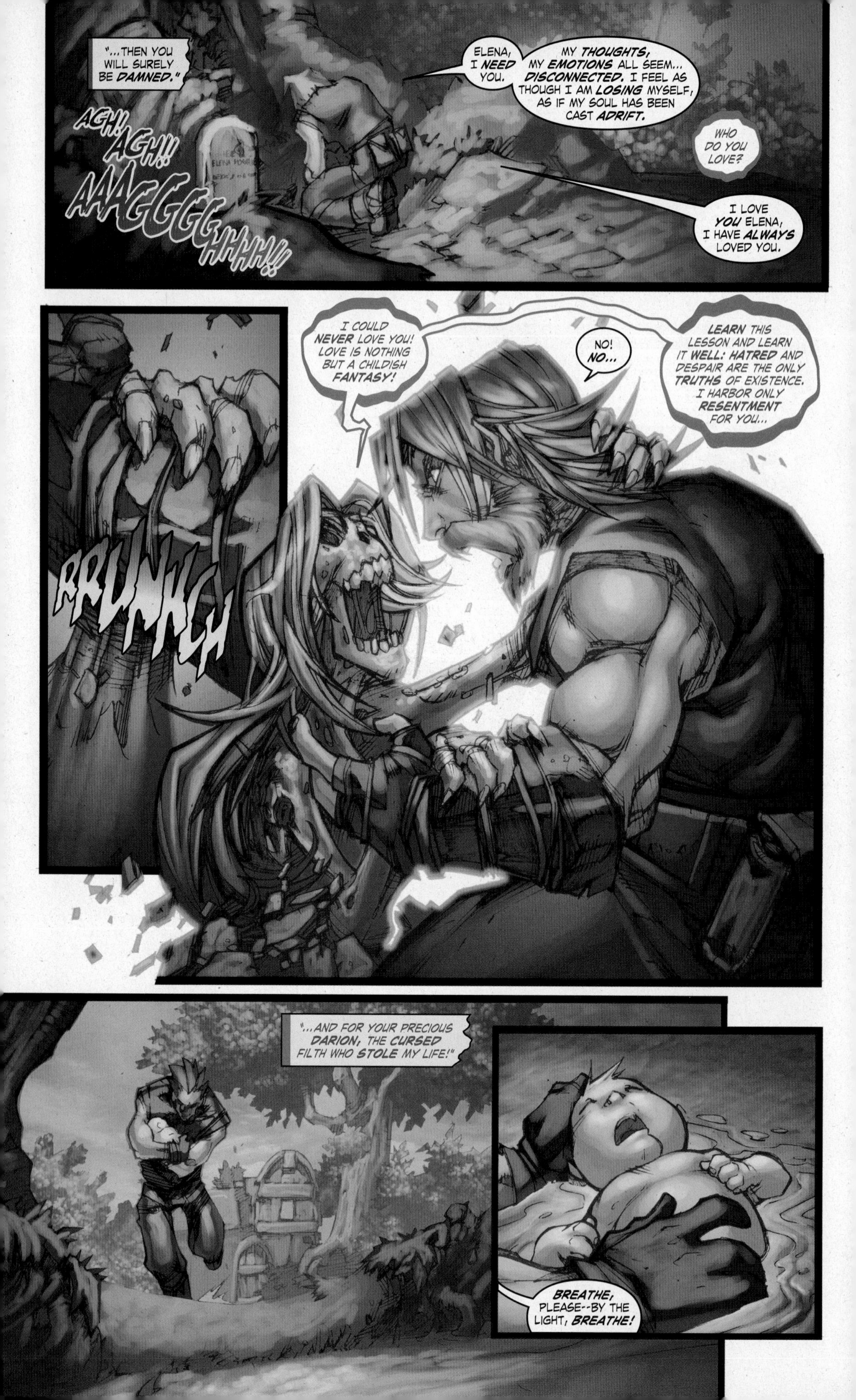
"...THEN YOU WILL SURELY BE DAMNED."
ELENA, I NEED YOU.
MY THOUGHTS, MY EMOTIONS ALL SEEM... DISCONNECTED. I FEEL AS THOUGH I AM LOSING MYSELF, AS IF MY SOUL HAS BEEN CAST ADRIFT.
AGH! AGH!! AAAGGGGHHHH!!
WHO DO YOU LOVE?
I LOVE YOU ELENA, I HAVE ALWAYS LOVED YOU.
I COULD NEVER LOVE YOU! LOVE IS NOTHING BUT A CHILDISH FANTASY!
NO! NO...
LEARN THIS LESSON AND LEARN IT WELL: HATRED AND DESPAIR ARE THE ONLY TRUTHS OF EXISTENCE. I HARBOR ONLY RESENTMENT FOR YOU...
RRUNKCH
"...AND FOR YOUR PRECIOUS DARION, THE CURSED FILTH WHO STOLE MY LIFE!"
BREATHE, PLEASE--BY THE LIGHT, BREATHE!

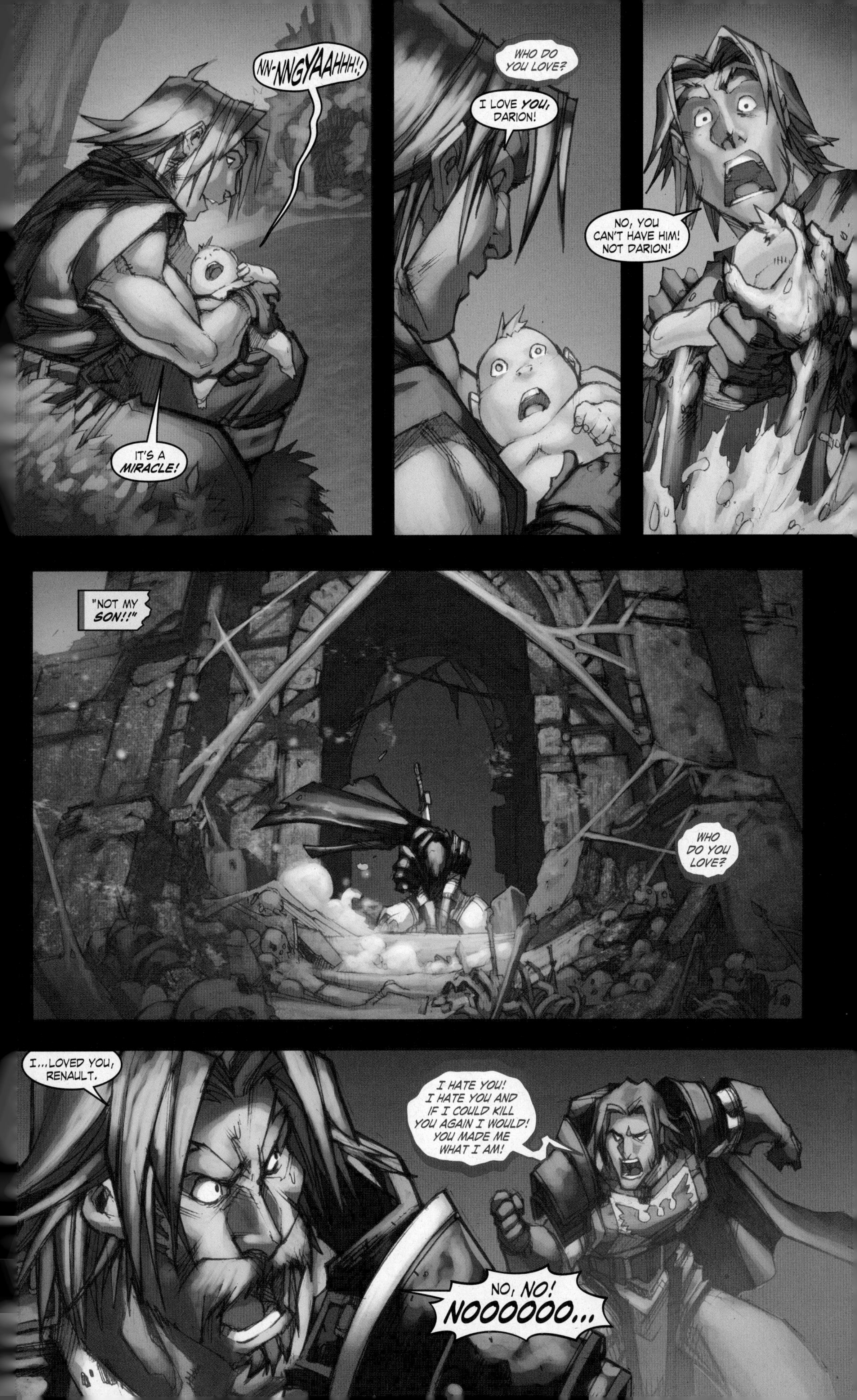
NN-NNGYAAHHH!!
IT'S A MIRACLE!
WHO DO YOU LOVE?
I LOVE YOU, DARION!
NO, YOU CAN'T HAVE HIM! NOT DARION!
"NOT MY SON!!"
WHO DO YOU LOVE?
I...LOVED YOU, RENAULT.
I HATE YOU! I HATE YOU AND IF I COULD KILL YOU AGAIN I WOULD! YOU MADE ME WHAT I AM!
NO, NO! NOOOOOO...

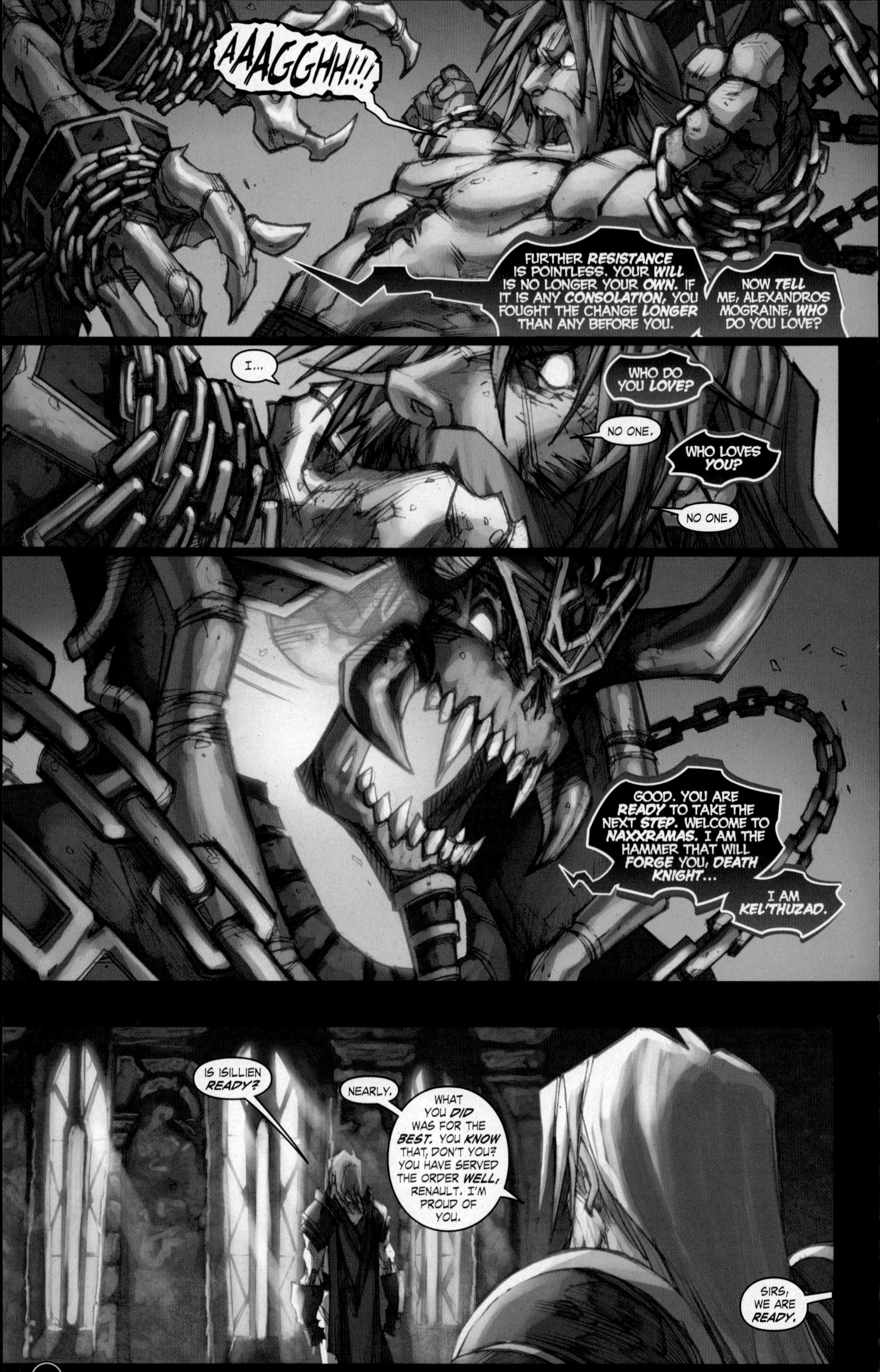
AAAGGHH!!!
FURTHER RESISTANCE IS POINTLESS. YOUR WILL IS NO LONGER YOUR OWN. IF IT IS ANY CONSOLATION, YOU FOUGHT THE CHANGE LONGER THAN ANY BEFORE YOU.
NOW TELL ME, ALEXANDROS MOGRAINE, WHO DO YOU LOVE?
I...
WHO DO YOU LOVE?
NO ONE.
WHO LOVES YOU?
NO ONE.
GOOD. YOU ARE READY TO TAKE THE NEXT STEP. WELCOME TO NAXXRAMAS. I AM THE HAMMER THAT WILL FORGE YOU, DEATH KNIGHT...
I AM KEL'THUZAD.
IS ISILLIEN READY?
NEARLY.
WHAT YOU DID WAS FOR THE BEST. YOU KNOW THAT, DON'T YOU? YOU HAVE SERVED THE ORDER WELL, RENAULT. I'M PROUD OF YOU.
SIRS, WE ARE READY.

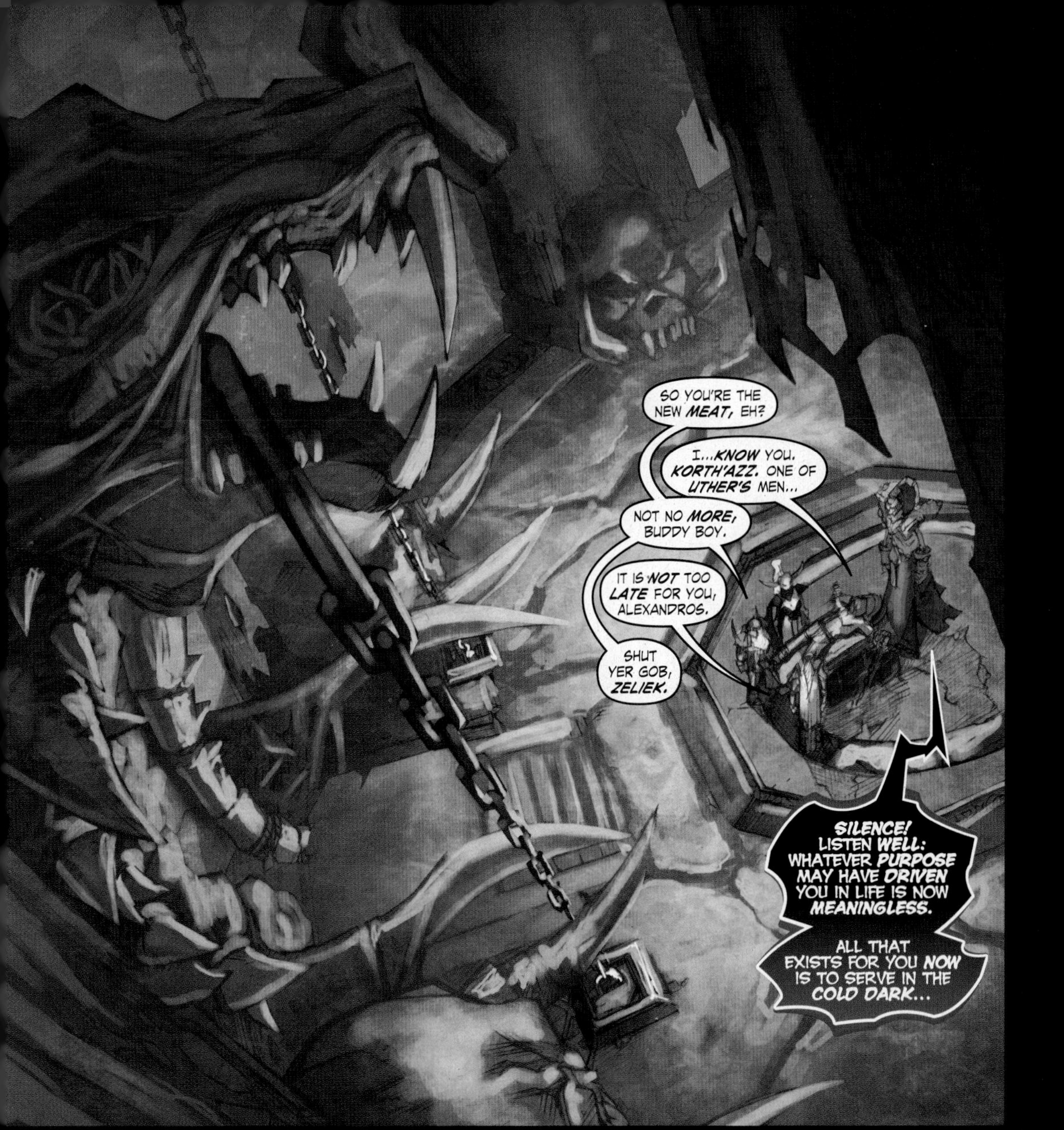

SO YOU'RE THE NEW **MEAT**, EH?
I...**KNOW** YOU. **KORTH'AZZ.** ONE OF **UTHER'S** MEN...
NOT NO **MORE**, BUDDY BOY.
IT IS **NOT** TOO **LATE** FOR YOU, ALEXANDROS.
SHUT YER GOB, **ZELIEK.**
SILENCE! LISTEN **WELL:** WHATEVER **PURPOSE** MAY HAVE **DRIVEN** YOU IN LIFE IS NOW **MEANINGLESS.**
ALL THAT EXISTS FOR YOU **NOW** IS TO SERVE IN THE **COLD DARK...**

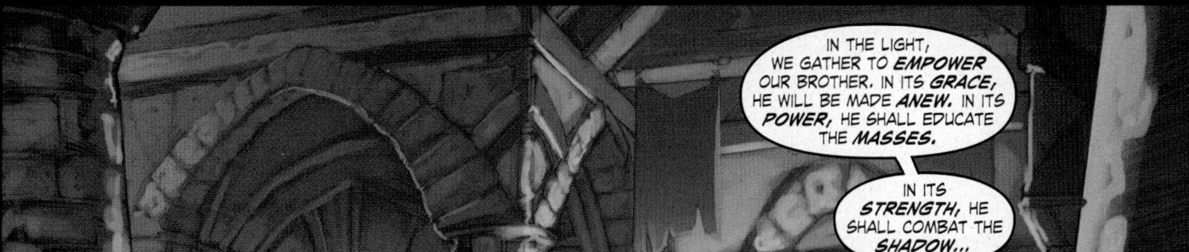

IN THE LIGHT, WE GATHER TO **EMPOWER** OUR BROTHER. IN ITS **GRACE,** HE WILL BE MADE **ANEW.** IN ITS **POWER,** HE SHALL EDUCATE THE **MASSES.**
IN ITS **STRENGTH,** HE SHALL COMBAT THE **SHADOW...**

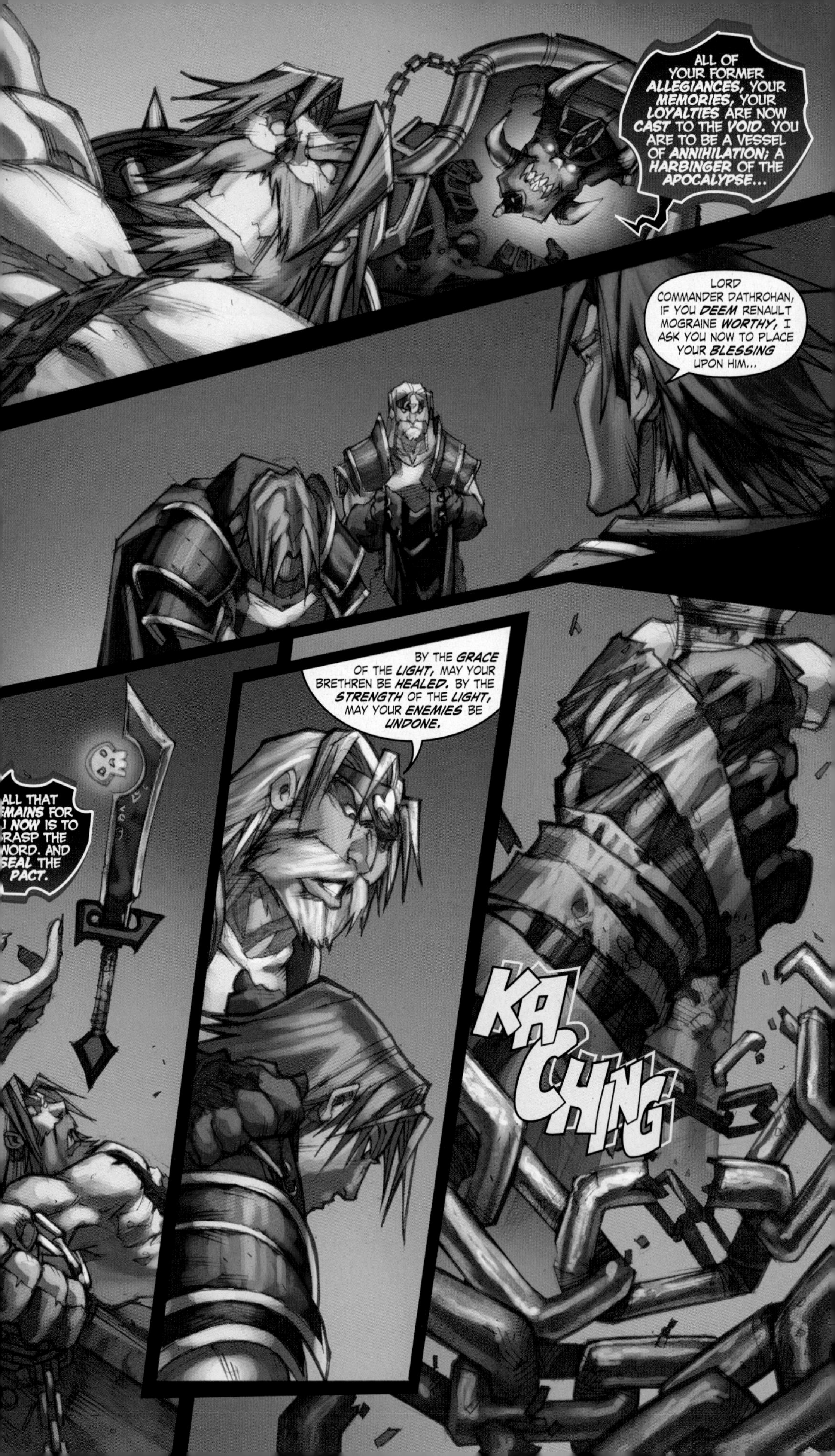
ALL OF YOUR FORMER ALLEGIANCES, YOUR MEMORIES, YOUR LOYALTIES ARE NOW CAST TO THE VOID. YOU ARE TO BE A VESSEL OF ANNIHILATION; A HARBINGER OF THE APOCALYPSE...
LORD COMMANDER DATHROHAN, IF YOU DEEM RENAULT MOGRAINE WORTHY, I ASK YOU NOW TO PLACE YOUR BLESSING UPON HIM...
BY THE GRACE OF THE LIGHT, MAY YOUR BRETHREN BE HEALED. BY THE STRENGTH OF THE LIGHT, MAY YOUR ENEMIES BE UNDONE.
ALL THAT EMAINS FOR U NOW IS TO RASP THE WORD. AND SEAL THE PACT.
KA CHING

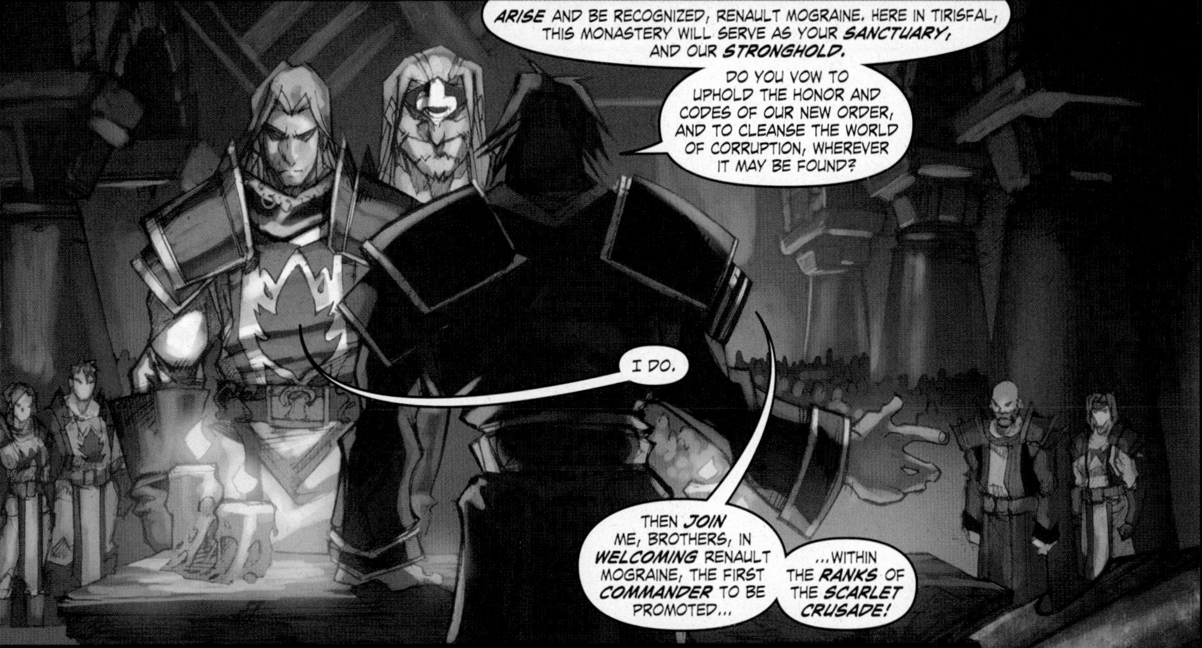
ARISE AND BE RECOGNIZED, RENAULT MOGRAINE. HERE IN TIRISFAL, THIS MONASTERY WILL SERVE AS YOUR SANCTUARY, AND OUR STRONGHOLD.
DO YOU VOW TO UPHOLD THE HONOR AND CODES OF OUR NEW ORDER, AND TO CLEANSE THE WORLD OF CORRUPTION, WHEREVER IT MAY BE FOUND?
I DO.
THEN JOIN ME, BROTHERS, IN WELCOMING RENAULT MOGRAINE, THE FIRST COMMANDER TO BE PROMOTED...
...WITHIN THE RANKS OF THE SCARLET CRUSADE!

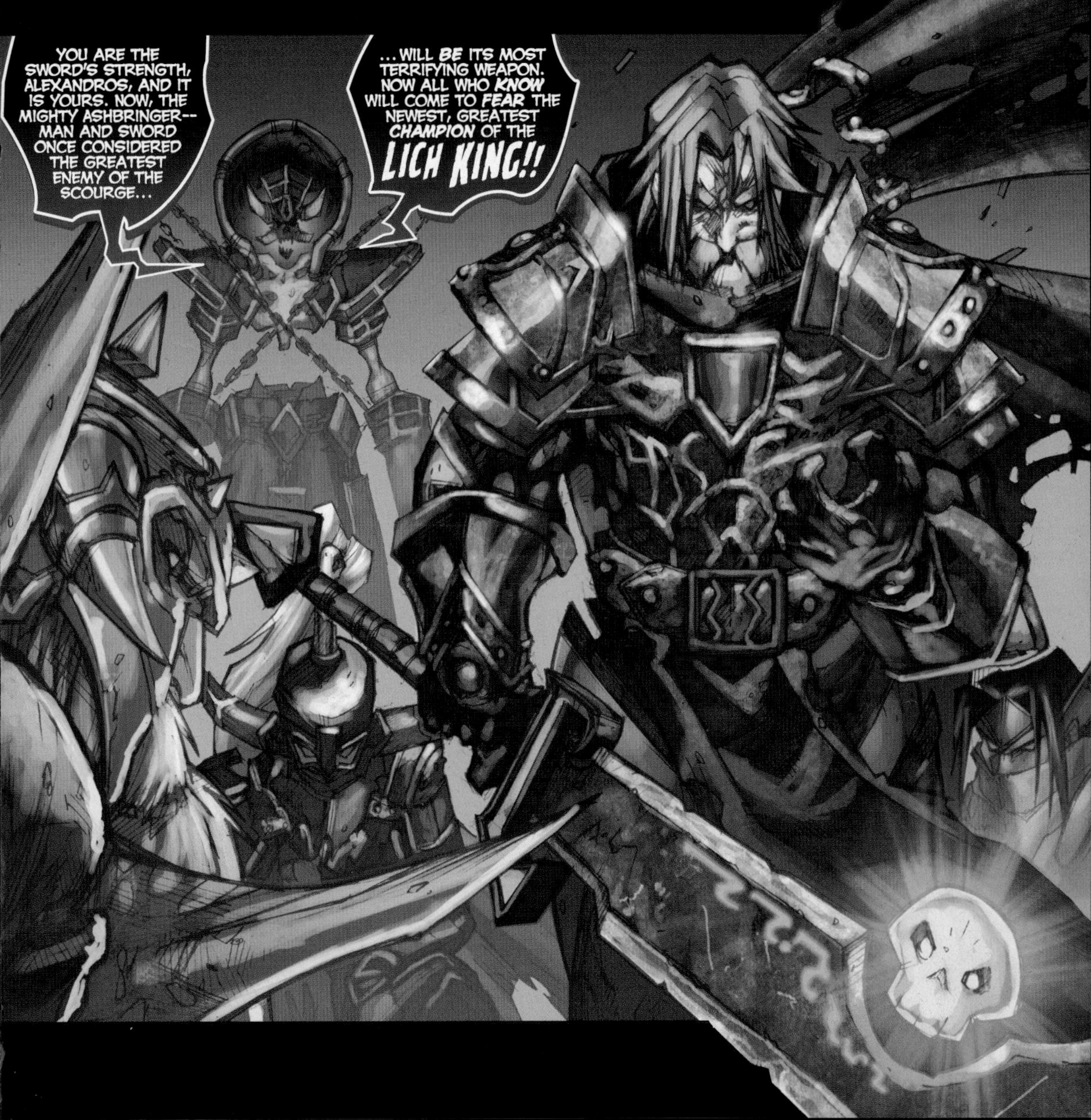
YOU ARE THE SWORD'S STRENGTH, ALEXANDROS, AND IT IS YOURS. NOW, THE MIGHTY ASHBRINGER--MAN AND SWORD ONCE CONSIDERED THE GREATEST ENEMY OF THE SCOURGE...
...WILL BE ITS MOST TERRIFYING WEAPON. NOW ALL WHO KNOW WILL COME TO FEAR THE NEWEST, GREATEST CHAMPION OF THE LICH KING!!

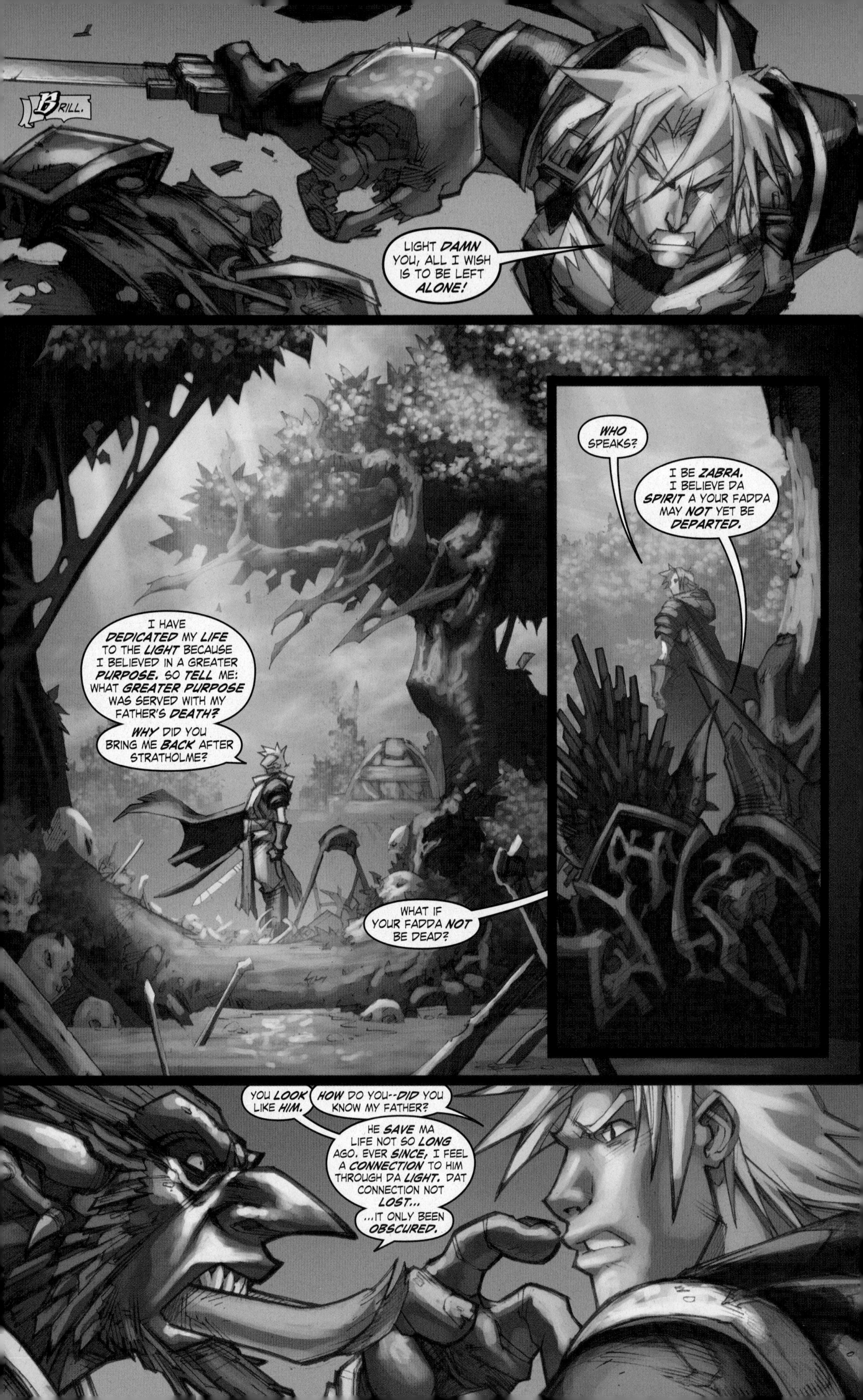

BRILL.
LIGHT DAMN YOU, ALL I WISH IS TO BE LEFT ALONE!
I HAVE DEDICATED MY LIFE TO THE LIGHT BECAUSE I BELIEVED IN A GREATER PURPOSE. SO TELL ME: WHAT GREATER PURPOSE WAS SERVED WITH MY FATHER'S DEATH?
WHY DID YOU BRING ME BACK AFTER STRATHOLME?
WHAT IF YOUR FADDA NOT BE DEAD?
WHO SPEAKS?
I BE ZABRA. I BELIEVE DA SPIRIT A YOUR FADDA MAY NOT YET BE DEPARTED.
YOU LOOK LIKE HIM.
HOW DO YOU--DID YOU KNOW MY FATHER?
HE SAVE MA LIFE NOT SO LONG AGO. EVER SINCE, I FEEL A CONNECTION TO HIM THROUGH DA LIGHT. DAT CONNECTION NOT LOST...
...IT ONLY BEEN OBSCURED.

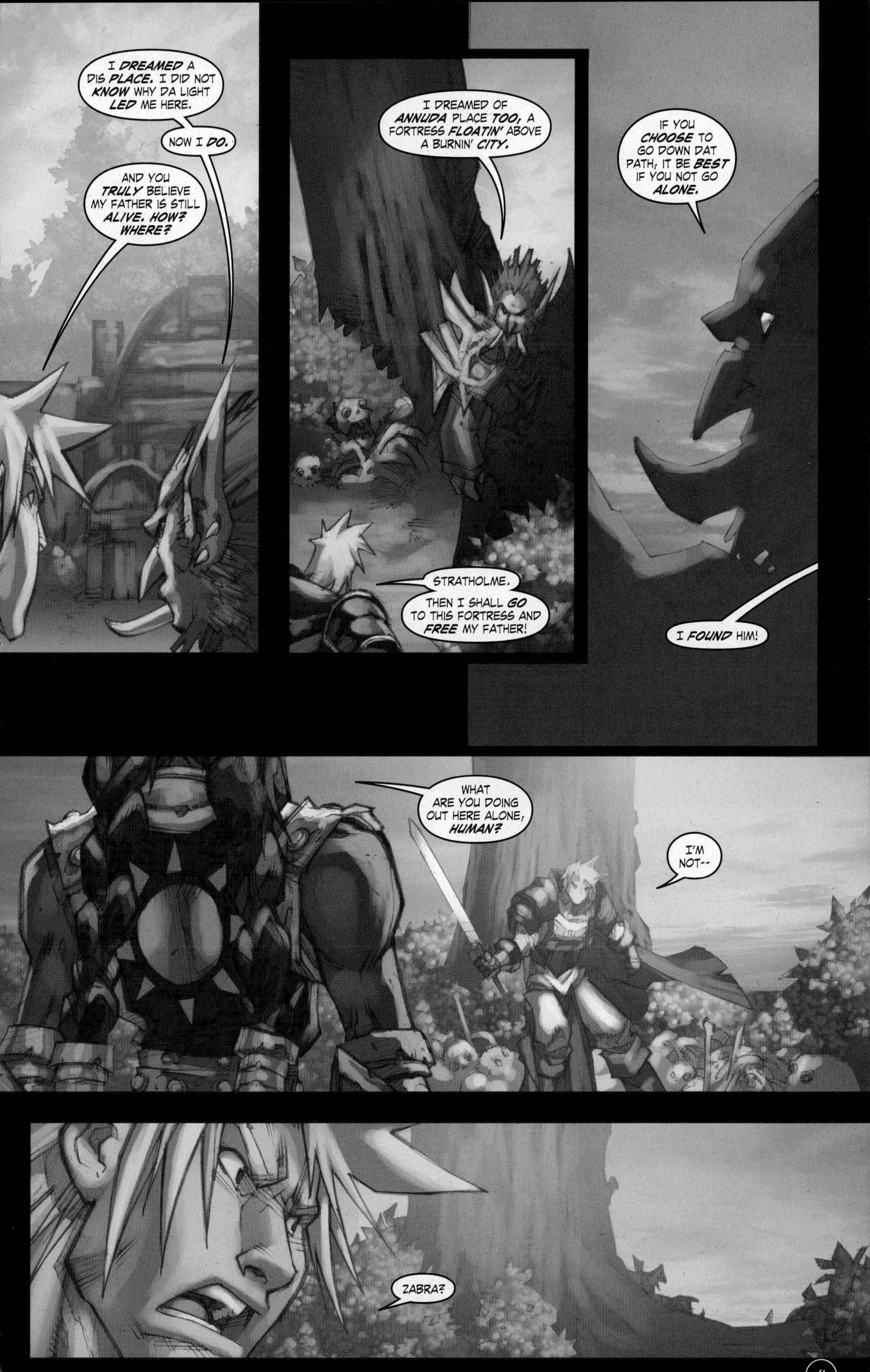
I DREAMED A DIS PLACE. I DID NOT KNOW WHY DA LIGHT LED ME HERE.
NOW I DO.
AND YOU TRULY BELIEVE MY FATHER IS STILL ALIVE. HOW? WHERE?
I DREAMED OF ANNUDA PLACE TOO, A FORTRESS FLOATIN' ABOVE A BURNIN' CITY.
STRATHOLME.
THEN I SHALL GO TO THIS FORTRESS AND FREE MY FATHER!
IF YOU CHOOSE TO GO DOWN DAT PATH, IT BE BEST IF YOU NOT GO ALONE.
I FOUND HIM!
WHAT ARE YOU DOING OUT HERE ALONE, HUMAN?
I'M NOT--
ZABRA?

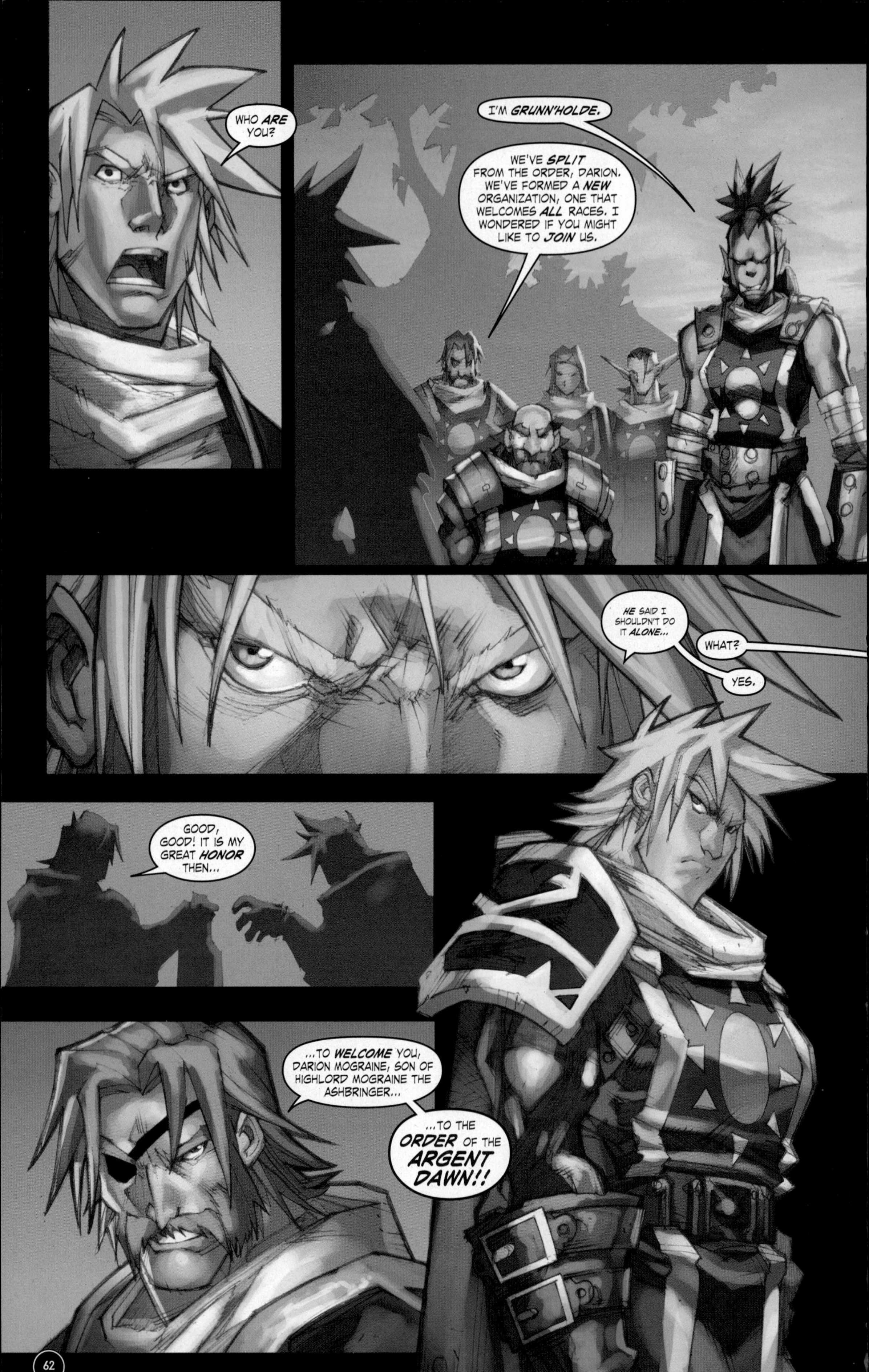

WHO ARE YOU?
I'M GRUNN'HOLDE.
WE'VE SPLIT FROM THE ORDER, DARION. WE'VE FORMED A NEW ORGANIZATION, ONE THAT WELCOMES ALL RACES. I WONDERED IF YOU MIGHT LIKE TO JOIN US.
HE SAID I SHOULDN'T DO IT ALONE...
WHAT?
YES.
GOOD, GOOD! IT IS MY GREAT HONOR THEN...
...TO WELCOME YOU, DARION MOGRAINE, SON OF HIGHLORD MOGRAINE THE ASHBRINGER...
...TO THE ORDER OF THE ARGENT DAWN!!

CHAPTER 3

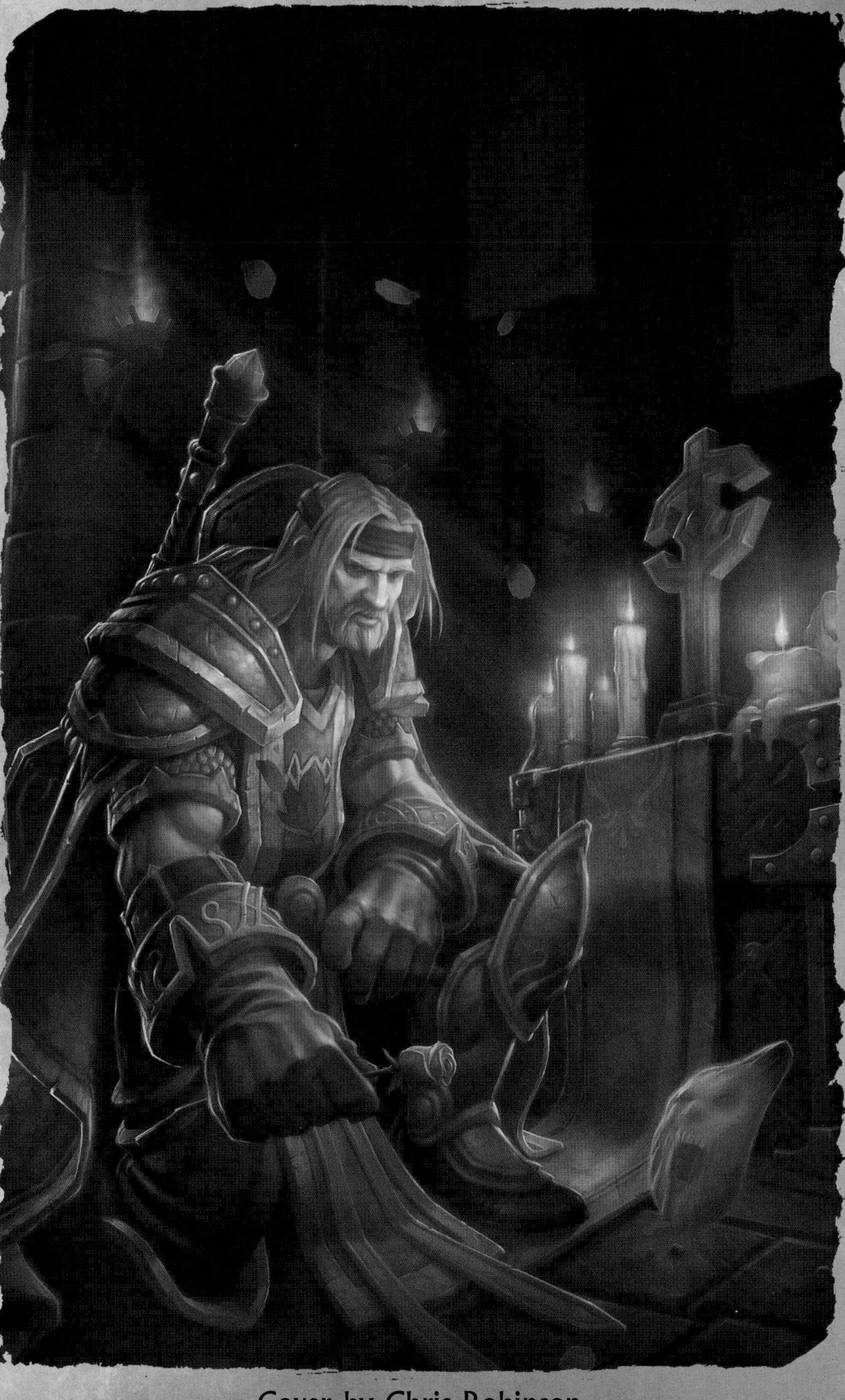

Cover by Chris Robinson

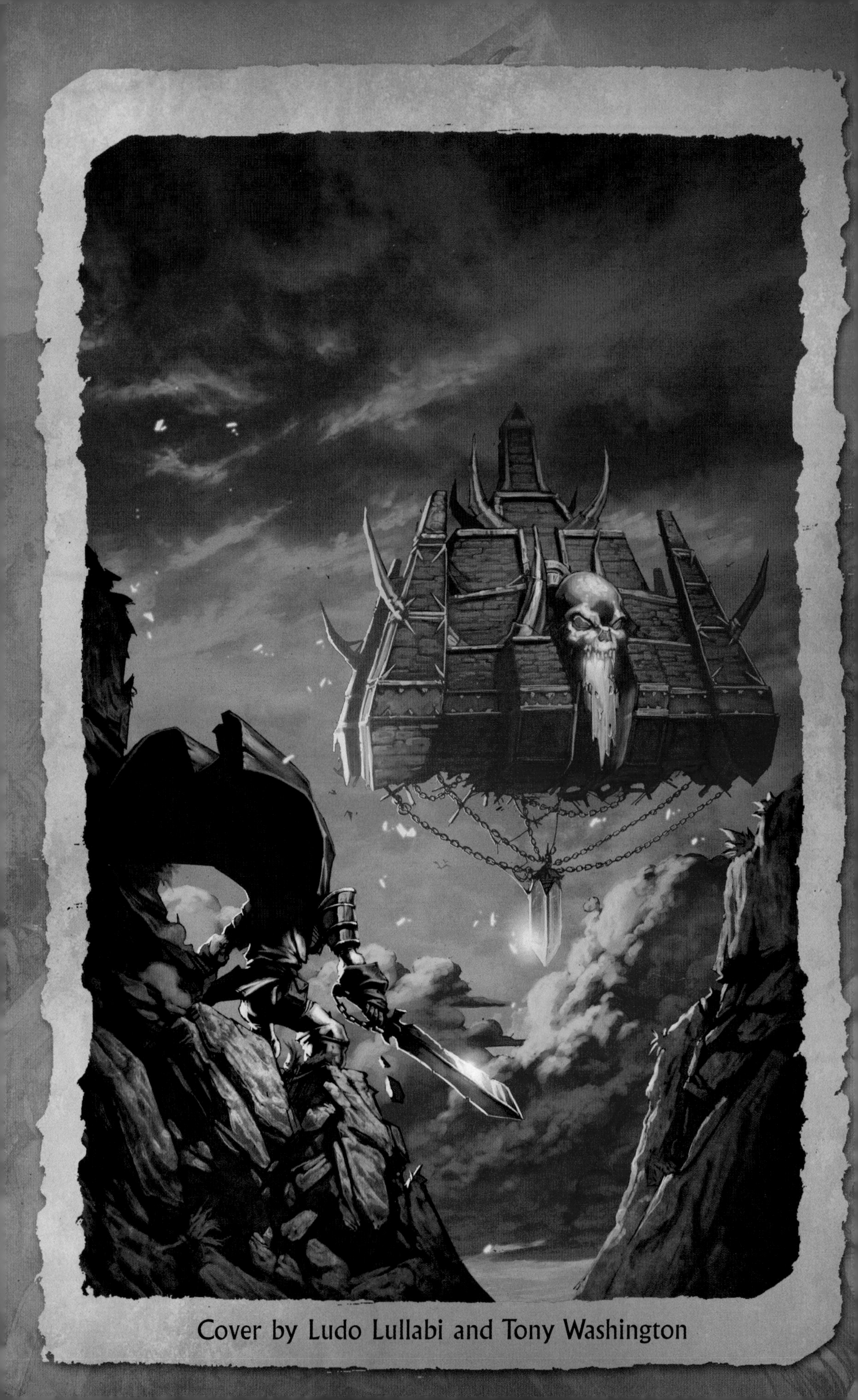

Cover by Ludo Lullabi and Tony Washington

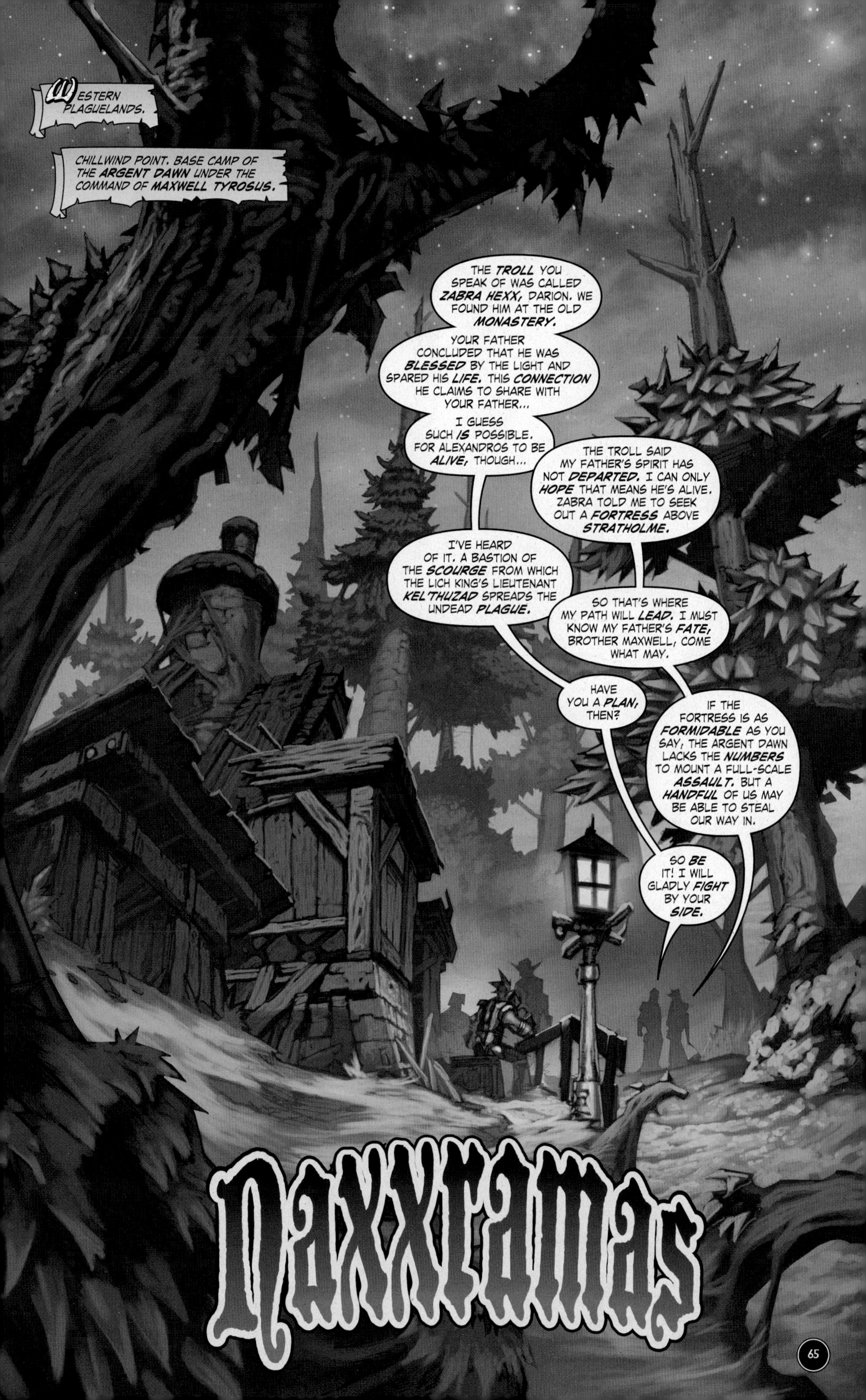
WESTERN PLAGUELANDS.
CHILLWIND POINT. BASE CAMP OF THE ARGENT DAWN UNDER THE COMMAND OF MAXWELL TYROSUS.
THE TROLL YOU SPEAK OF WAS CALLED ZABRA HEXX, DARION. WE FOUND HIM AT THE OLD MONASTERY.
YOUR FATHER CONCLUDED THAT HE WAS BLESSED BY THE LIGHT AND SPARED HIS LIFE. THIS CONNECTION HE CLAIMS TO SHARE WITH YOUR FATHER...
I GUESS SUCH IS POSSIBLE. FOR ALEXANDROS TO BE ALIVE, THOUGH...
THE TROLL SAID MY FATHER'S SPIRIT HAS NOT DEPARTED. I CAN ONLY HOPE THAT MEANS HE'S ALIVE. ZABRA TOLD ME TO SEEK OUT A FORTRESS ABOVE STRATHOLME.
I'VE HEARD OF IT. A BASTION OF THE SCOURGE FROM WHICH THE LICH KING'S LIEUTENANT KEL'THUZAD SPREADS THE UNDEAD PLAGUE.
SO THAT'S WHERE MY PATH WILL LEAD. I MUST KNOW MY FATHER'S FATE, BROTHER MAXWELL, COME WHAT MAY.
HAVE YOU A PLAN, THEN?
IF THE FORTRESS IS AS FORMIDABLE AS YOU SAY, THE ARGENT DAWN LACKS THE NUMBERS TO MOUNT A FULL-SCALE ASSAULT. BUT A HANDFUL OF US MAY BE ABLE TO STEAL OUR WAY IN.
SO BE IT! I WILL GLADLY FIGHT BY YOUR SIDE.
NAXXRAMAS

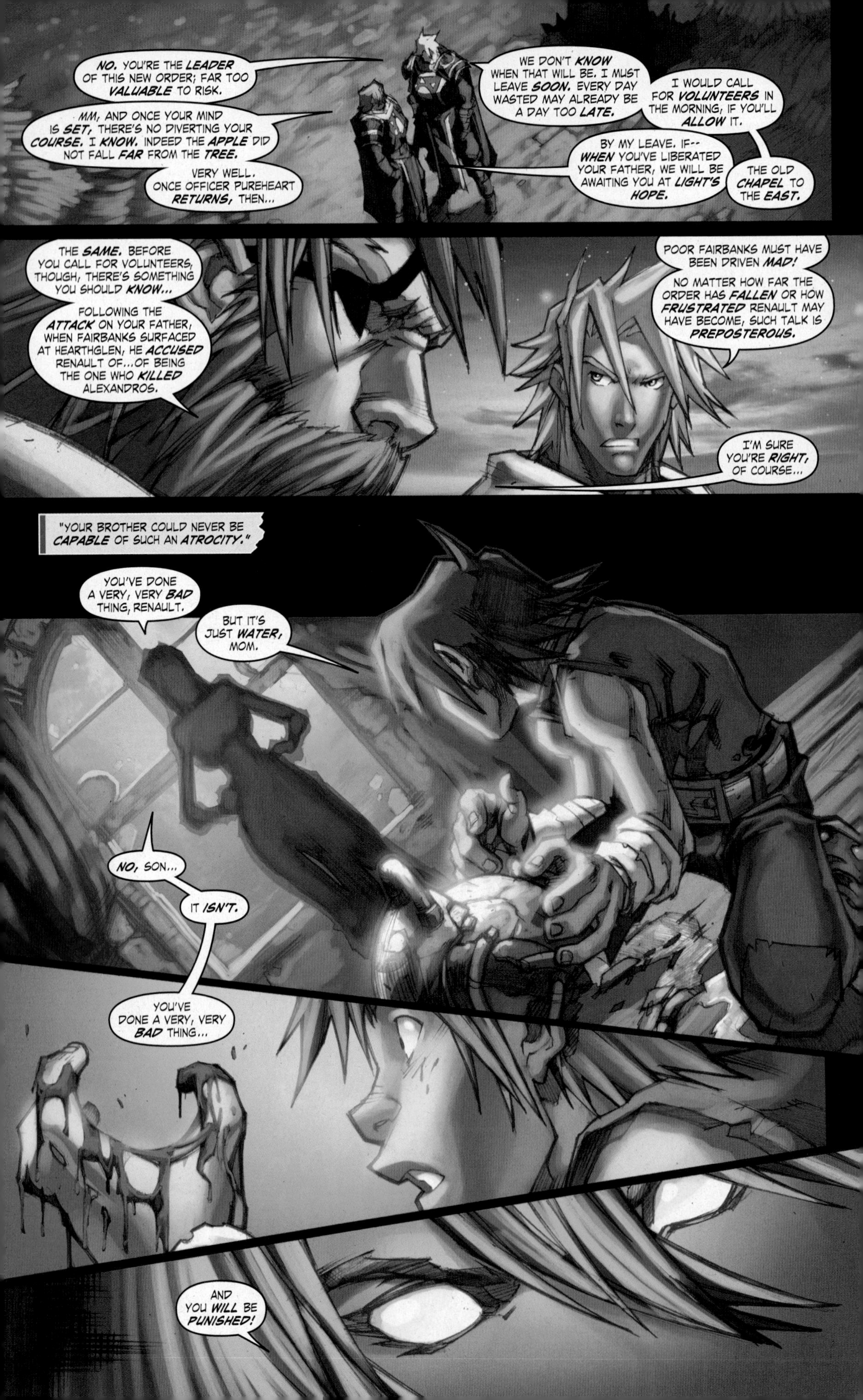

NO. YOU'RE THE LEADER OF THIS NEW ORDER; FAR TOO VALUABLE TO RISK.
MM, AND ONCE YOUR MIND IS SET, THERE'S NO DIVERTING YOUR COURSE. I KNOW. INDEED THE APPLE DID NOT FALL FAR FROM THE TREE.
VERY WELL. ONCE OFFICER PUREHEART RETURNS, THEN...
WE DON'T KNOW WHEN THAT WILL BE. I MUST LEAVE SOON. EVERY DAY WASTED MAY ALREADY BE A DAY TOO LATE.
I WOULD CALL FOR VOLUNTEERS IN THE MORNING, IF YOU'LL ALLOW IT.
BY MY LEAVE. IF-- WHEN YOU'VE LIBERATED YOUR FATHER, WE WILL BE AWAITING YOU AT LIGHT'S HOPE.
THE OLD CHAPEL TO THE EAST.
THE SAME. BEFORE YOU CALL FOR VOLUNTEERS, THOUGH, THERE'S SOMETHING YOU SHOULD KNOW...
FOLLOWING THE ATTACK ON YOUR FATHER, WHEN FAIRBANKS SURFACED AT HEARTHGLEN, HE ACCUSED RENAULT OF...OF BEING THE ONE WHO KILLED ALEXANDROS.
POOR FAIRBANKS MUST HAVE BEEN DRIVEN MAD!
NO MATTER HOW FAR THE ORDER HAS FALLEN OR HOW FRUSTRATED RENAULT MAY HAVE BECOME, SUCH TALK IS PREPOSTEROUS.
I'M SURE YOU'RE RIGHT, OF COURSE...
"YOUR BROTHER COULD NEVER BE CAPABLE OF SUCH AN ATROCITY."
YOU'VE DONE A VERY, VERY BAD THING, RENAULT.
BUT IT'S JUST WATER, MOM.
NO, SON...
IT ISN'T.
YOU'VE DONE A VERY, VERY BAD THING...
AND YOU WILL BE PUNISHED!

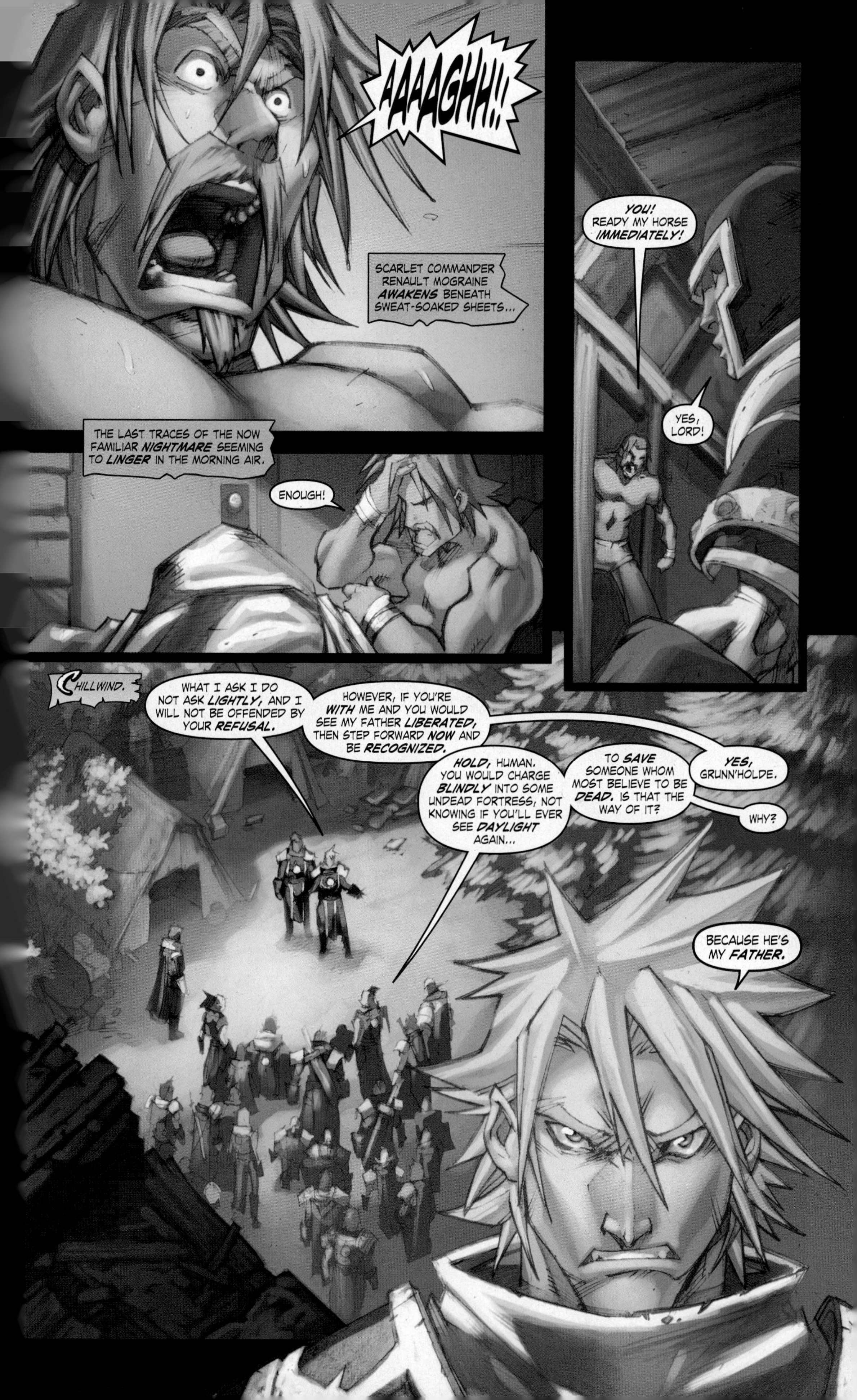
AAAAGHH!!
SCARLET COMMANDER RENAULT MOGRAINE AWAKENS BENEATH SWEAT-SOAKED SHEETS...
YOU! READY MY HORSE IMMEDIATELY!
YES, LORD!
THE LAST TRACES OF THE NOW FAMILIAR NIGHTMARE SEEMING TO LINGER IN THE MORNING AIR.
ENOUGH!
CHILLWIND.
WHAT I ASK I DO NOT ASK LIGHTLY, AND I WILL NOT BE OFFENDED BY YOUR REFUSAL.
HOWEVER, IF YOU'RE WITH ME AND YOU WOULD SEE MY FATHER LIBERATED, THEN STEP FORWARD NOW AND BE RECOGNIZED.
HOLD, HUMAN. YOU WOULD CHARGE BLINDLY INTO SOME UNDEAD FORTRESS, NOT KNOWING IF YOU'LL EVER SEE DAYLIGHT AGAIN...
TO SAVE SOMEONE WHOM MOST BELIEVE TO BE DEAD. IS THAT THE WAY OF IT?
YES, GRUNN'HOLDE.
WHY?
BECAUSE HE'S MY FATHER.

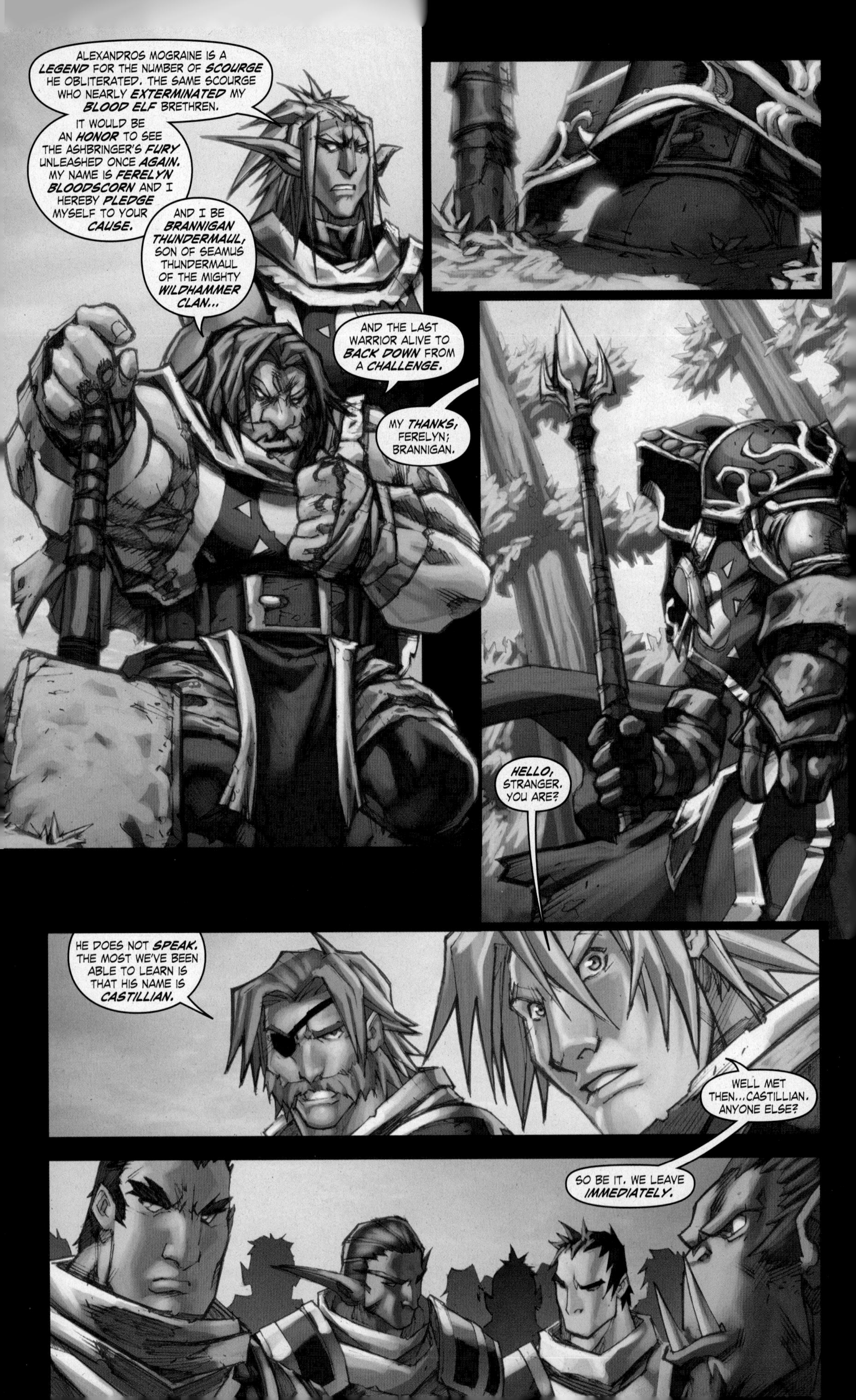
ALEXANDROS MOGRAINE IS A LEGEND FOR THE NUMBER OF SCOURGE HE OBLITERATED. THE SAME SCOURGE WHO NEARLY EXTERMINATED MY BLOOD ELF BRETHREN.
IT WOULD BE AN HONOR TO SEE THE ASHBRINGER'S FURY UNLEASHED ONCE AGAIN. MY NAME IS FERELYN BLOODSCORN AND I HEREBY PLEDGE MYSELF TO YOUR CAUSE.
AND I BE BRANNIGAN THUNDERMAUL, SON OF SEAMUS THUNDERMAUL OF THE MIGHTY WILDHAMMER CLAN...
AND THE LAST WARRIOR ALIVE TO BACK DOWN FROM A CHALLENGE.
MY THANKS, FERELYN; BRANNIGAN.
HELLO, STRANGER. YOU ARE?
HE DOES NOT SPEAK. THE MOST WE'VE BEEN ABLE TO LEARN IS THAT HIS NAME IS CASTILLIAN.
WELL MET THEN...CASTILLIAN. ANYONE ELSE?
SO BE IT. WE LEAVE IMMEDIATELY.

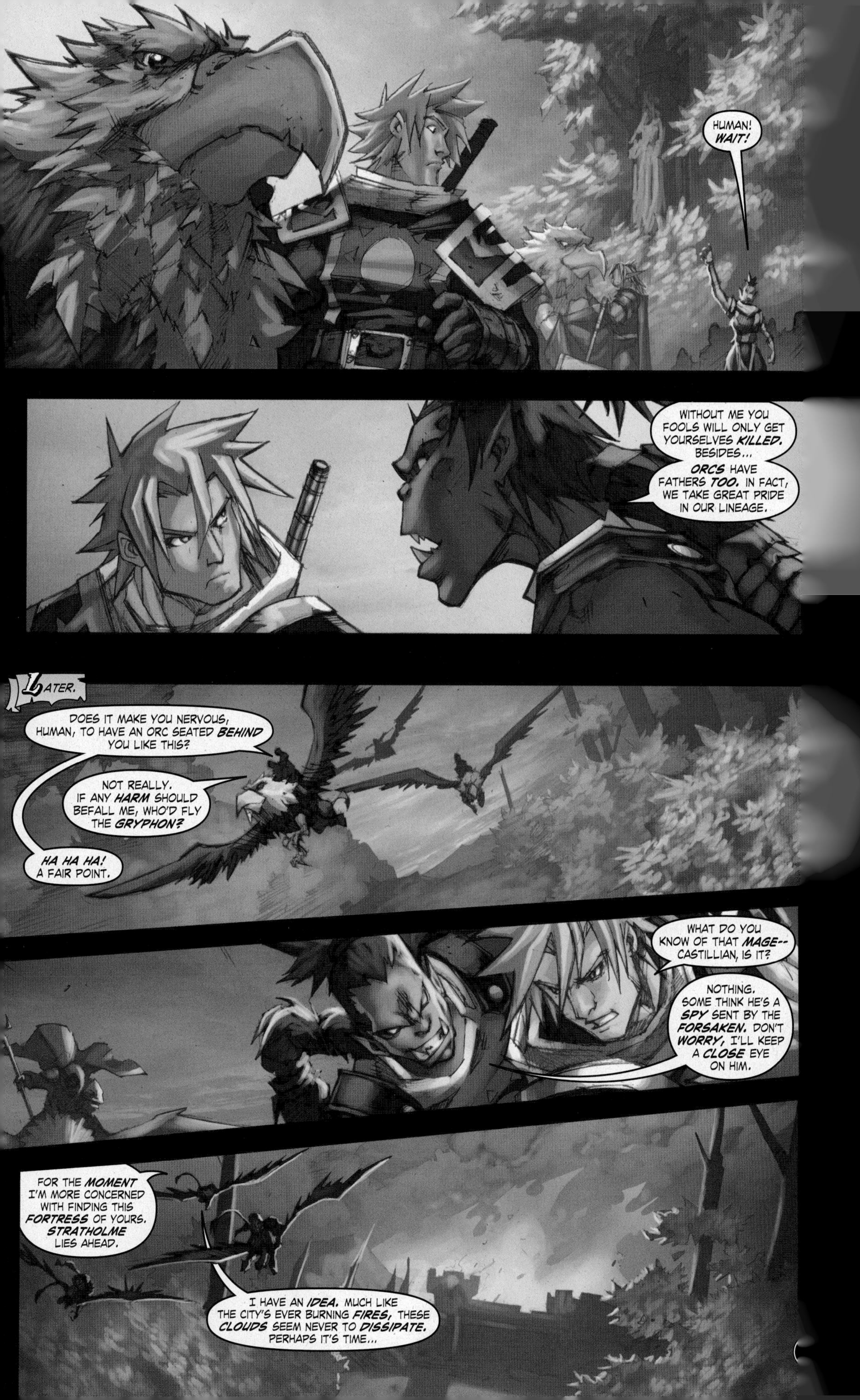
HUMAN! WAIT!
WITHOUT ME YOU FOOLS WILL ONLY GET YOURSELVES KILLED. BESIDES... ORCS HAVE FATHERS TOO. IN FACT, WE TAKE GREAT PRIDE IN OUR LINEAGE.
LATER.
DOES IT MAKE YOU NERVOUS, HUMAN, TO HAVE AN ORC SEATED BEHIND YOU LIKE THIS?
NOT REALLY. IF ANY HARM SHOULD BEFALL ME, WHO'D FLY THE GRYPHON?
HA HA HA! A FAIR POINT.
WHAT DO YOU KNOW OF THAT MAGE--CASTILLIAN, IS IT?
NOTHING. SOME THINK HE'S A SPY SENT BY THE FORSAKEN. DON'T WORRY, I'LL KEEP A CLOSE EYE ON HIM.
FOR THE MOMENT I'M MORE CONCERNED WITH FINDING THIS FORTRESS OF YOURS. STRATHOLME LIES AHEAD.
I HAVE AN IDEA. MUCH LIKE THE CITY'S EVER BURNING FIRES, THESE CLOUDS SEEM NEVER TO DISSIPATE. PERHAPS IT'S TIME...

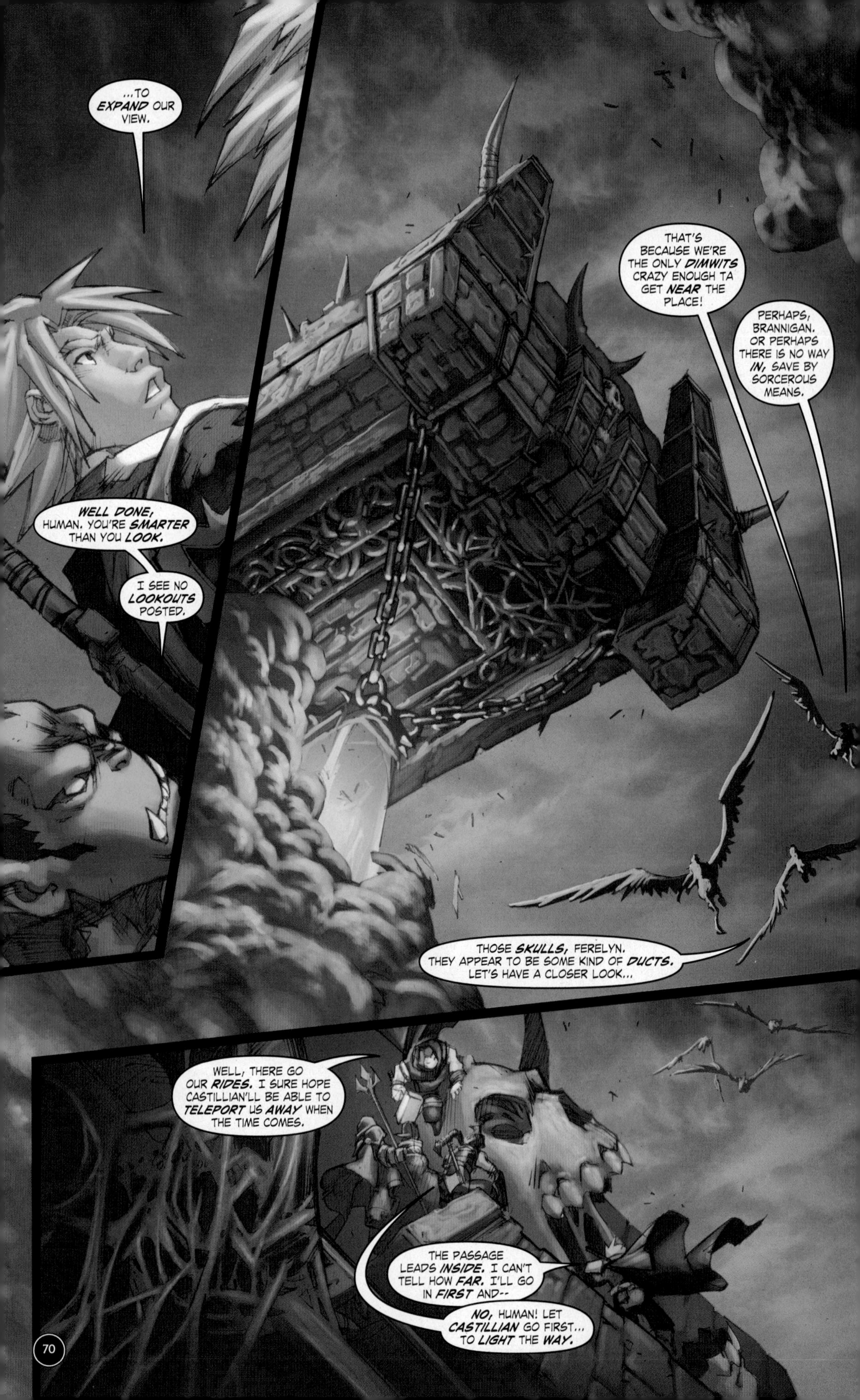
...TO EXPAND OUR VIEW.
WELL DONE, HUMAN. YOU'RE SMARTER THAN YOU LOOK.
I SEE NO LOOKOUTS POSTED.
THAT'S BECAUSE WE'RE THE ONLY DIMWITS CRAZY ENOUGH TA GET NEAR THE PLACE!
PERHAPS, BRANNIGAN. OR PERHAPS THERE IS NO WAY IN, SAVE BY SORCEROUS MEANS.
THOSE SKULLS, FERELYN. THEY APPEAR TO BE SOME KIND OF DUCTS. LET'S HAVE A CLOSER LOOK...
WELL, THERE GO OUR RIDES. I SURE HOPE CASTILLIAN'LL BE ABLE TO TELEPORT US AWAY WHEN THE TIME COMES.
THE PASSAGE LEADS INSIDE. I CAN'T TELL HOW FAR. I'LL GO IN FIRST AND--
NO, HUMAN! LET CASTILLIAN GO FIRST... TO LIGHT THE WAY.

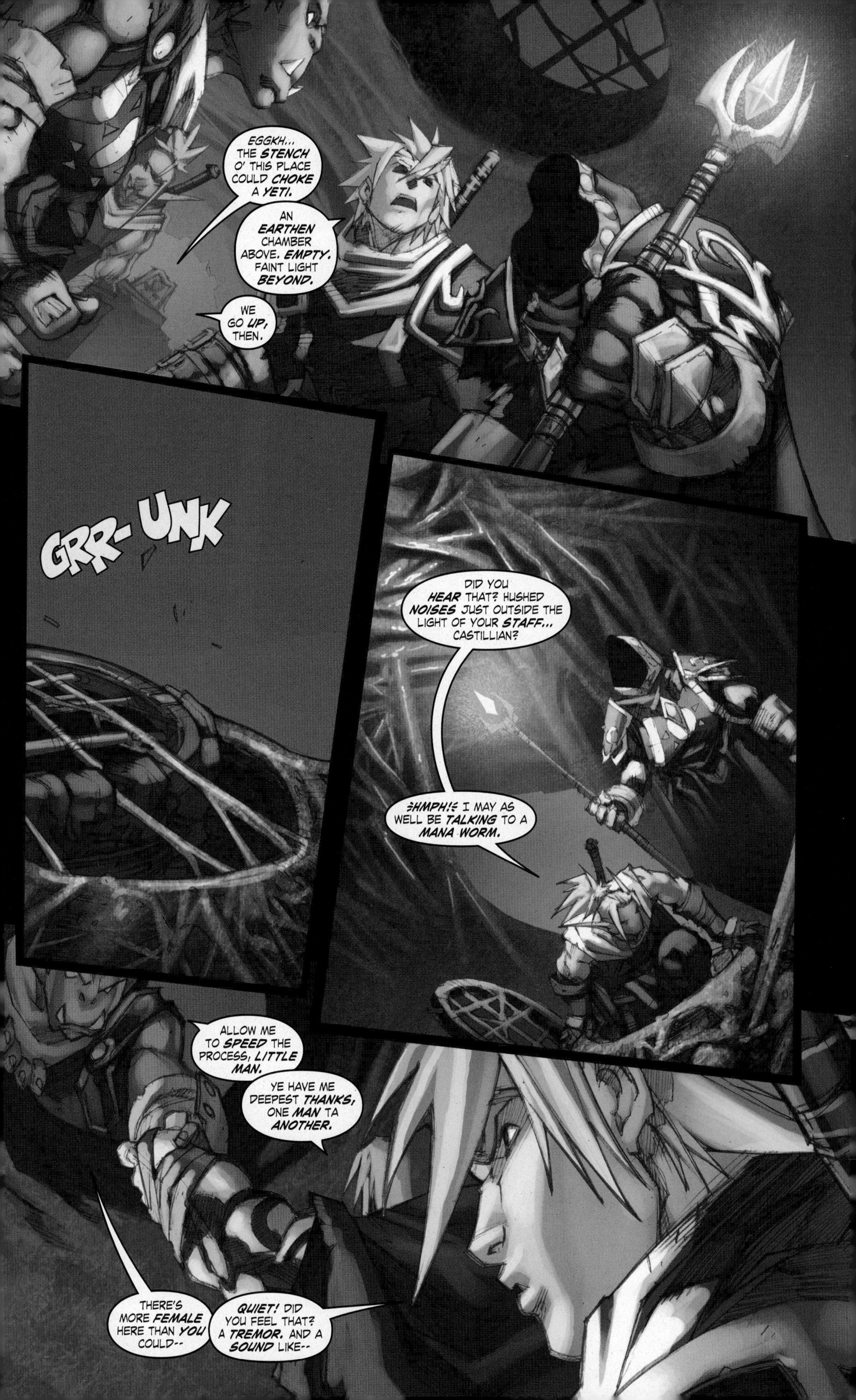

EGGKH... THE STENCH O' THIS PLACE COULD CHOKE A YETI.
AN EARTHEN CHAMBER ABOVE. EMPTY. FAINT LIGHT BEYOND.
WE GO UP, THEN.
GRR-UNK
DID YOU HEAR THAT? HUSHED NOISES JUST OUTSIDE THE LIGHT OF YOUR STAFF... CASTILLIAN?
SHMPH!? I MAY AS WELL BE TALKING TO A MANA WORM.
ALLOW ME TO SPEED THE PROCESS, LITTLE MAN.
YE HAVE ME DEEPEST THANKS, ONE MAN TA ANOTHER.
THERE'S MORE FEMALE HERE THAN YOU COULD--
QUIET! DID YOU FEEL THAT? A TREMOR. AND A SOUND LIKE--

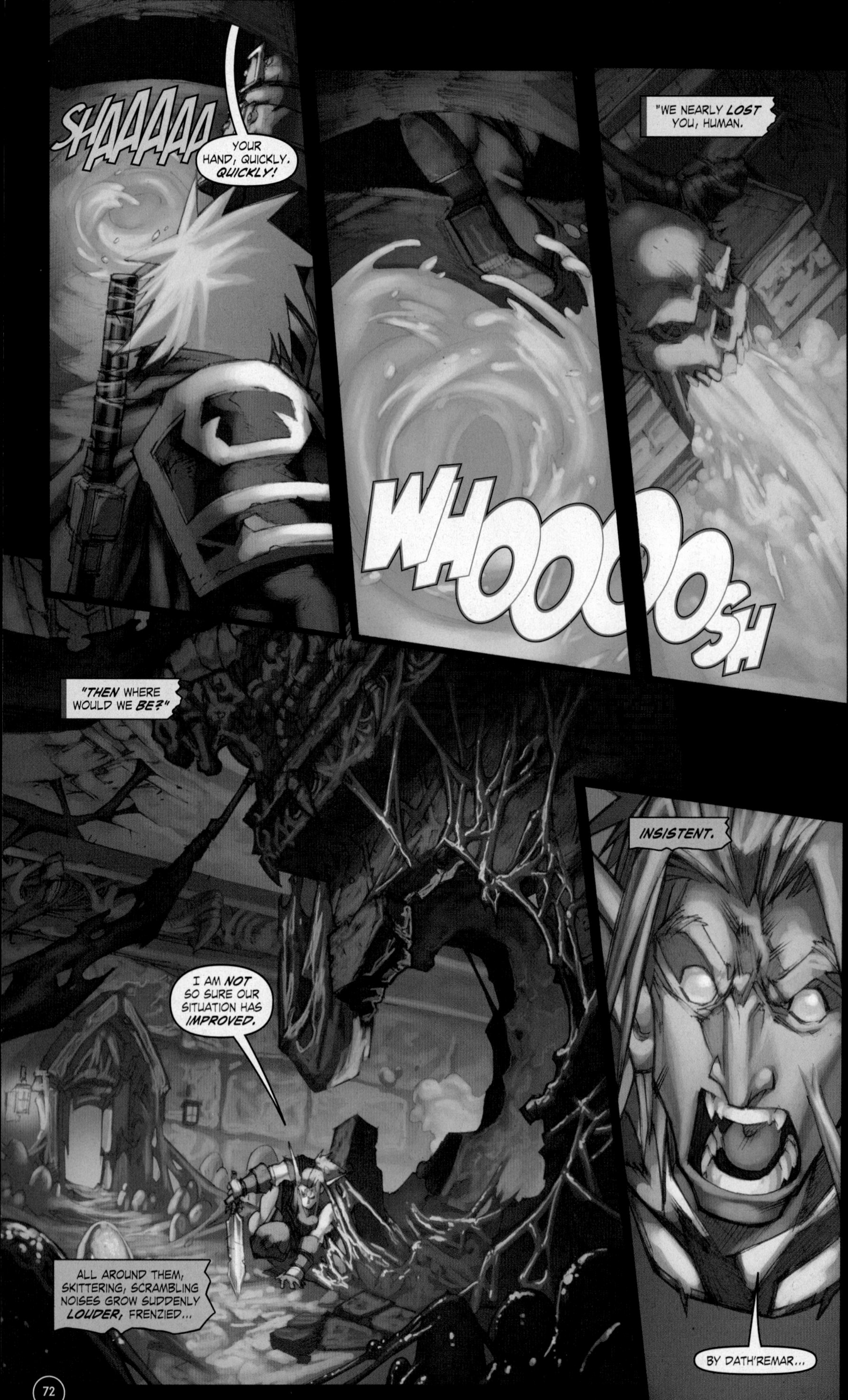
SHAAAAA
YOUR HAND, QUICKLY. QUICKLY!
WHOOOOOSH
"WE NEARLY LOST YOU, HUMAN.
"THEN WHERE WOULD WE BE?"
I AM NOT SO SURE OUR SITUATION HAS IMPROVED.
ALL AROUND THEM, SKITTERING, SCRAMBLING NOISES GROW SUDDENLY LOUDER, FRENZIED...
INSISTENT.
BY DATH'REMAR...

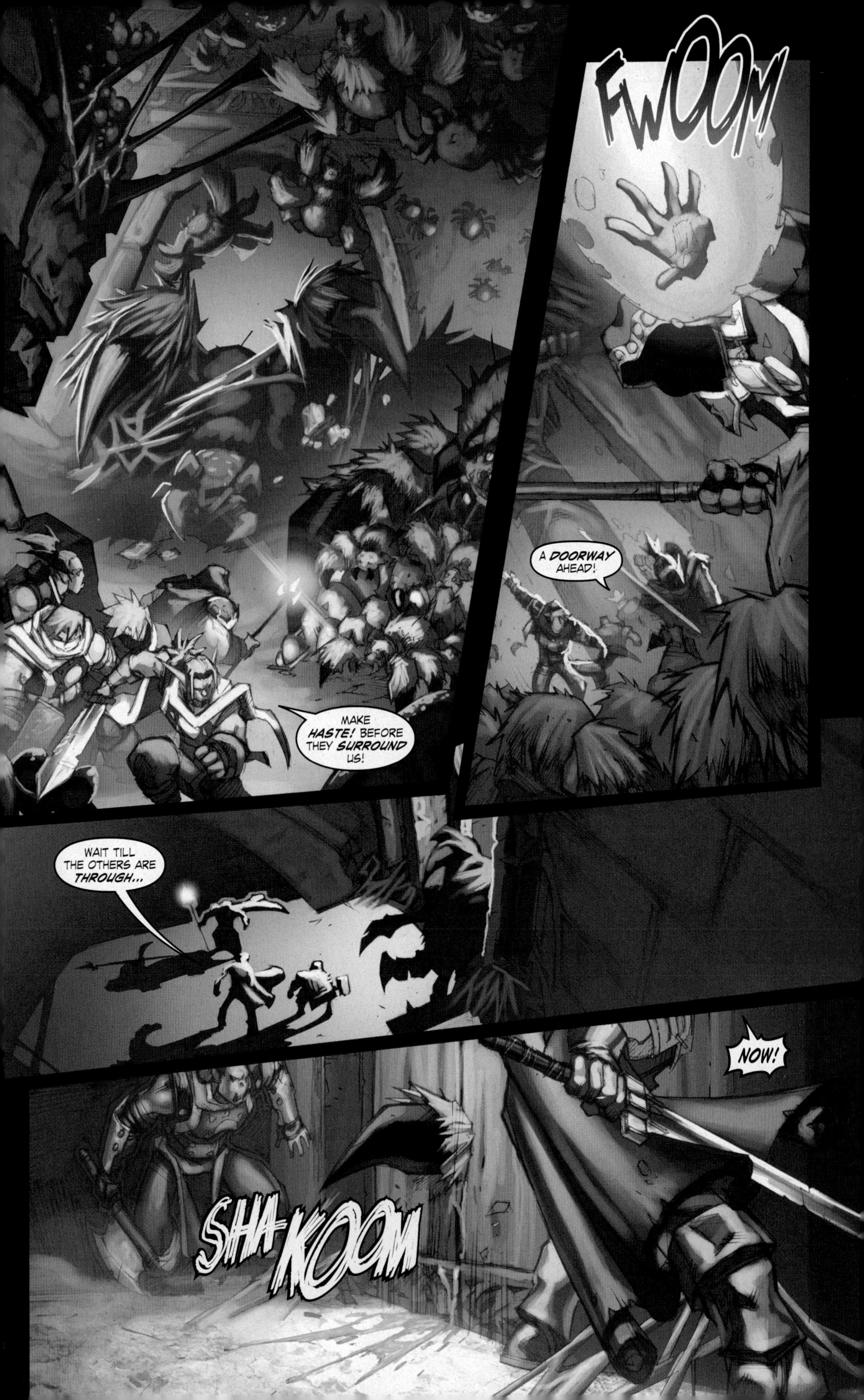
FWOOM
MAKE HASTE! BEFORE THEY SURROUND US!
A DOORWAY AHEAD!
WAIT TILL THE OTHERS ARE THROUGH...
NOW!
SHA-KOOM

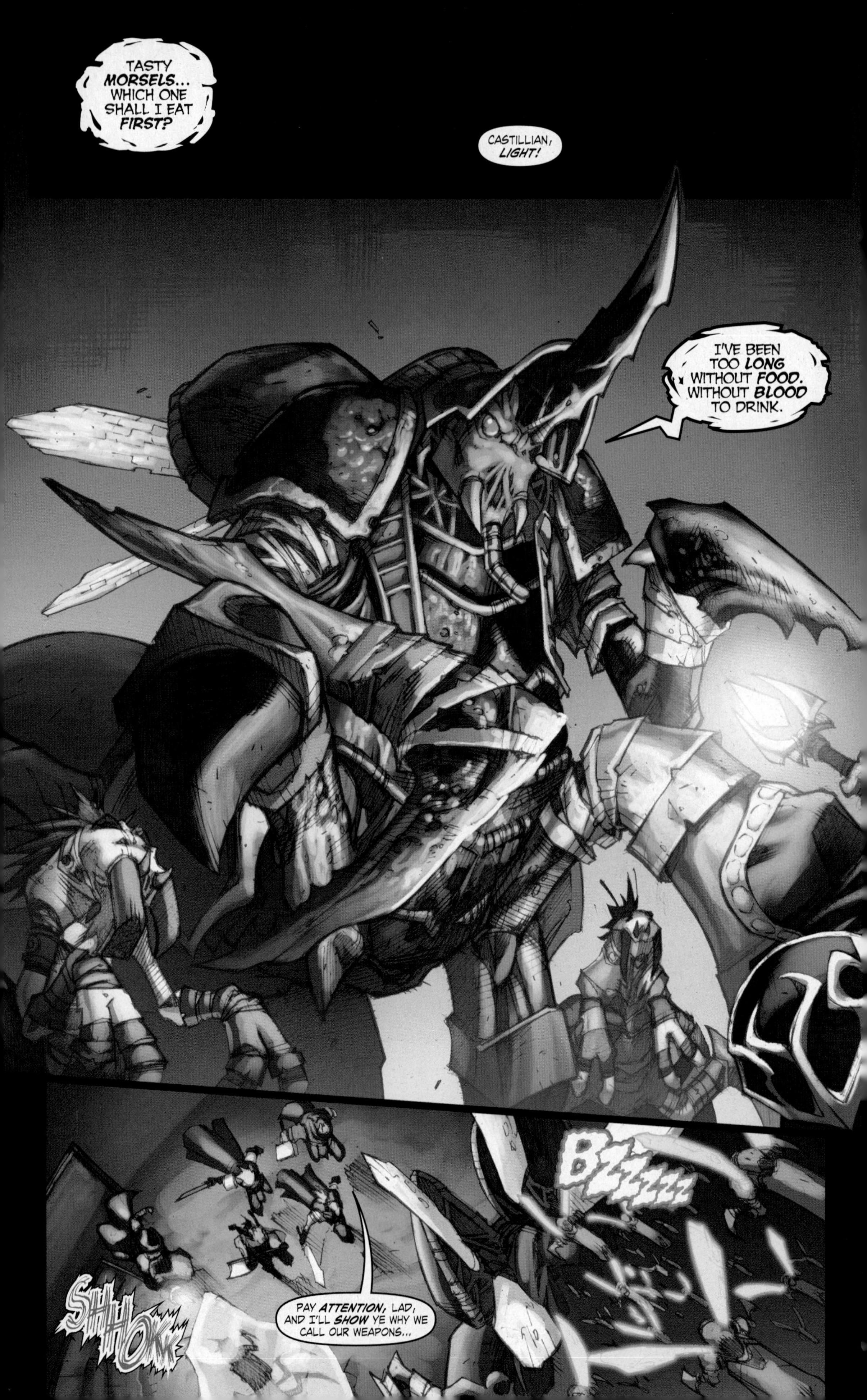
TASTY MORSELS... WHICH ONE SHALL I EAT FIRST?
CASTILLIAN, LIGHT!
I'VE BEEN TOO LONG WITHOUT FOOD. WITHOUT BLOOD TO DRINK.
BZZZZZ
SHHOKK
PAY ATTENTION, LAD, AND I'LL SHOW YE WHY WE CALL OUR WEAPONS...

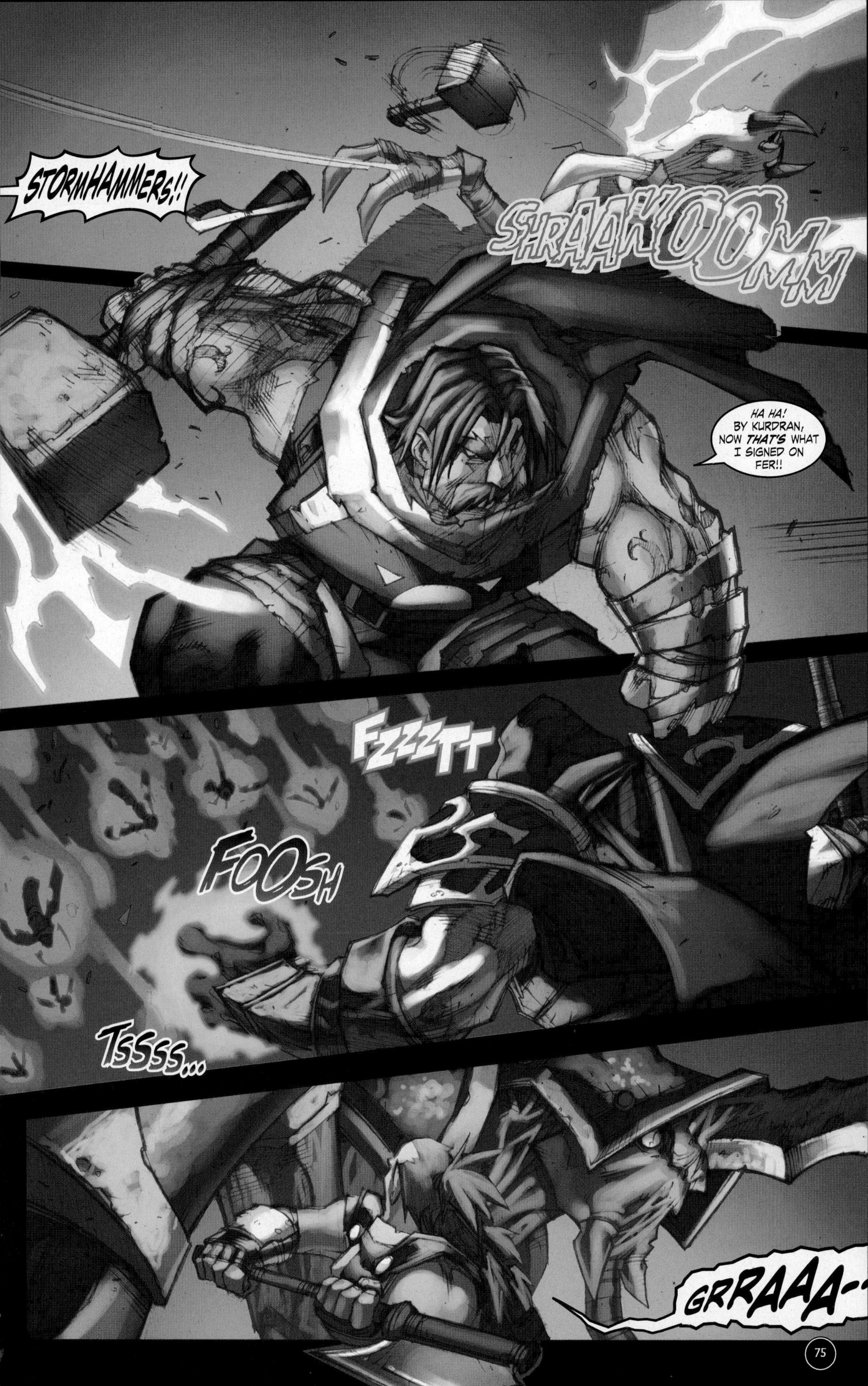

STORMHAMMERS!!
SHRAAKOOMM
HA HA! BY KURDRAN, NOW THAT'S WHAT I SIGNED ON FER!!
FZZZTT
FOOSH
TSSSS...
GRRAAA--

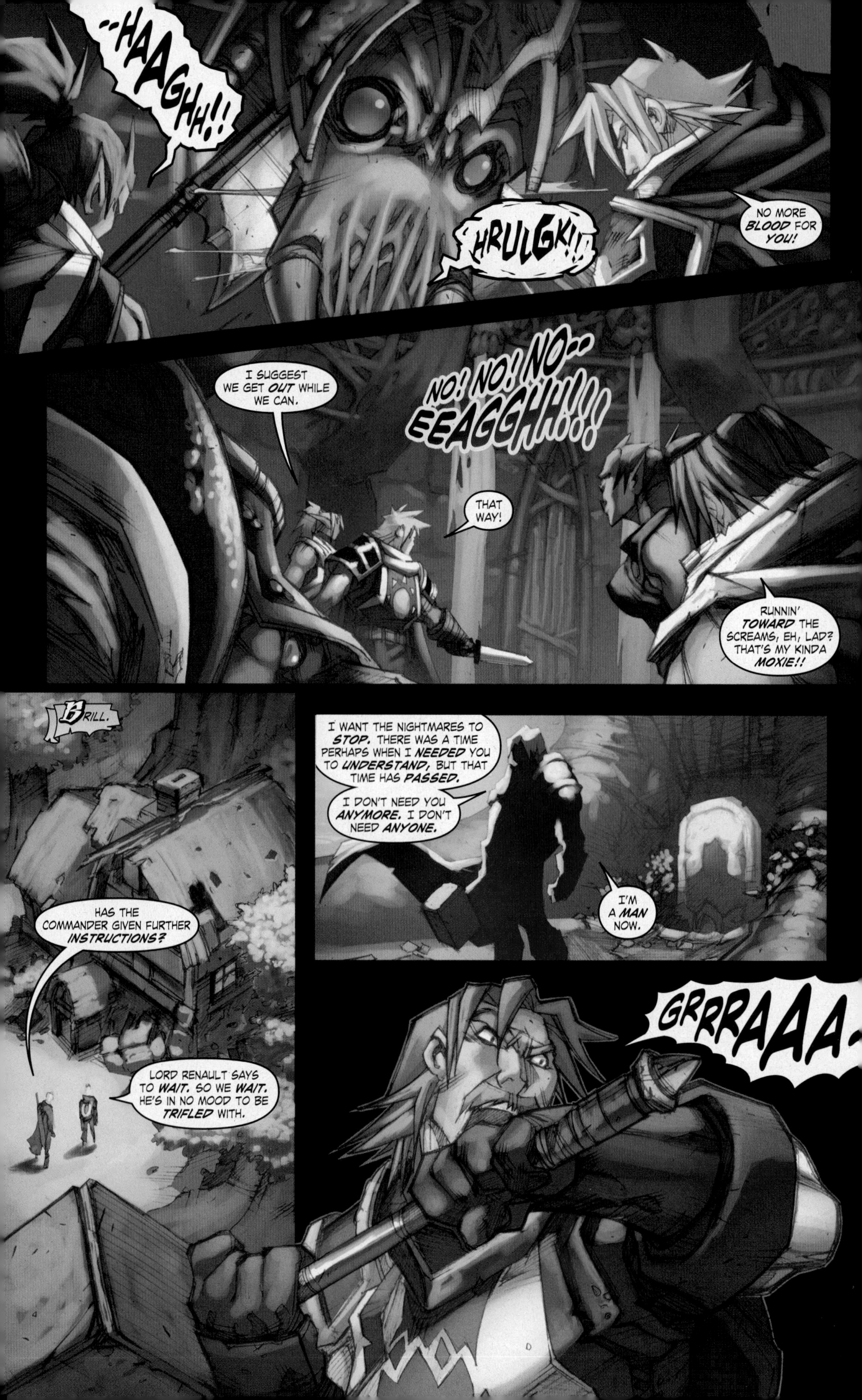
--HAAGHH!!
HRULGK!!
NO MORE BLOOD FOR YOU!
I SUGGEST WE GET OUT WHILE WE CAN.
NO! NO! NO-- EEAGGHH!!!!
THAT WAY!
RUNNIN' TOWARD THE SCREAMS, EH, LAD? THAT'S MY KINDA MOXIE!!
BRILL.
HAS THE COMMANDER GIVEN FURTHER INSTRUCTIONS?
LORD RENAULT SAYS TO WAIT. SO WE WAIT. HE'S IN NO MOOD TO BE TRIFLED WITH.
I WANT THE NIGHTMARES TO STOP. THERE WAS A TIME PERHAPS WHEN I NEEDED YOU TO UNDERSTAND, BUT THAT TIME HAS PASSED.
I DON'T NEED YOU ANYMORE. I DON'T NEED ANYONE.
I'M A MAN NOW.
GRRRAAAA-

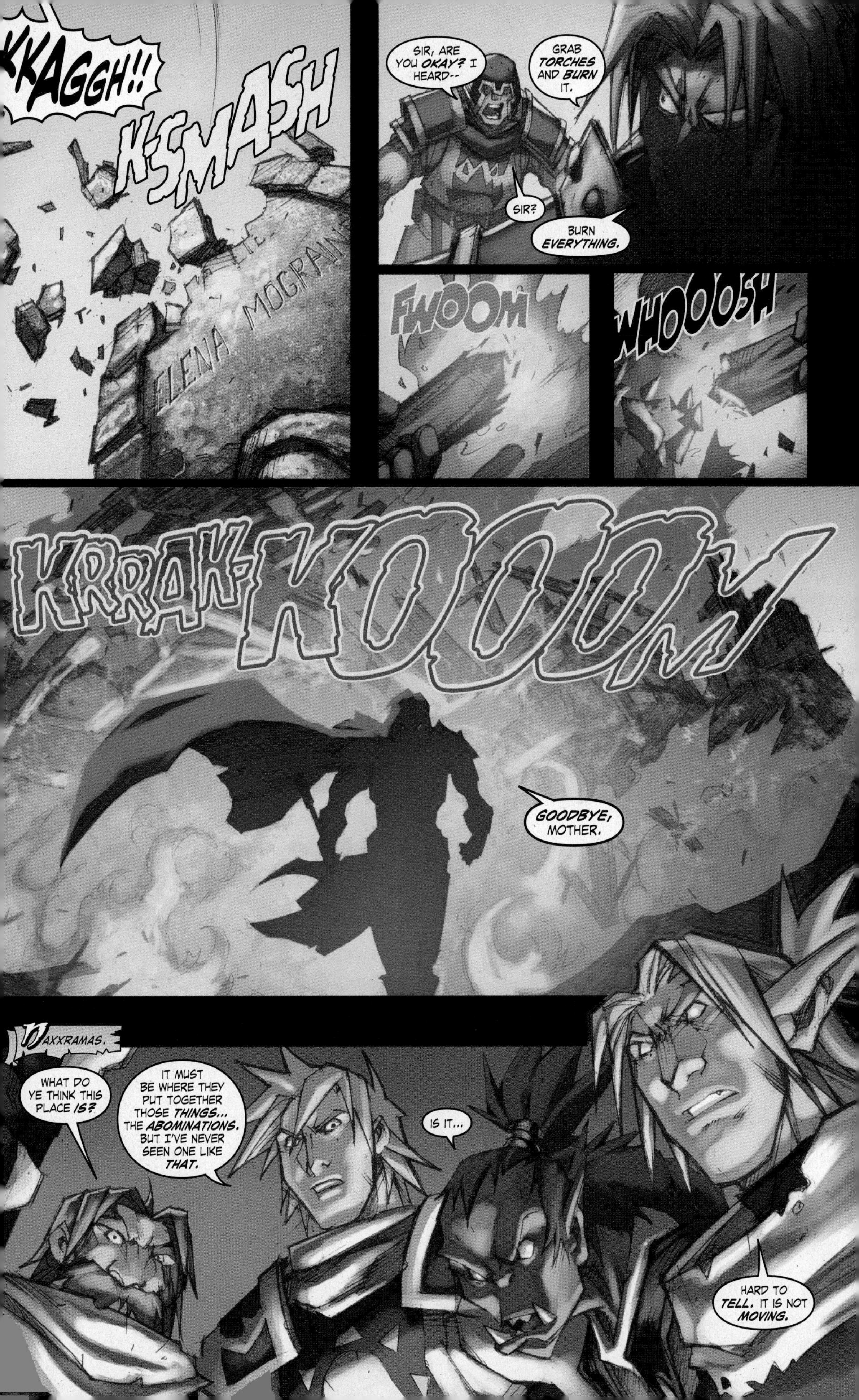
KKAGGH!!
K-SMASH
ELENA MOGRAINE
SIR, ARE YOU OKAY? I HEARD--
GRAB TORCHES AND BURN IT.
SIR?
BURN EVERYTHING.
FWOOM
WHOOOOSH
KRRAK-KOOOOM
GOODBYE, MOTHER.
NAXXRAMAS.
WHAT DO YE THINK THIS PLACE IS?
IT MUST BE WHERE THEY PUT TOGETHER THOSE THINGS... THE ABOMINATIONS. BUT I'VE NEVER SEEN ONE LIKE THAT.
IS IT...
HARD TO TELL. IT IS NOT MOVING.

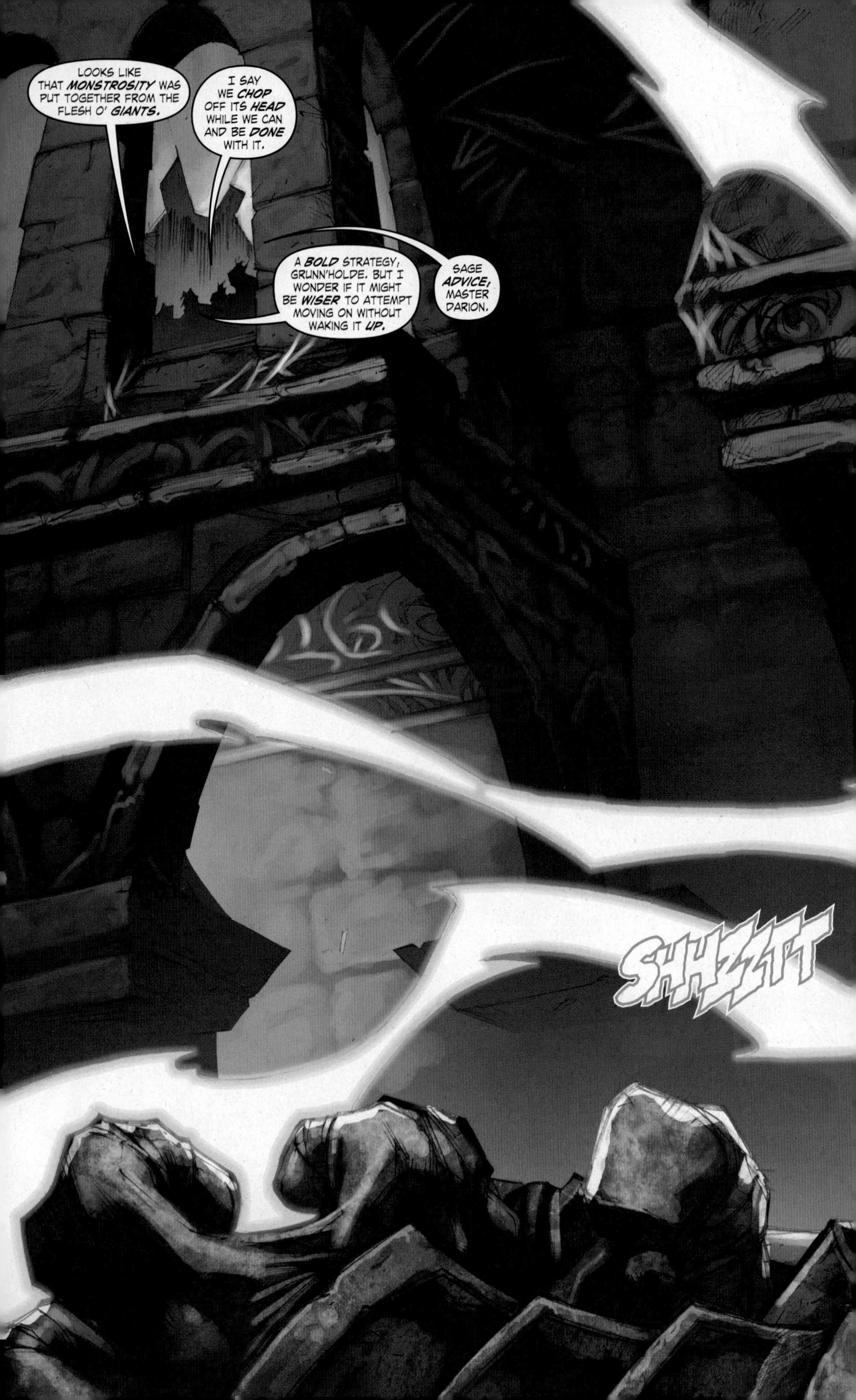
LOOKS LIKE THAT MONSTROSITY WAS PUT TOGETHER FROM THE FLESH O' GIANTS.
I SAY WE CHOP OFF ITS HEAD WHILE WE CAN AND BE DONE WITH IT.
A BOLD STRATEGY, GRUNN'HOLDE. BUT I WONDER IF IT MIGHT BE WISER TO ATTEMPT MOVING ON WITHOUT WAKING IT UP.
SAGE ADVICE, MASTER DARION.
SHZZTT

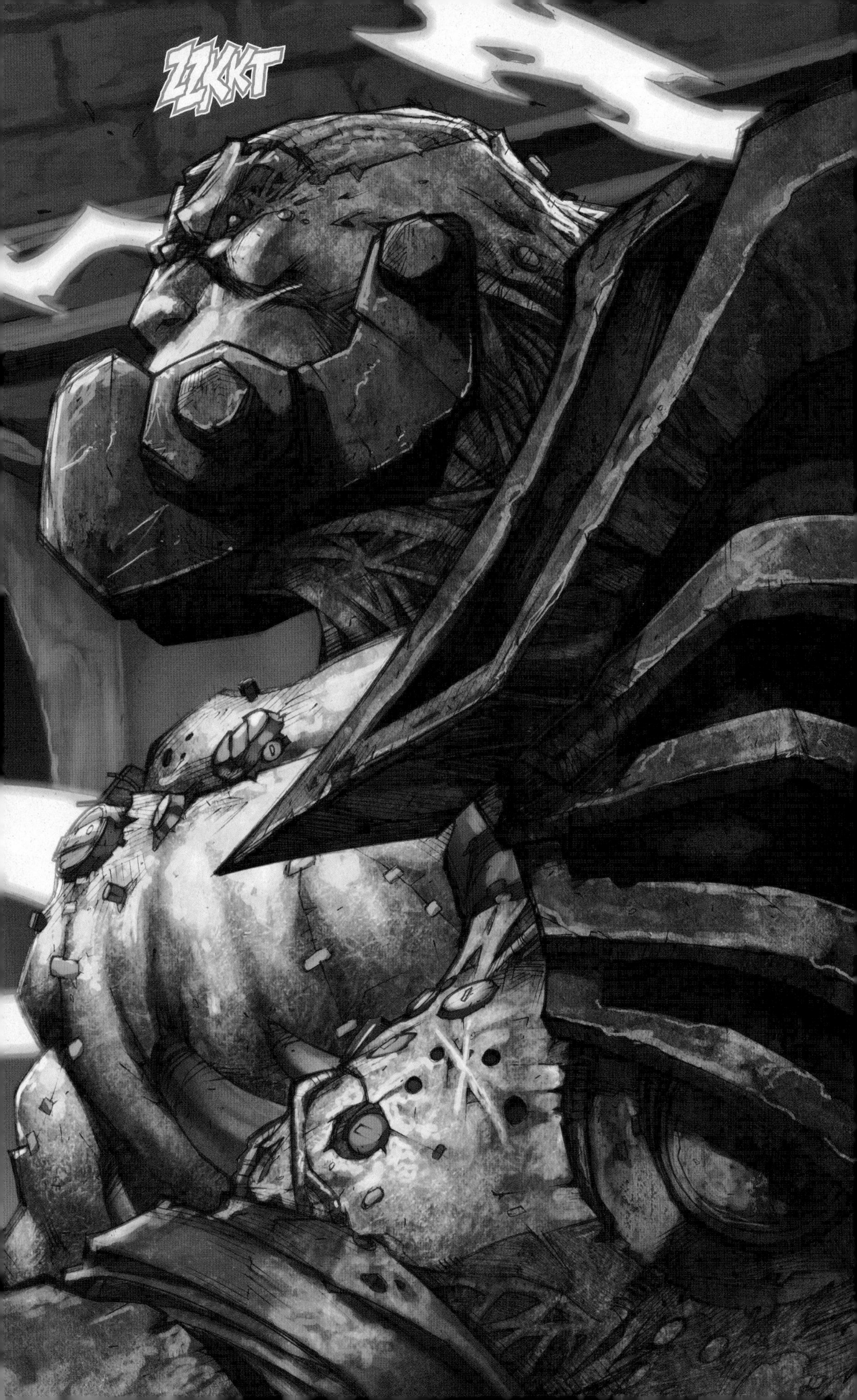
ZZKKT

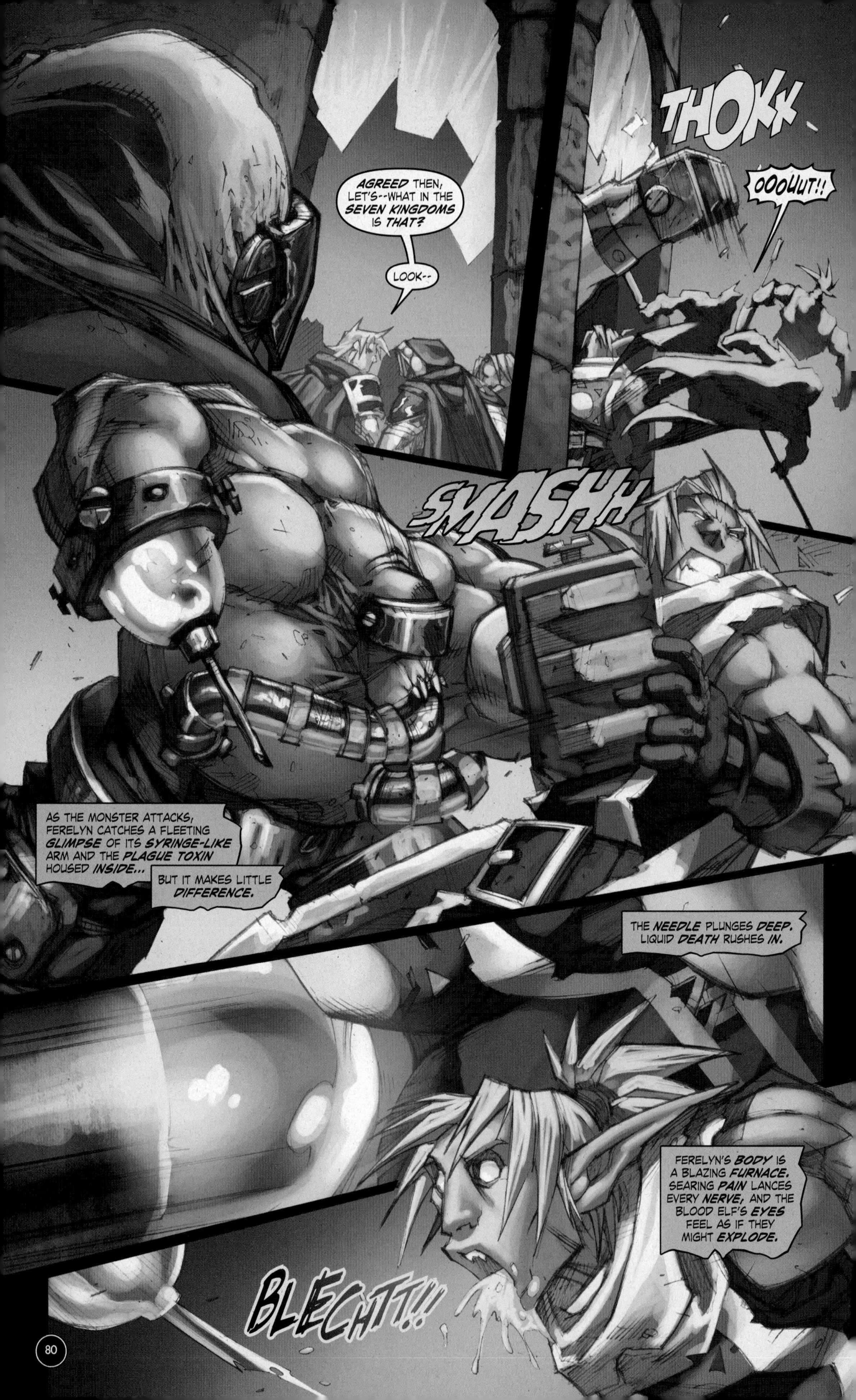
AGREED THEN, LET'S--WHAT IN THE SEVEN KINGDOMS IS THAT?
LOOK--
THOKK
OOOUUT!!
SMASHH
AS THE MONSTER ATTACKS, FERELYN CATCHES A FLEETING GLIMPSE OF ITS SYRINGE-LIKE ARM AND THE PLAGUE TOXIN HOUSED INSIDE...
BUT IT MAKES LITTLE DIFFERENCE.
THE NEEDLE PLUNGES DEEP. LIQUID DEATH RUSHES IN.
FERELYN'S BODY IS A BLAZING FURNACE. SEARING PAIN LANCES EVERY NERVE, AND THE BLOOD ELF'S EYES FEEL AS IF THEY MIGHT EXPLODE.
BLECHTT!!

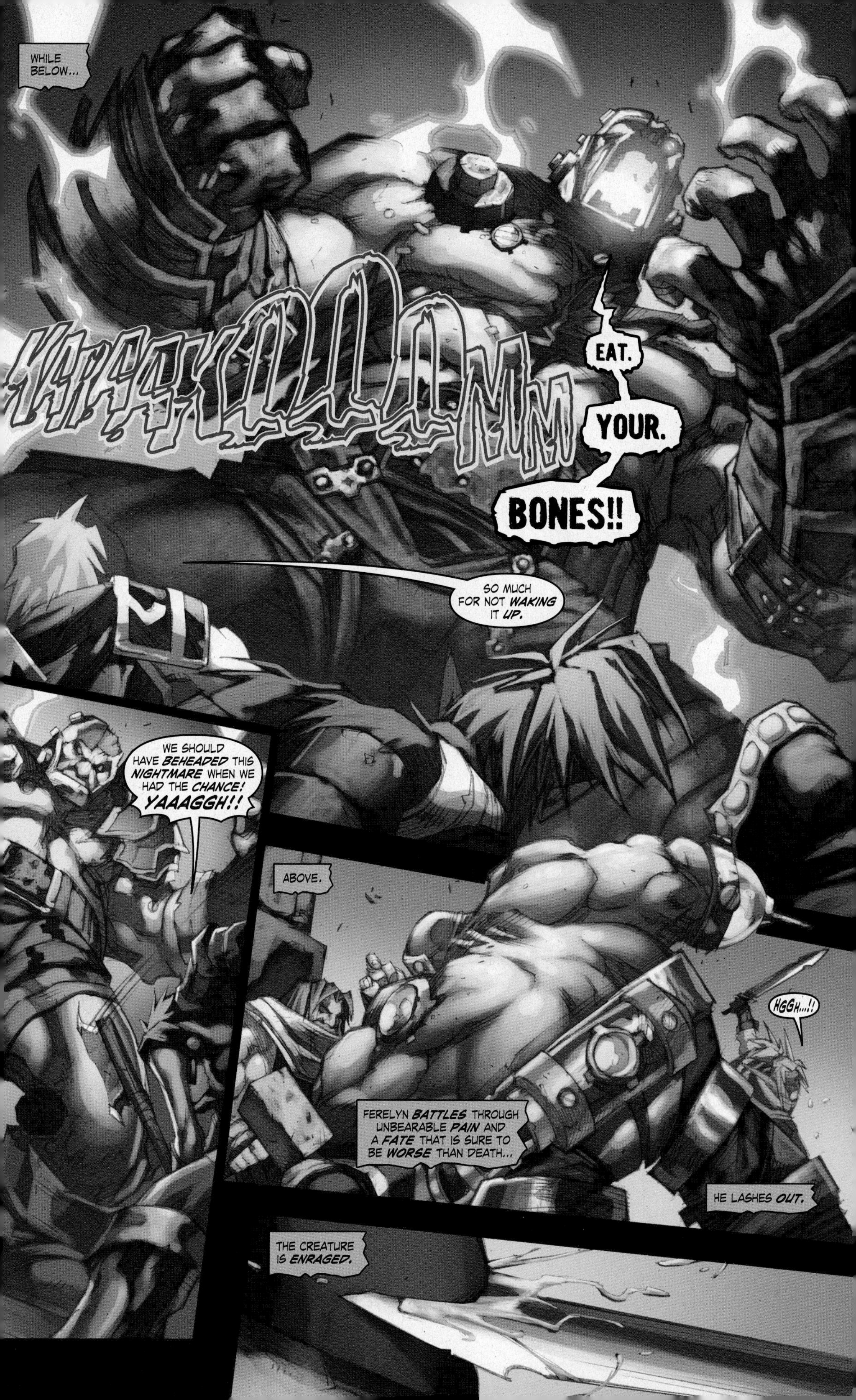
WHILE BELOW...
EAT.
YOUR.
BONES!!
SO MUCH FOR NOT WAKING IT UP.
WE SHOULD HAVE BEHEADED THIS NIGHTMARE WHEN WE HAD THE CHANCE! YAAAGGH!!
ABOVE.
HGGH...!!
FERELYN BATTLES THROUGH UNBEARABLE PAIN AND A FATE THAT IS SURE TO BE WORSE THAN DEATH...
HE LASHES OUT.
THE CREATURE IS ENRAGED.

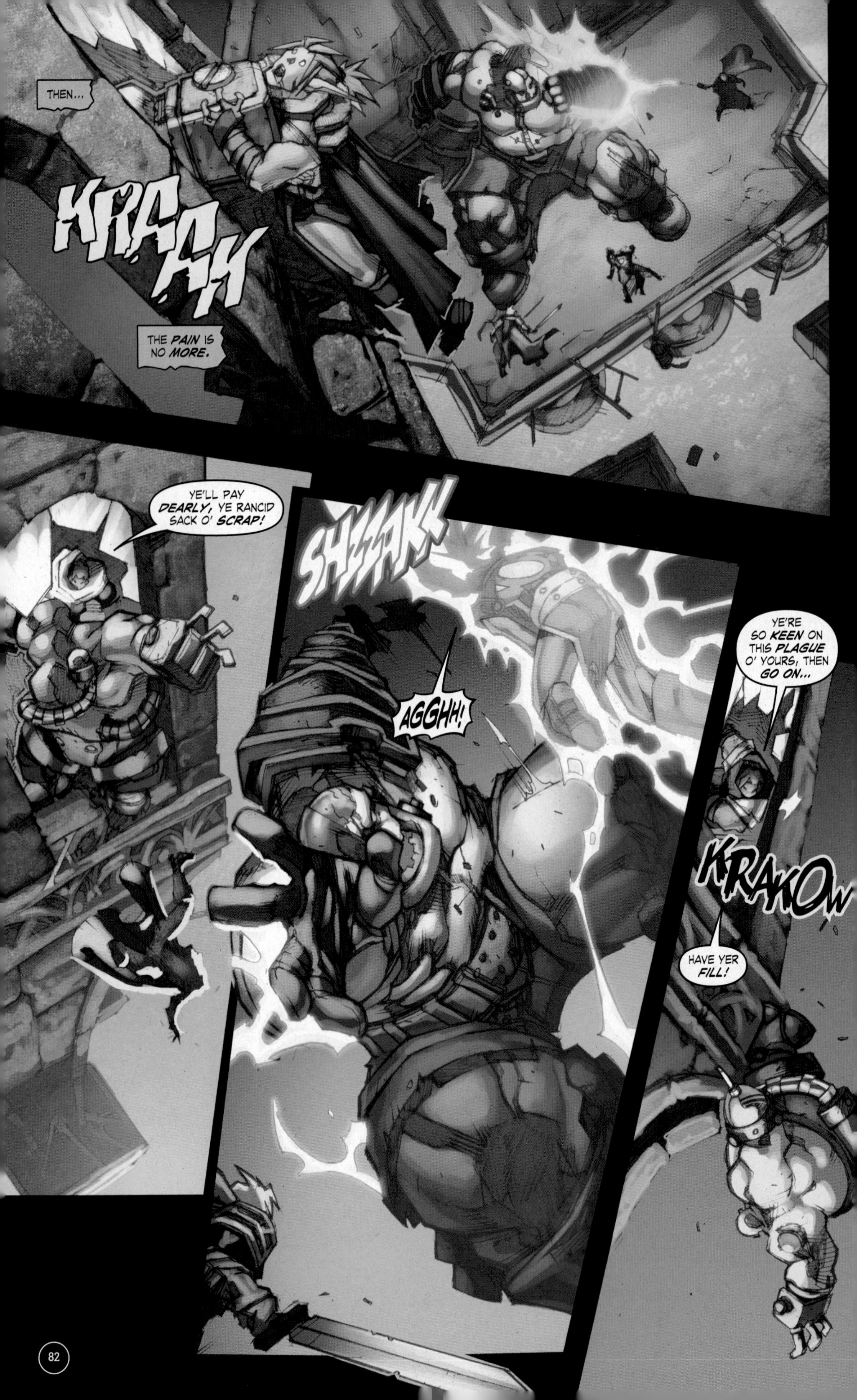
THEN...
KRRAAKK
THE PAIN IS NO MORE.
YE'LL PAY DEARLY, YE RANCID SACK O' SCRAP!
SHRAAK!
AGGHH!
YE'RE SO KEEN ON THIS PLAGUE O' YOURS, THEN GO ON...
KRAKOW
HAVE YER FILL!

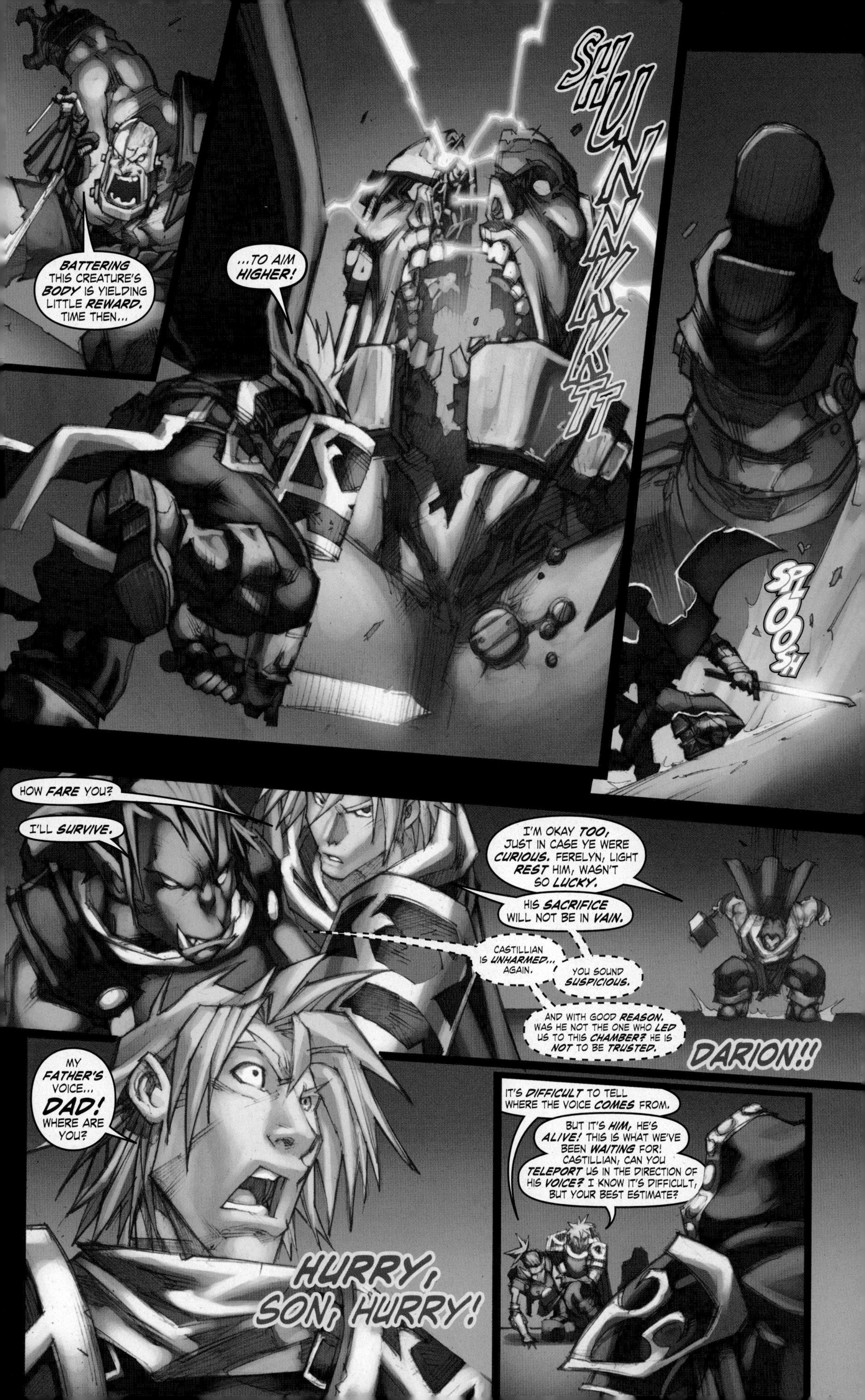
BATTERING THIS CREATURE'S BODY IS YIELDING LITTLE REWARD. TIME THEN...
...TO AIM HIGHER!
SHUNNNKKKATT
SPLOOOSH
HOW FARE YOU?
I'LL SURVIVE.
I'M OKAY TOO, JUST IN CASE YE WERE CURIOUS. FERELYN, LIGHT REST HIM, WASN'T SO LUCKY.
HIS SACRIFICE WILL NOT BE IN VAIN.
CASTILLIAN IS UNHARMED... AGAIN.
YOU SOUND SUSPICIOUS.
AND WITH GOOD REASON. WAS HE NOT THE ONE WHO LED US TO THIS CHAMBER? HE IS NOT TO BE TRUSTED.
DARION!!
MY FATHER'S VOICE... DAD! WHERE ARE YOU?
HURRY, SON, HURRY!
IT'S DIFFICULT TO TELL WHERE THE VOICE COMES FROM.
BUT IT'S HIM, HE'S ALIVE! THIS IS WHAT WE'VE BEEN WAITING FOR! CASTILLIAN, CAN YOU TELEPORT US IN THE DIRECTION OF HIS VOICE? I KNOW IT'S DIFFICULT, BUT YOUR BEST ESTIMATE?

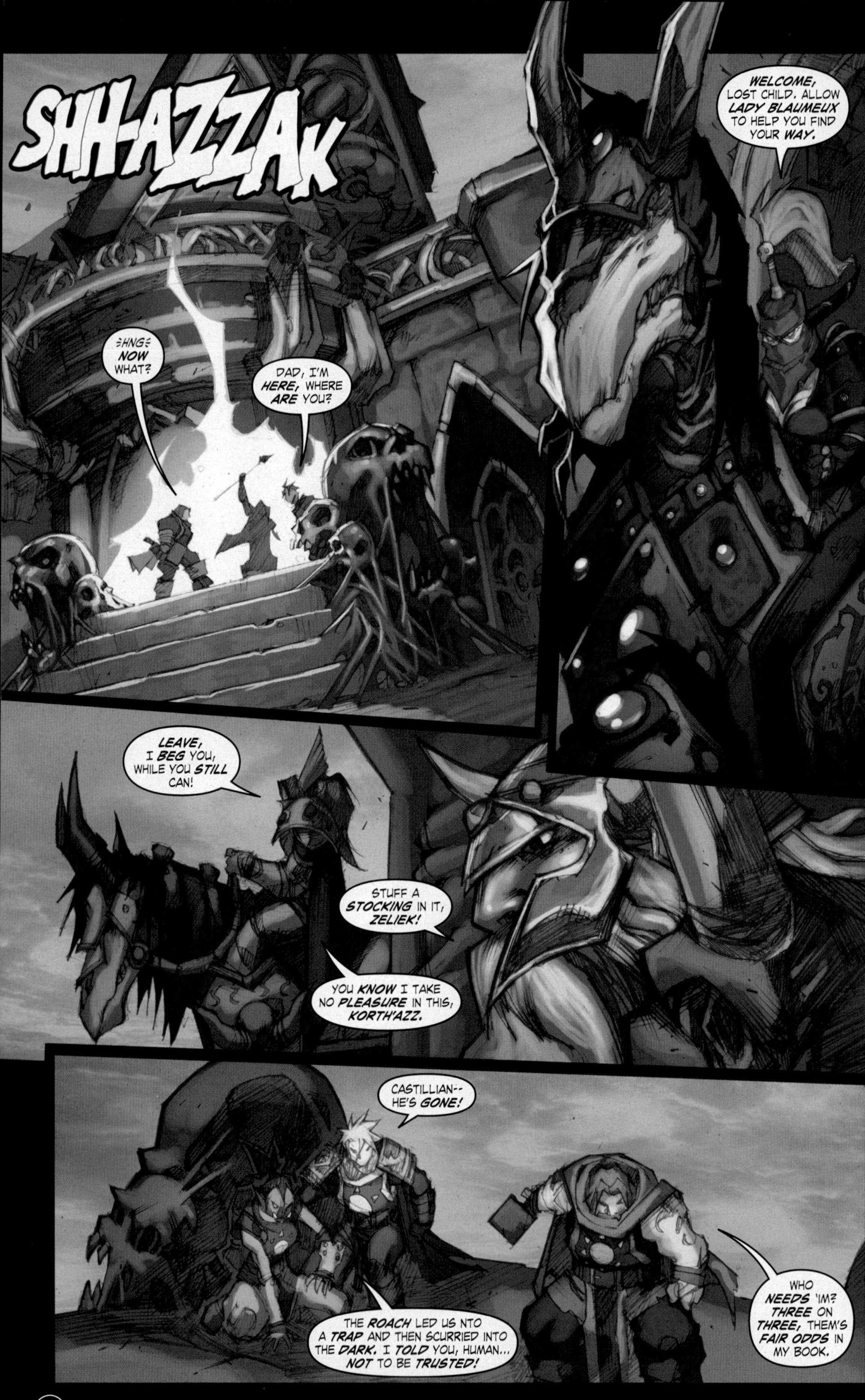
SHH-AZZAK
HNG NOW WHAT?
DAD, I'M HERE, WHERE ARE YOU?
WELCOME, LOST CHILD. ALLOW LADY BLAUMEUX TO HELP YOU FIND YOUR WAY.
LEAVE, I BEG YOU, WHILE YOU STILL CAN!
STUFF A STOCKING IN IT, ZELIEK!
YOU KNOW I TAKE NO PLEASURE IN THIS, KORTH'AZZ.
CASTILLIAN-- HE'S GONE!
THE ROACH LED US NTO A TRAP AND THEN SCURRIED INTO THE DARK. I TOLD YOU, HUMAN... NOT TO BE TRUSTED!
WHO NEEDS 'IM? THREE ON THREE, THEM'S FAIR ODDS IN MY BOOK.

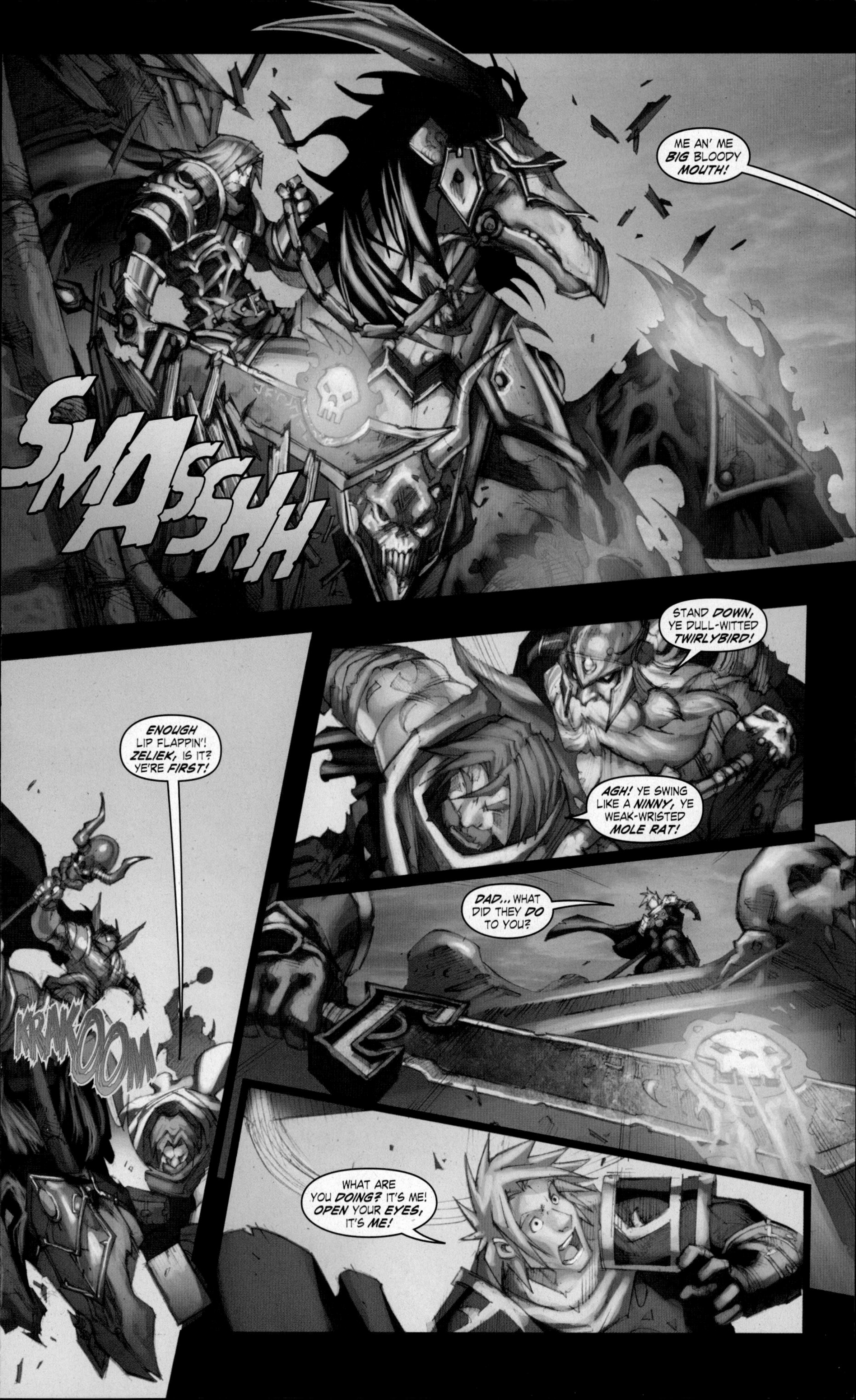
SMASSHH
ME AN' ME BIG BLOODY MOUTH!
ENOUGH LIP FLAPPIN'! ZELIEK, IS IT? YE'RE FIRST!
KRAKOOM
STAND DOWN, YE DULL-WITTED TWIRLYBIRD!
AGH! YE SWING LIKE A NINNY, YE WEAK-WRISTED MOLE RAT!
DAD... WHAT DID THEY DO TO YOU?
WHAT ARE YOU DOING? IT'S ME! OPEN YOUR EYES, IT'S ME!

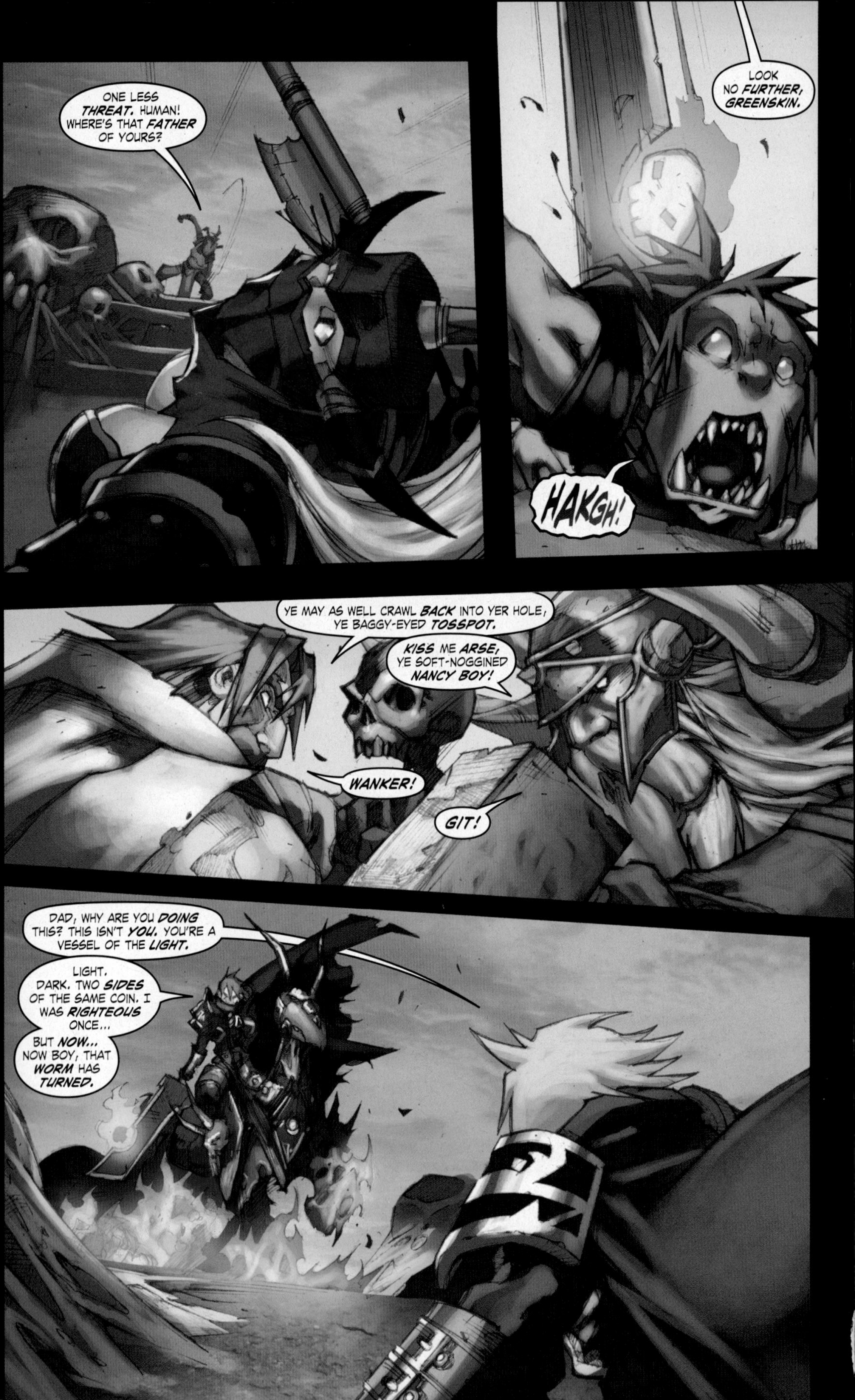
ONE LESS THREAT. HUMAN! WHERE'S THAT FATHER OF YOURS?
LOOK NO FURTHER, GREENSKIN.
HAKGH!
YE MAY AS WELL CRAWL BACK INTO YER HOLE, YE BAGGY-EYED TOSSPOT.
KISS ME ARSE, YE SOFT-NOGGINED NANCY BOY!
WANKER!
GIT!
DAD, WHY ARE YOU DOING THIS? THIS ISN'T YOU. YOU'RE A VESSEL OF THE LIGHT.
LIGHT. DARK. TWO SIDES OF THE SAME COIN. I WAS RIGHTEOUS ONCE...
BUT NOW... NOW BOY, THAT WORM HAS TURNED.

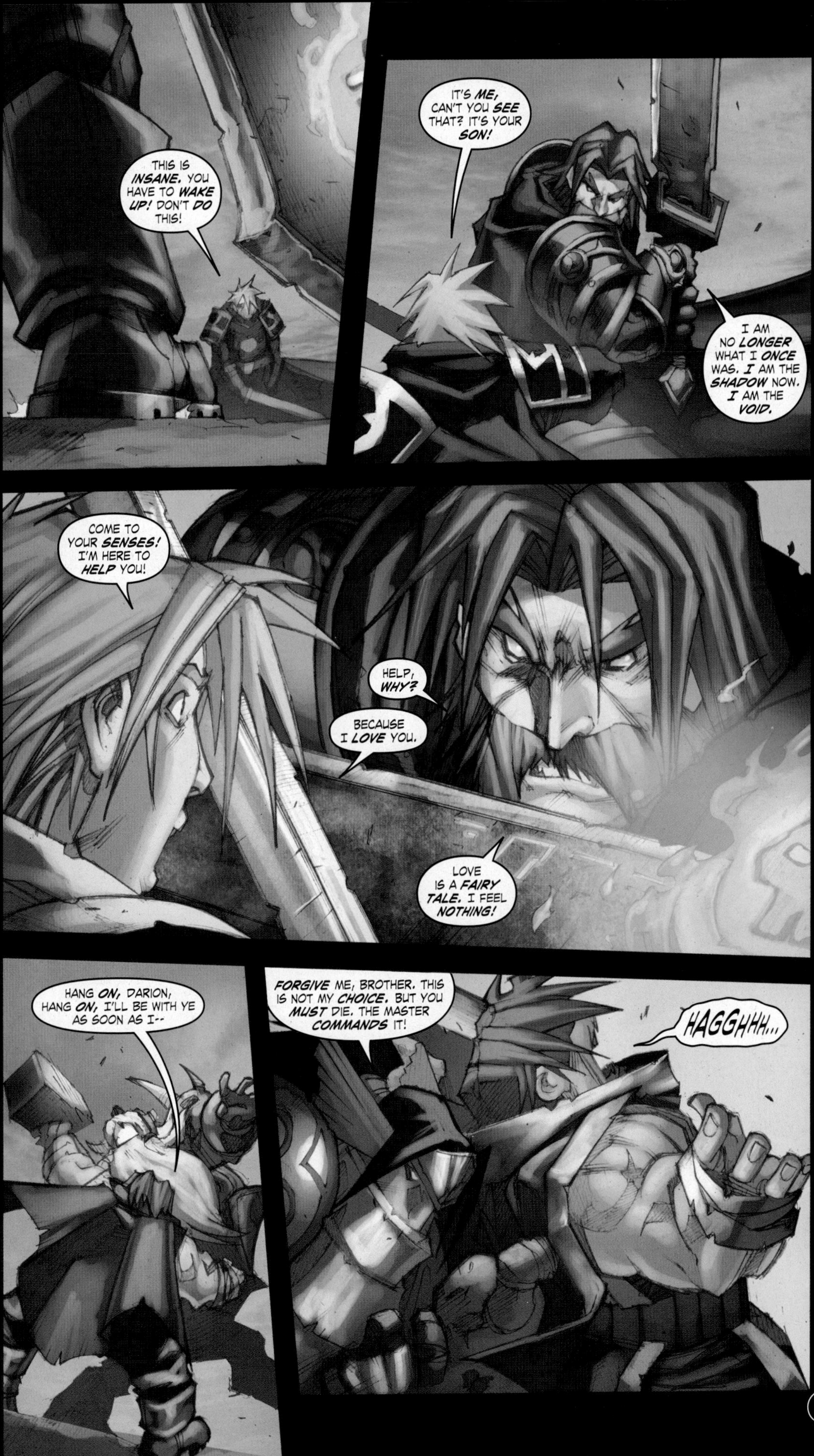
THIS IS INSANE. YOU HAVE TO WAKE UP! DON'T DO THIS!
IT'S ME, CAN'T YOU SEE THAT? IT'S YOUR SON!
I AM NO LONGER WHAT I ONCE WAS. I AM THE SHADOW NOW. I AM THE VOID.
COME TO YOUR SENSES! I'M HERE TO HELP YOU!
HELP, WHY?
BECAUSE I LOVE YOU.
LOVE IS A FAIRY TALE. I FEEL NOTHING!
HANG ON, DARION, HANG ON, I'LL BE WITH YE AS SOON AS I--
FORGIVE ME, BROTHER. THIS IS NOT MY CHOICE. BUT YOU MUST DIE. THE MASTER COMMANDS IT!
HAGGHHH...

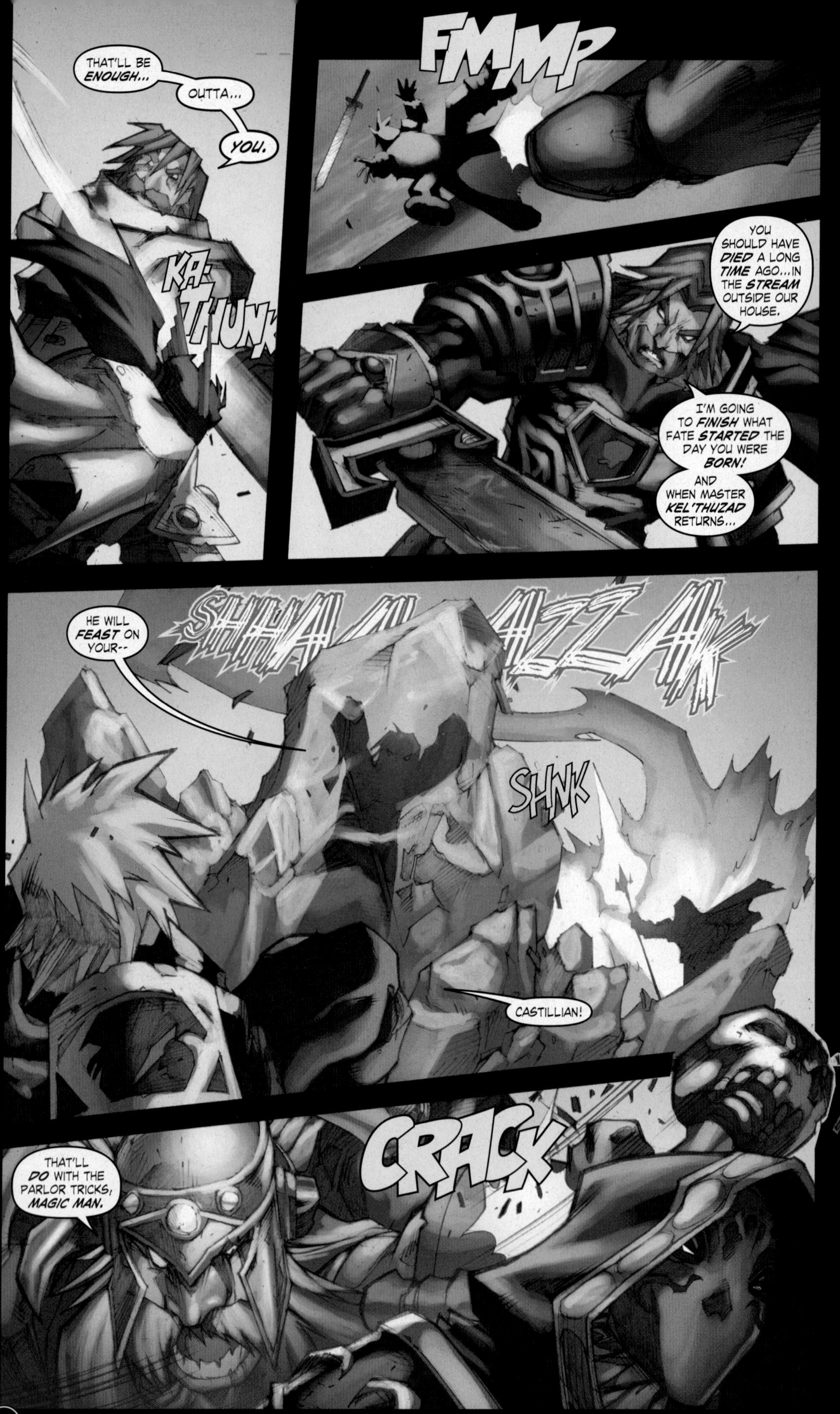
THAT'LL BE ENOUGH...
OUTTA...
YOU.
KA-THUNK
FMMP
YOU SHOULD HAVE DIED A LONG TIME AGO...IN THE STREAM OUTSIDE OUR HOUSE.
I'M GOING TO FINISH WHAT FATE STARTED THE DAY YOU WERE BORN!
AND WHEN MASTER KEL'THUZAD RETURNS...
HE WILL FEAST ON YOUR--
SHHAAAAZZZAK
SHNK
CASTILLIAN!
THAT'LL DO WITH THE PARLOR TRICKS, MAGIC MAN.
CRACK

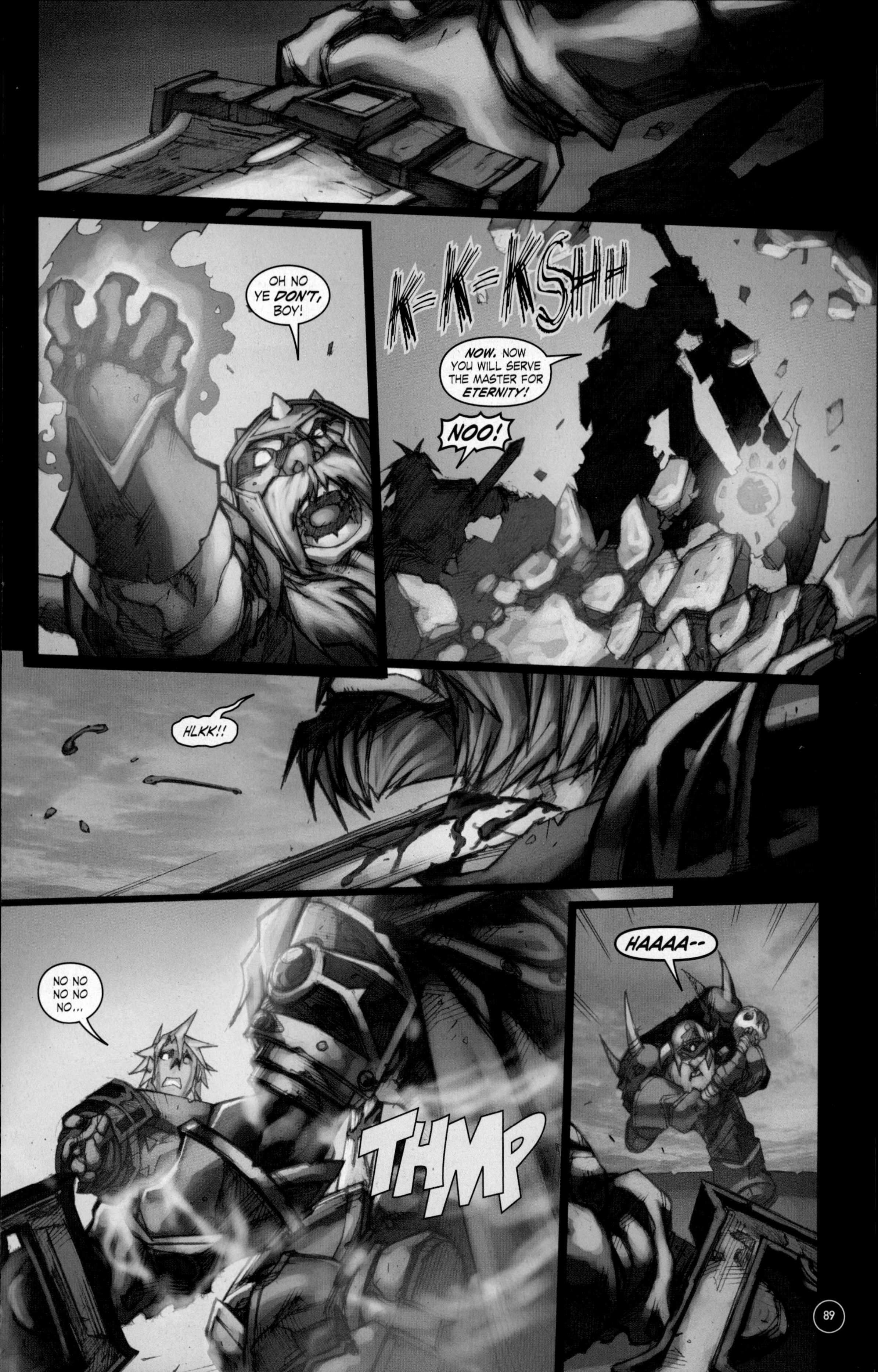
OH NO YE DON'T, BOY!
K-K-KSHH
NOW. NOW YOU WILL SERVE THE MASTER FOR ETERNITY!
NOO!
HLKK!!
NO NO NO NO NO...
THMP
HAAAA--

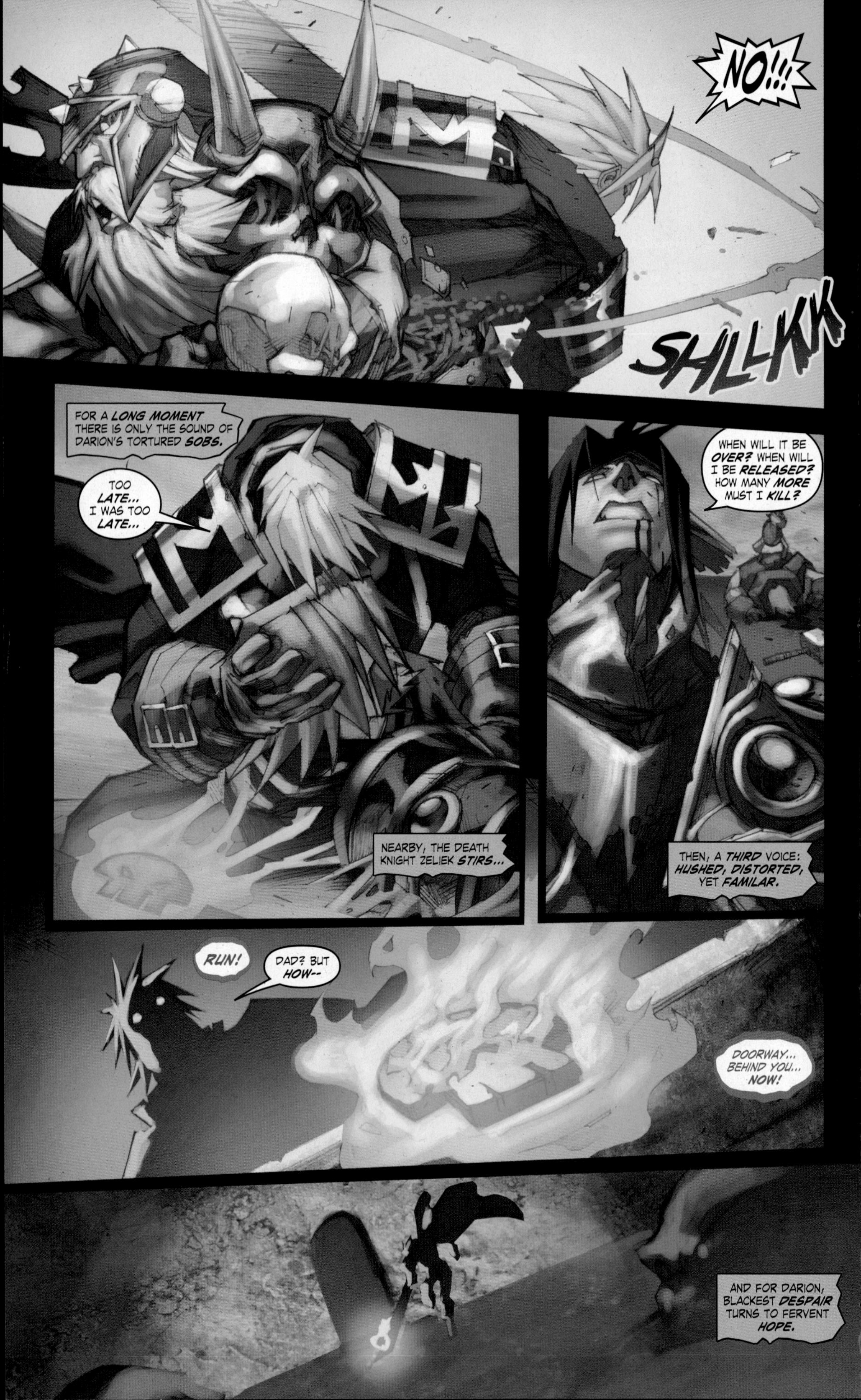

NO!!!
SHLLKK
FOR A LONG MOMENT THERE IS ONLY THE SOUND OF DARION'S TORTURED SOBS.
TOO LATE... I WAS TOO LATE...
NEARBY, THE DEATH KNIGHT ZELIEK STIRS...
WHEN WILL IT BE OVER? WHEN WILL I BE RELEASED? HOW MANY MORE MUST I KILL?
THEN, A THIRD VOICE: HUSHED, DISTORTED, YET FAMILAR.
RUN!
DAD? BUT HOW--
DOORWAY... BEHIND YOU... NOW!
AND FOR DARION, BLACKEST DESPAIR TURNS TO FERVENT HOPE.

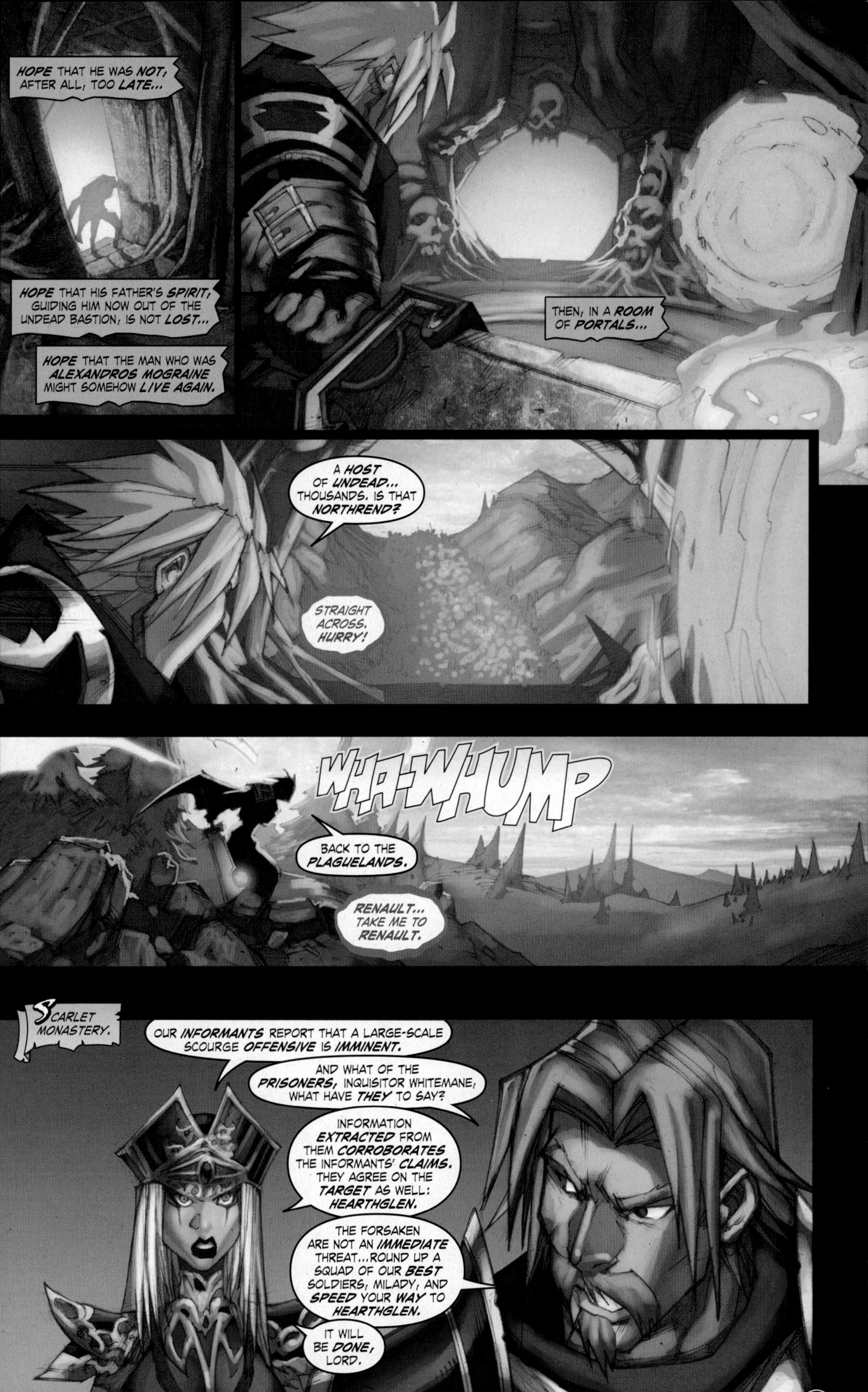
HOPE THAT HE WAS NOT, AFTER ALL, TOO LATE...
HOPE THAT HIS FATHER'S SPIRIT, GUIDING HIM NOW OUT OF THE UNDEAD BASTION, IS NOT LOST...
HOPE THAT THE MAN WHO WAS ALEXANDROS MOGRAINE MIGHT SOMEHOW LIVE AGAIN.
THEN, IN A ROOM OF PORTALS...
A HOST OF UNDEAD... THOUSANDS. IS THAT NORTHREND?
STRAIGHT ACROSS. HURRY!
WHA-WHUMP
BACK TO THE PLAGUELANDS.
RENAULT... TAKE ME TO RENAULT.
SCARLET MONASTERY.
OUR INFORMANTS REPORT THAT A LARGE-SCALE SCOURGE OFFENSIVE IS IMMINENT.
AND WHAT OF THE PRISONERS, INQUISITOR WHITEMANE, WHAT HAVE THEY TO SAY?
INFORMATION EXTRACTED FROM THEM CORROBORATES THE INFORMANTS' CLAIMS. THEY AGREE ON THE TARGET AS WELL: HEARTHGLEN.
THE FORSAKEN ARE NOT AN IMMEDIATE THREAT...ROUND UP A SQUAD OF OUR BEST SOLDIERS, MILADY, AND SPEED YOUR WAY TO HEARTHGLEN.
IT WILL BE DONE, LORD.

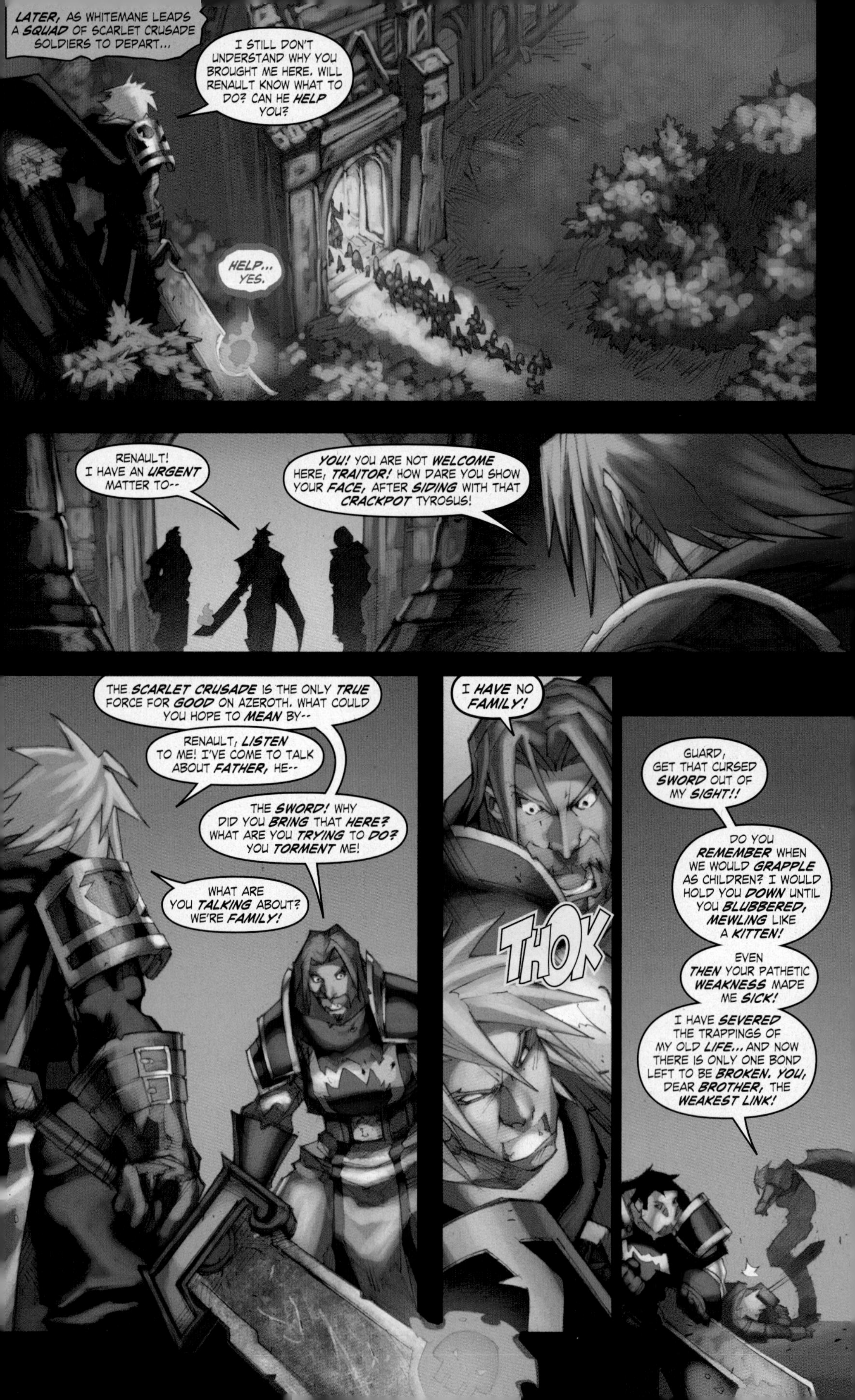

LATER, AS WHITEMANE LEADS A SQUAD OF SCARLET CRUSADE SOLDIERS TO DEPART...
I STILL DON'T UNDERSTAND WHY YOU BROUGHT ME HERE. WILL RENAULT KNOW WHAT TO DO? CAN HE HELP YOU?
HELP... YES.
RENAULT! I HAVE AN URGENT MATTER TO--
YOU! YOU ARE NOT WELCOME HERE, TRAITOR! HOW DARE YOU SHOW YOUR FACE, AFTER SIDING WITH THAT CRACKPOT TYROSUS!
THE SCARLET CRUSADE IS THE ONLY TRUE FORCE FOR GOOD ON AZEROTH. WHAT COULD YOU HOPE TO MEAN BY--
RENAULT, LISTEN TO ME! I'VE COME TO TALK ABOUT FATHER, HE--
THE SWORD! WHY DID YOU BRING THAT HERE? WHAT ARE YOU TRYING TO DO? YOU TORMENT ME!
WHAT ARE YOU TALKING ABOUT? WE'RE FAMILY!
I HAVE NO FAMILY!
THOK
GUARD, GET THAT CURSED SWORD OUT OF MY SIGHT!!
DO YOU REMEMBER WHEN WE WOULD GRAPPLE AS CHILDREN? I WOULD HOLD YOU DOWN UNTIL YOU BLUBBERED, MEWLING LIKE A KITTEN!
EVEN THEN YOUR PATHETIC WEAKNESS MADE ME SICK!
I HAVE SEVERED THE TRAPPINGS OF MY OLD LIFE... AND NOW THERE IS ONLY ONE BOND LEFT TO BE BROKEN. YOU, DEAR BROTHER, THE WEAKEST LINK!

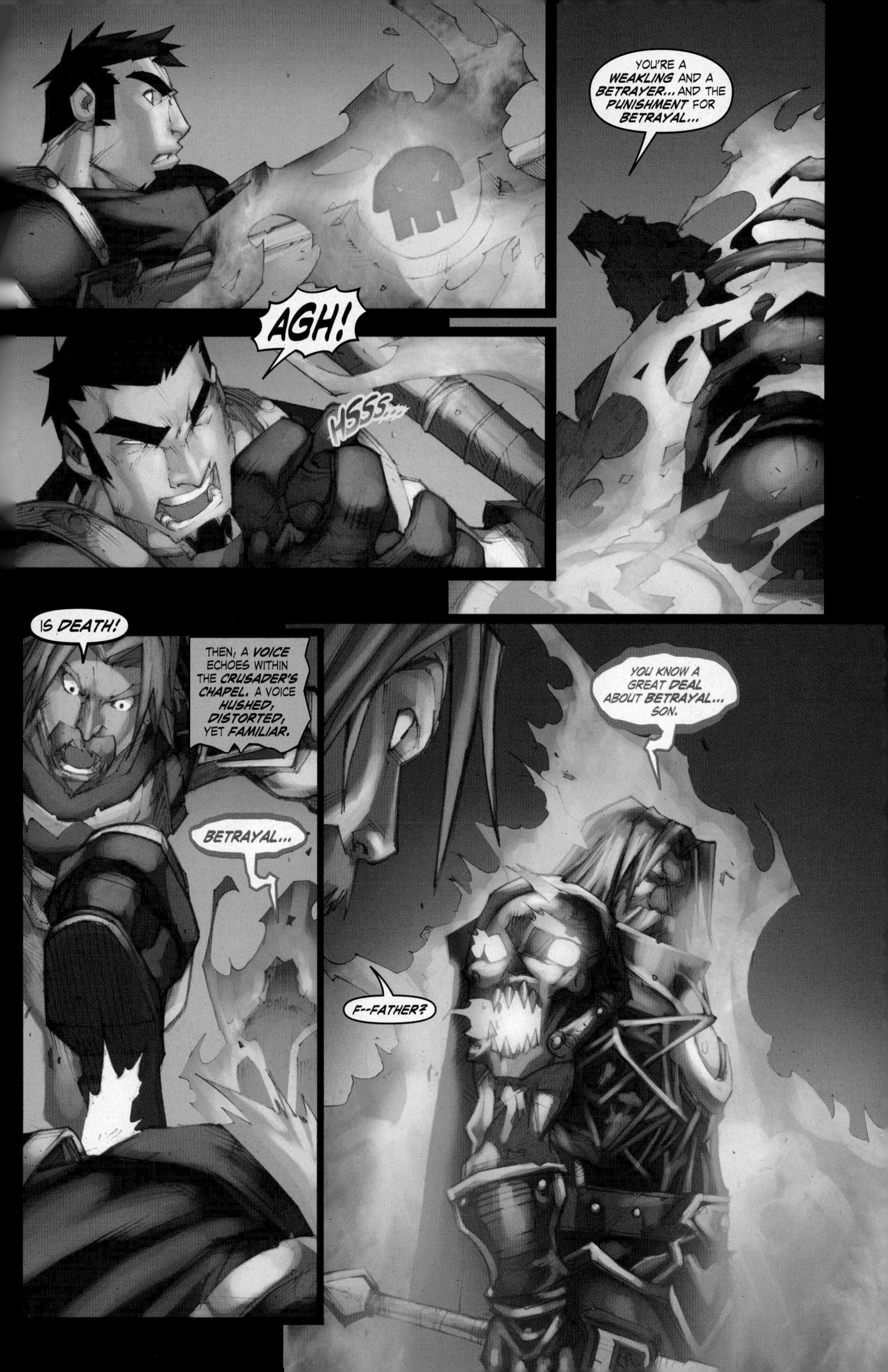
AGH!
HSSS...
YOU'RE A WEAKLING AND A BETRAYER... AND THE PUNISHMENT FOR BETRAYAL...
IS DEATH!
THEN, A VOICE ECHOES WITHIN THE CRUSADER'S CHAPEL. A VOICE HUSHED, DISTORTED, YET FAMILIAR.
BETRAYAL...
YOU KNOW A GREAT DEAL ABOUT BETRAYAL... SON.
F--FATHER?

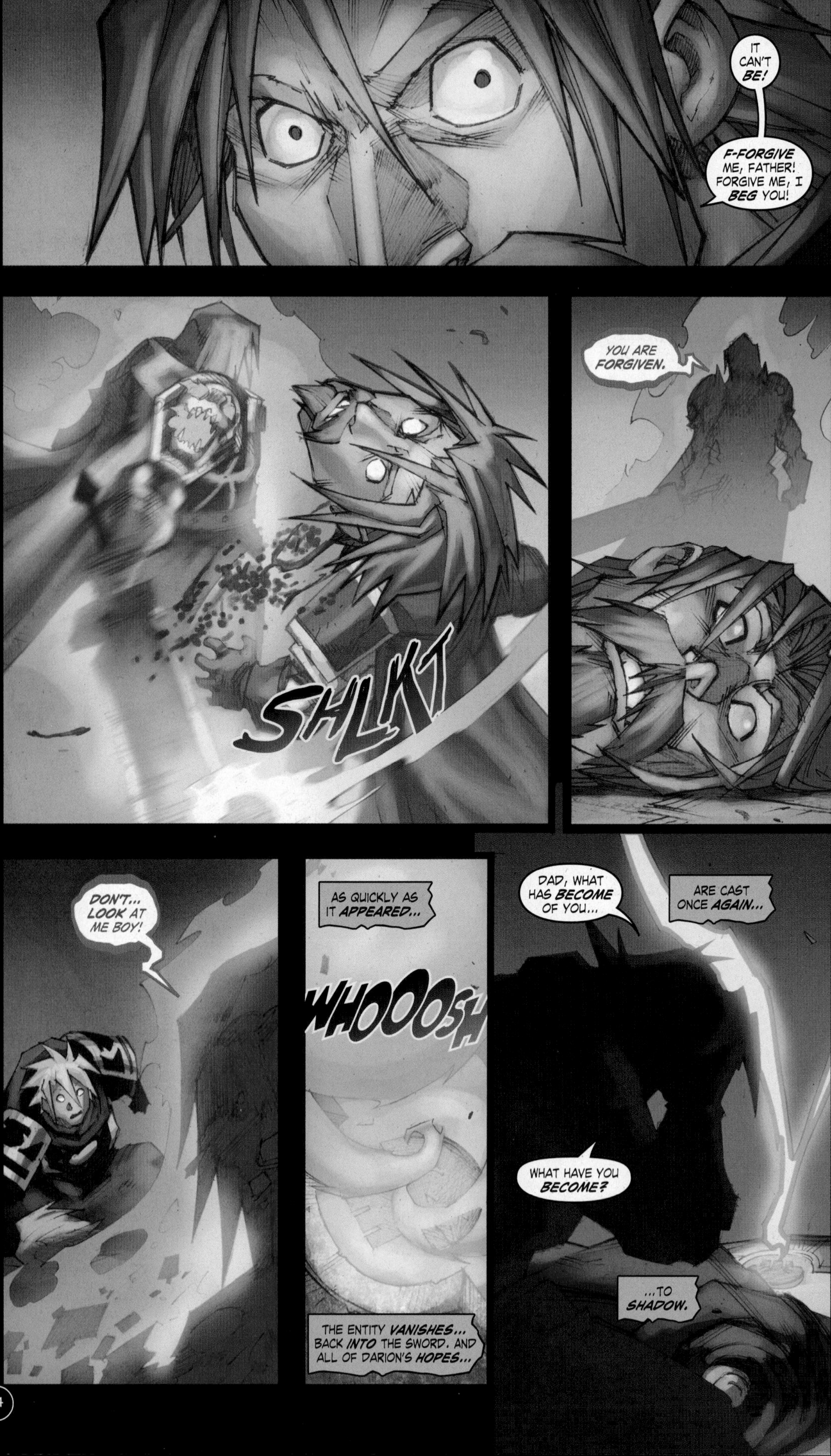

IT CAN'T BE!
F-FORGIVE ME, FATHER! FORGIVE ME, I BEG YOU!
SHLKT
YOU ARE FORGIVEN.
DON'T... LOOK AT ME BOY!
AS QUICKLY AS IT APPEARED...
WHOOOSH
THE ENTITY VANISHES... BACK INTO THE SWORD. AND ALL OF DARION'S HOPES...
DAD, WHAT HAS BECOME OF YOU...
ARE CAST ONCE AGAIN...
WHAT HAVE YOU BECOME?
...TO SHADOW.

CHAPTER 4

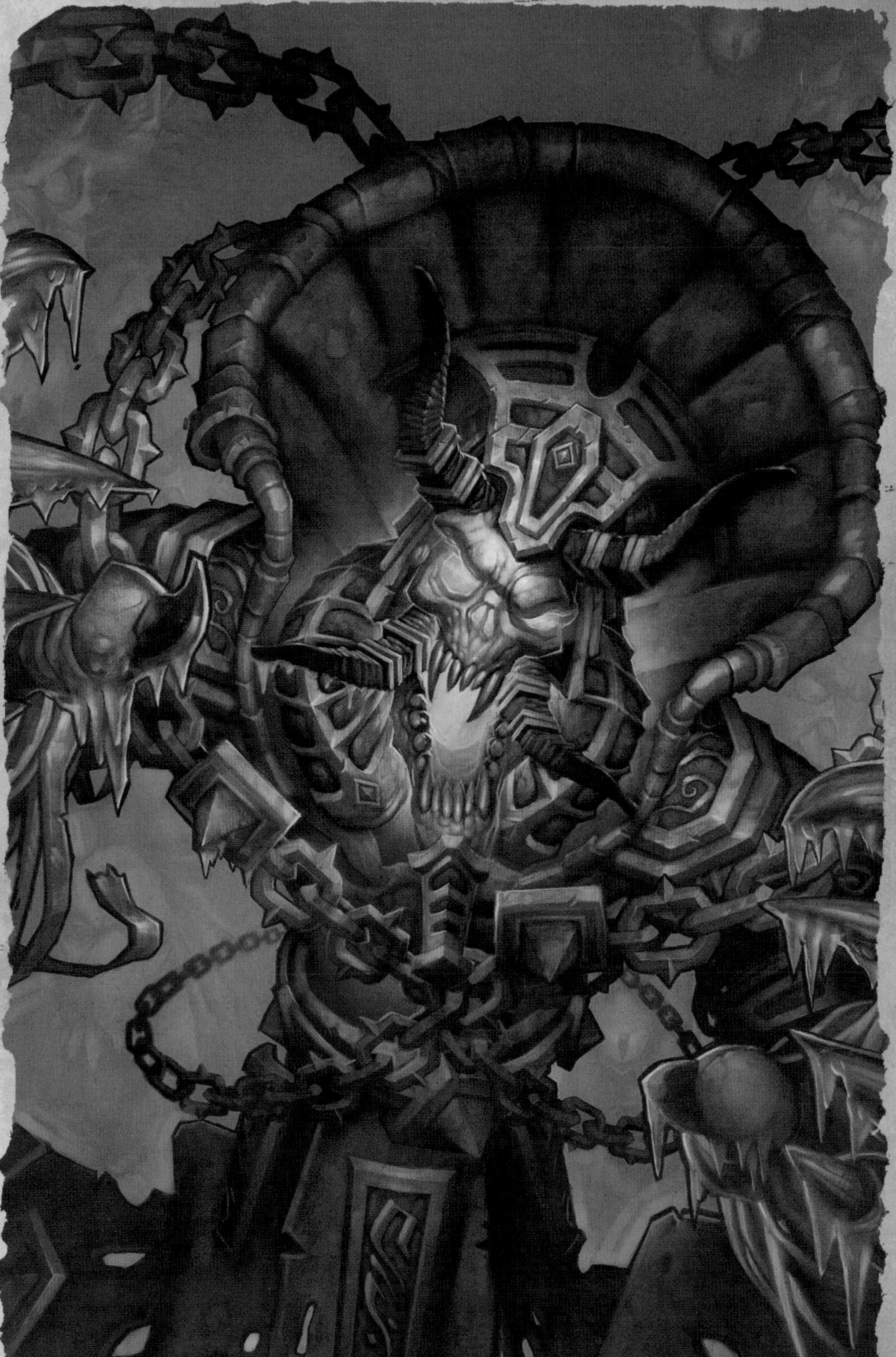

Cover by Chris Robinson

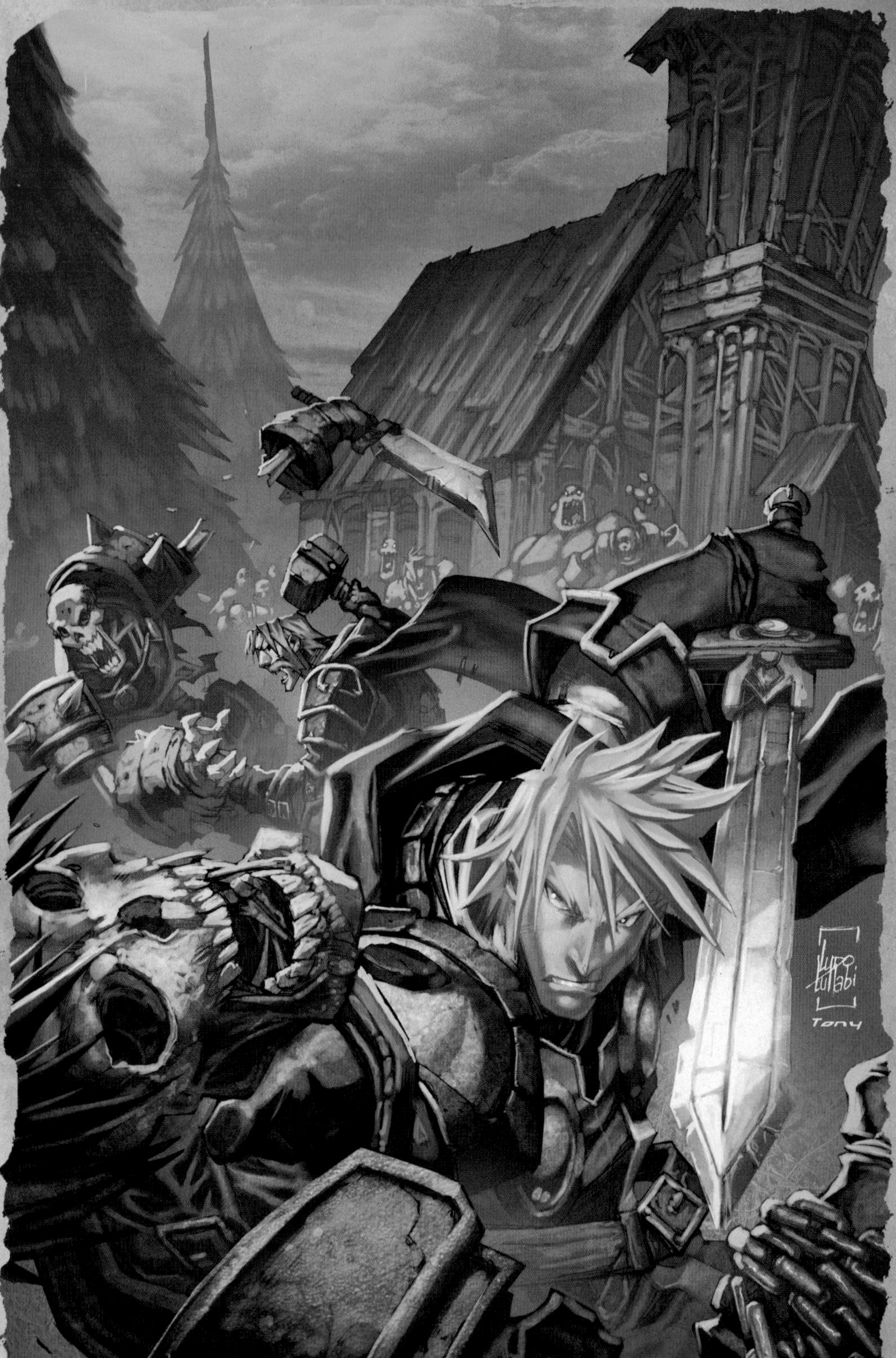
Ludo Lullabi
Tony

Cover by Ludo Lullabi and Tony Washington

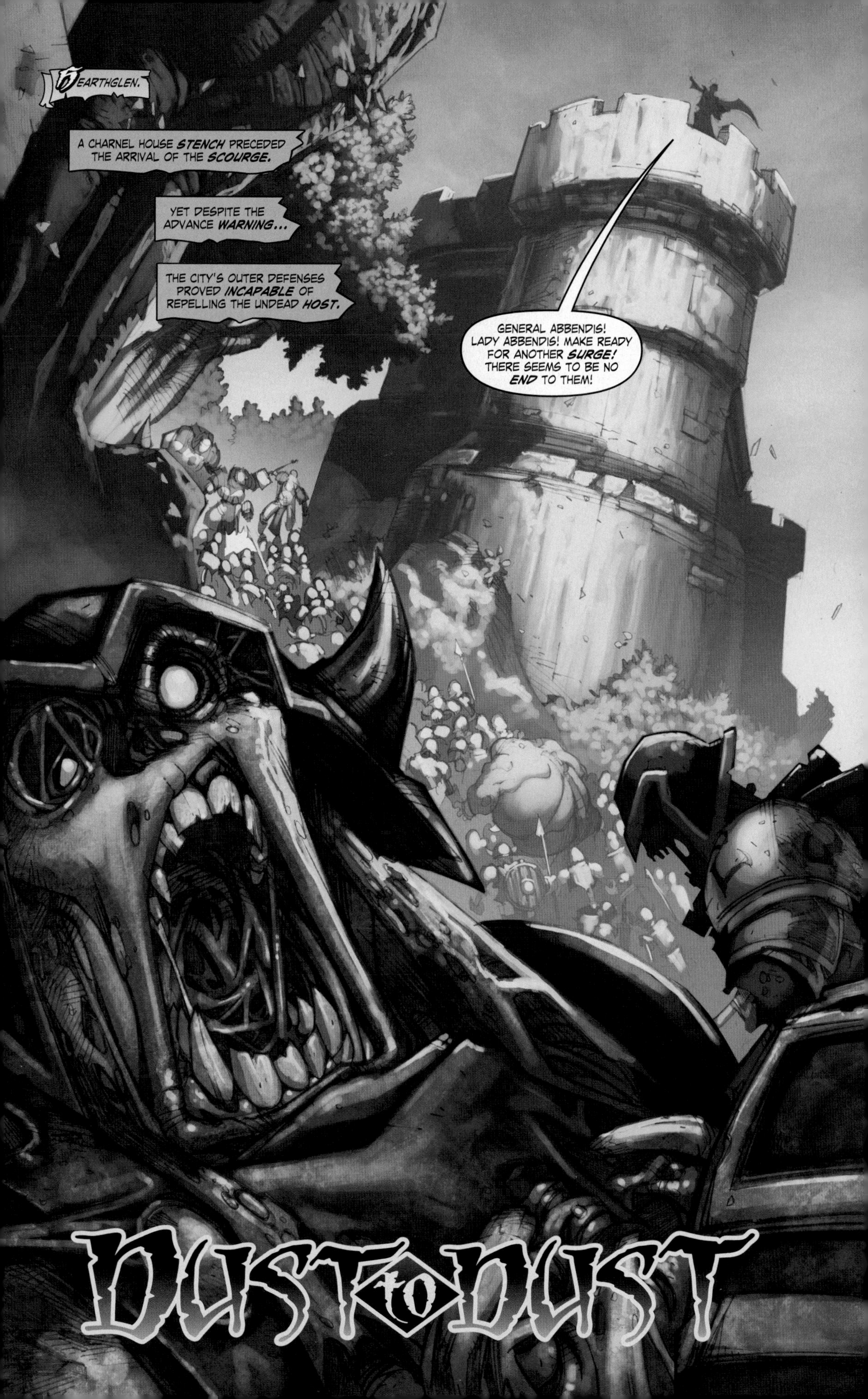

HEARTHGLEN.
A CHARNEL HOUSE STENCH PRECEDED THE ARRIVAL OF THE SCOURGE.
YET DESPITE THE ADVANCE WARNING...
THE CITY'S OUTER DEFENSES PROVED INCAPABLE OF REPELLING THE UNDEAD HOST.
GENERAL ABBENDIS! LADY ABBENDIS! MAKE READY FOR ANOTHER SURGE! THERE SEEMS TO BE NO END TO THEM!
DUST TO DUST

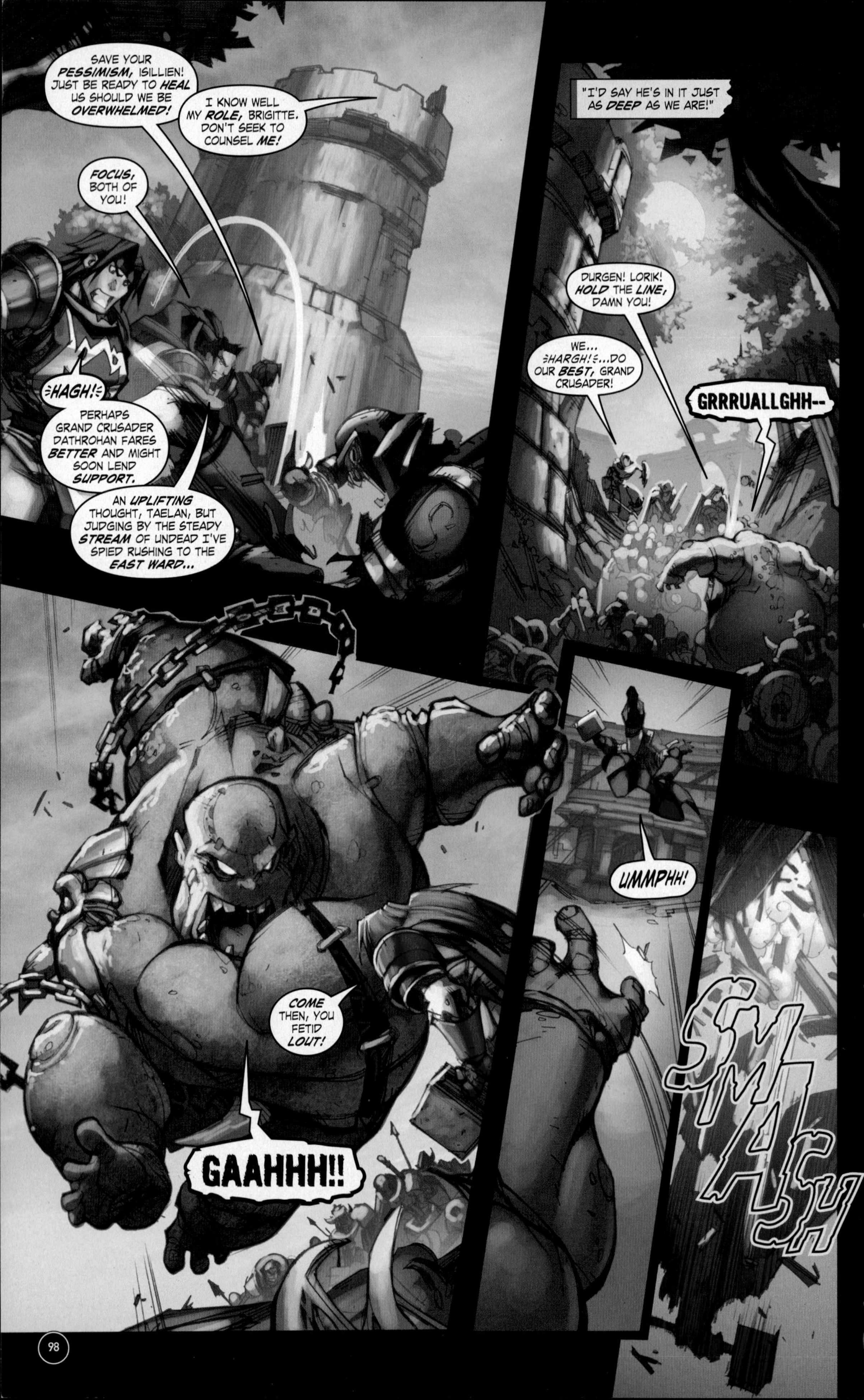

SAVE YOUR PESSIMISM, ISILLIEN! JUST BE READY TO HEAL US SHOULD WE BE OVERWHELMED!
I KNOW WELL MY ROLE, BRIGITTE. DON'T SEEK TO COUNSEL ME!
FOCUS, BOTH OF YOU!
HAGH!
PERHAPS GRAND CRUSADER DATHROHAN FARES BETTER AND MIGHT SOON LEND SUPPORT.
AN UPLIFTING THOUGHT, TAELAN, BUT JUDGING BY THE STEADY STREAM OF UNDEAD I'VE SPIED RUSHING TO THE EAST WARD...
"I'D SAY HE'S IN IT JUST AS DEEP AS WE ARE!"
DURGEN! LORIK! HOLD THE LINE, DAMN YOU!
WE... HARGH! ...DO OUR BEST, GRAND CRUSADER!
GRRRUALLGHH--
COME THEN, YOU FETID LOUT!
GAAHHH!!
UMMPHH!
SMASH

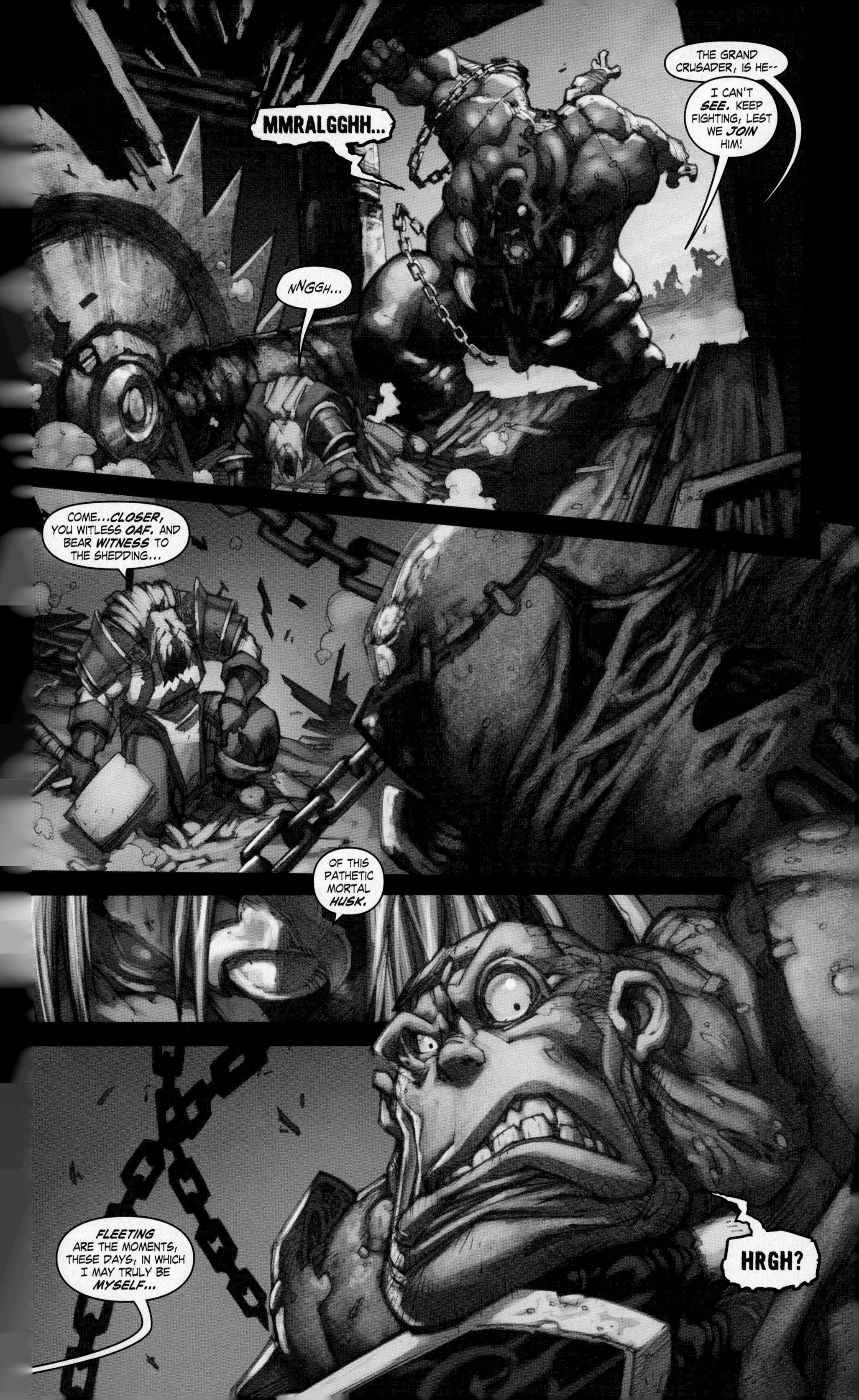
MMRALGGHH...
THE GRAND CRUSADER, IS HE--
I CAN'T SEE. KEEP FIGHTING, LEST WE JOIN HIM!
NNGGH...
COME...CLOSER, YOU WITLESS OAF. AND BEAR WITNESS TO THE SHEDDING...
OF THIS PATHETIC MORTAL HUSK.
FLEETING ARE THE MOMENTS, THESE DAYS, IN WHICH I MAY TRULY BE MYSELF...
HRGH?

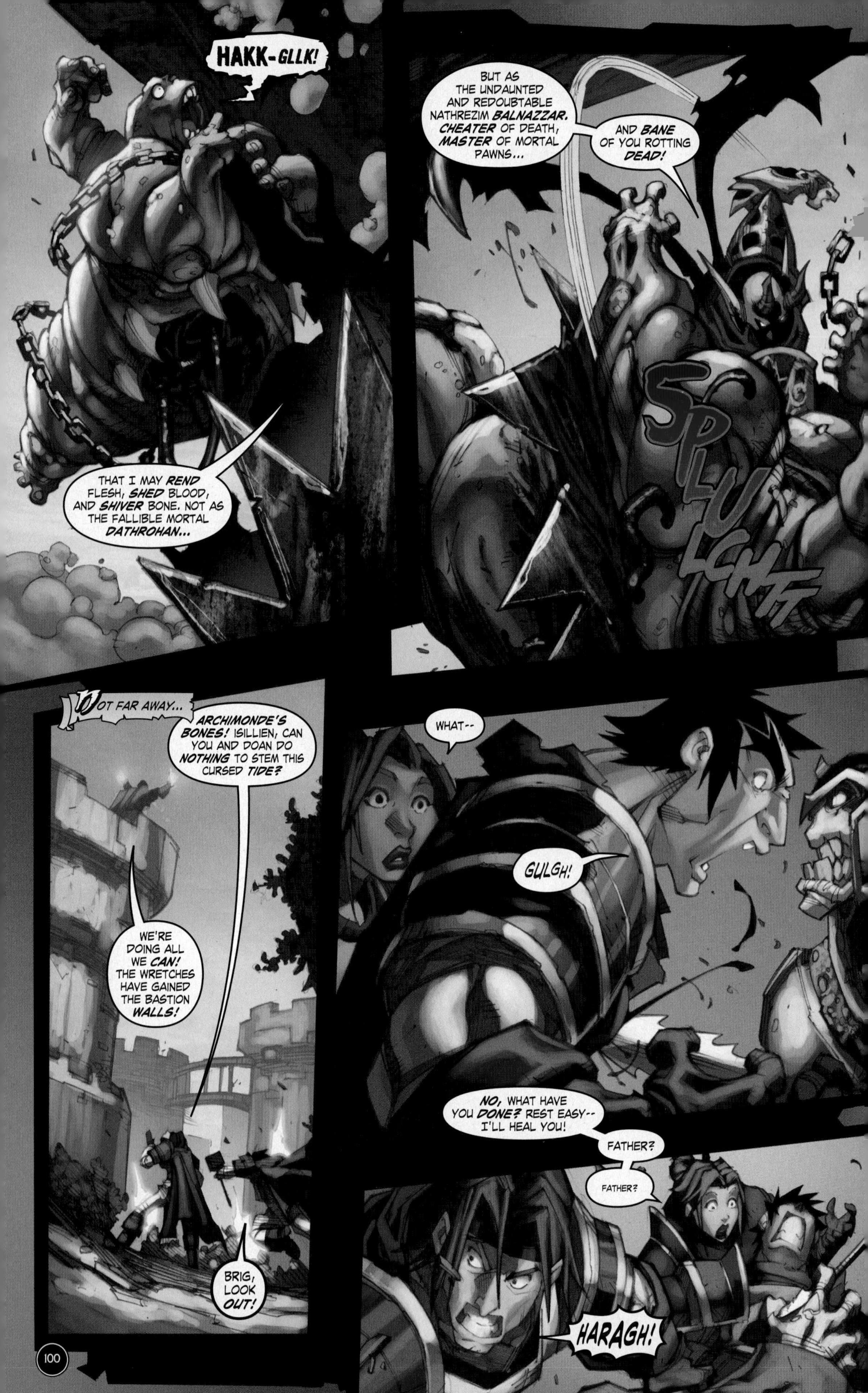
HAKK-GLLK!
THAT I MAY REND FLESH, SHED BLOOD, AND SHIVER BONE. NOT AS THE FALLIBLE MORTAL DATHROHAN...
BUT AS THE UNDAUNTED AND REDOUBTABLE NATHREZIM BALNAZZAR. CHEATER OF DEATH, MASTER OF MORTAL PAWNS...
AND BANE OF YOU ROTTING DEAD!
SPLULCHT
NOT FAR AWAY...
ARCHIMONDE'S BONES! ISILLIEN, CAN YOU AND DOAN DO NOTHING TO STEM THIS CURSED TIDE?
WE'RE DOING ALL WE CAN! THE WRETCHES HAVE GAINED THE BASTION WALLS!
BRIG, LOOK OUT!
WHAT--
GULGH!
NO, WHAT HAVE YOU DONE? REST EASY-- I'LL HEAL YOU!
FATHER?
FATHER?
HARAGH!

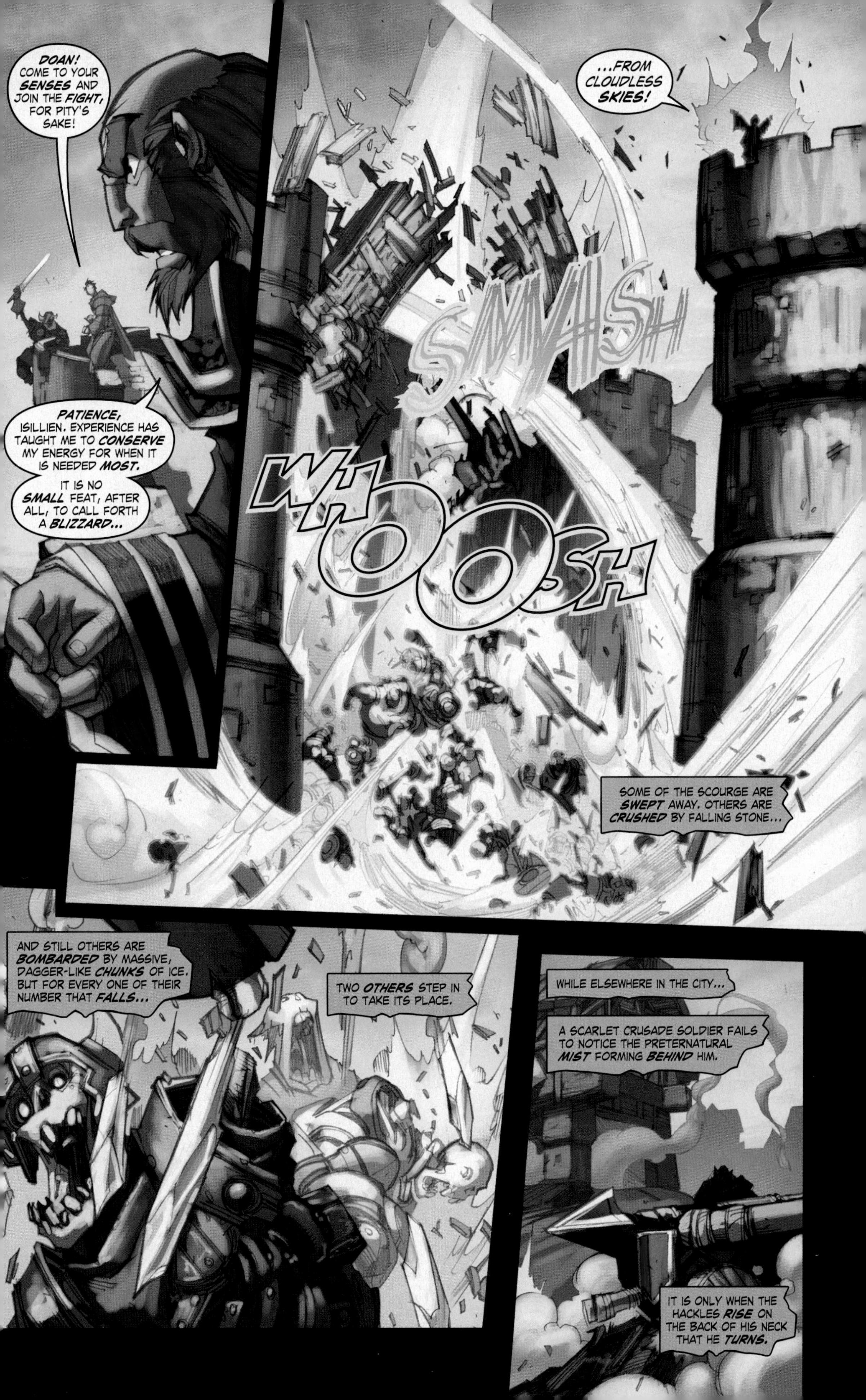
DOAN! COME TO YOUR SENSES AND JOIN THE FIGHT, FOR PITY'S SAKE!
PATIENCE, ISILLIEN. EXPERIENCE HAS TAUGHT ME TO CONSERVE MY ENERGY FOR WHEN IT IS NEEDED MOST.
IT IS NO SMALL FEAT, AFTER ALL, TO CALL FORTH A BLIZZARD...
...FROM CLOUDLESS SKIES!
SMASH
WHOOOSH
SOME OF THE SCOURGE ARE SWEPT AWAY. OTHERS ARE CRUSHED BY FALLING STONE...
AND STILL OTHERS ARE BOMBARDED BY MASSIVE, DAGGER-LIKE CHUNKS OF ICE. BUT FOR EVERY ONE OF THEIR NUMBER THAT FALLS...
TWO OTHERS STEP IN TO TAKE ITS PLACE.
WHILE ELSEWHERE IN THE CITY...
A SCARLET CRUSADE SOLDIER FAILS TO NOTICE THE PRETERNATURAL MIST FORMING BEHIND HIM.
IT IS ONLY WHEN THE HACKLES RISE ON THE BACK OF HIS NECK THAT HE TURNS.

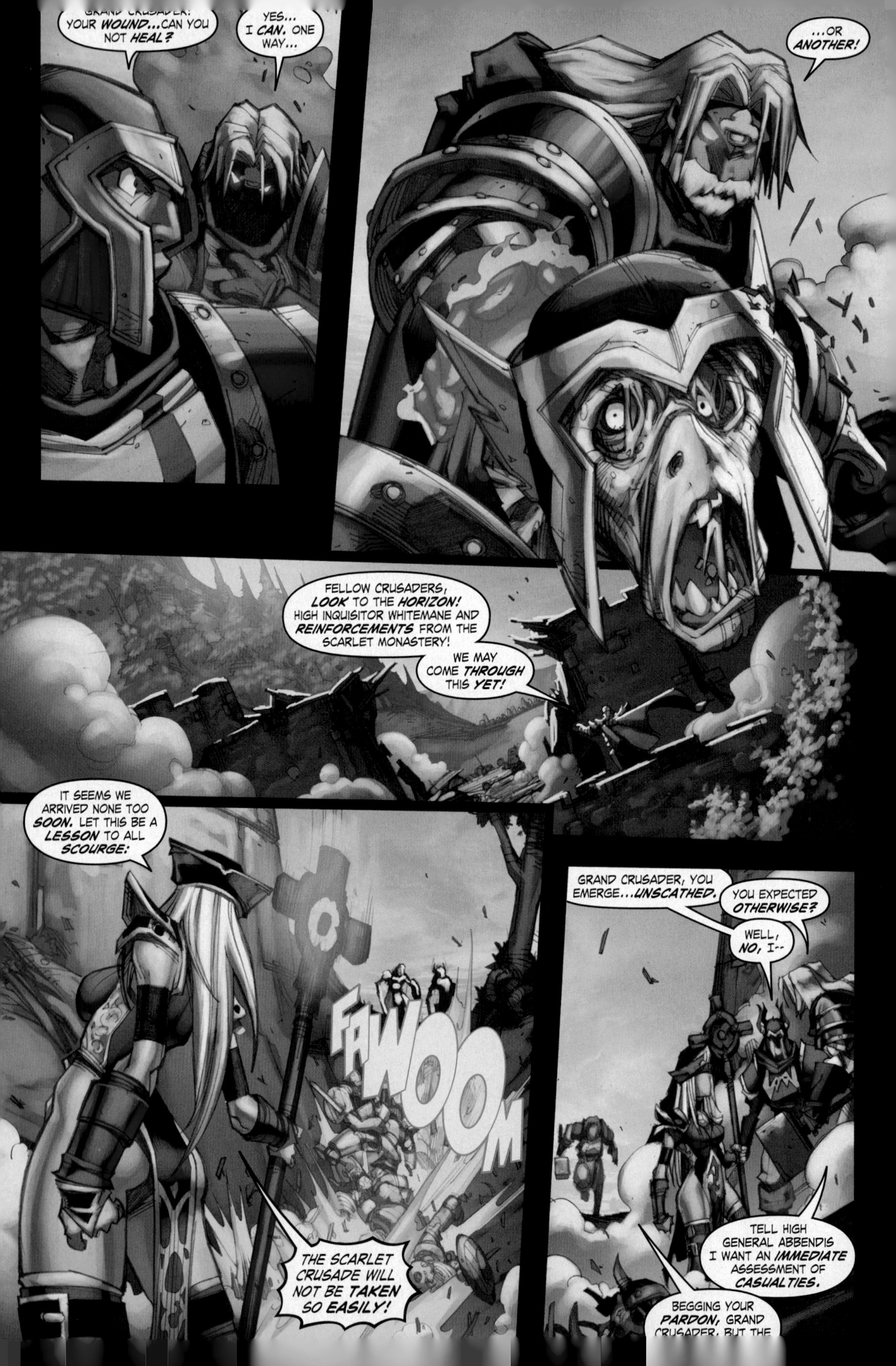

GRAND CRUSADER! YOUR WOUND...CAN YOU NOT HEAL?
YES... I CAN. ONE WAY...
...OR ANOTHER!
FELLOW CRUSADERS, LOOK TO THE HORIZON! HIGH INQUISITOR WHITEMANE AND REINFORCEMENTS FROM THE SCARLET MONASTERY!
WE MAY COME THROUGH THIS YET!
IT SEEMS WE ARRIVED NONE TOO SOON. LET THIS BE A LESSON TO ALL SCOURGE:
FAWOOM
THE SCARLET CRUSADE WILL NOT BE TAKEN SO EASILY!
GRAND CRUSADER, YOU EMERGE...UNSCATHED.
YOU EXPECTED OTHERWISE?
WELL, NO, I--
TELL HIGH GENERAL ABBENDIS I WANT AN IMMEDIATE ASSESSMENT OF CASUALTIES.
BEGGING YOUR PARDON, GRAND CRUSADER, BUT THE

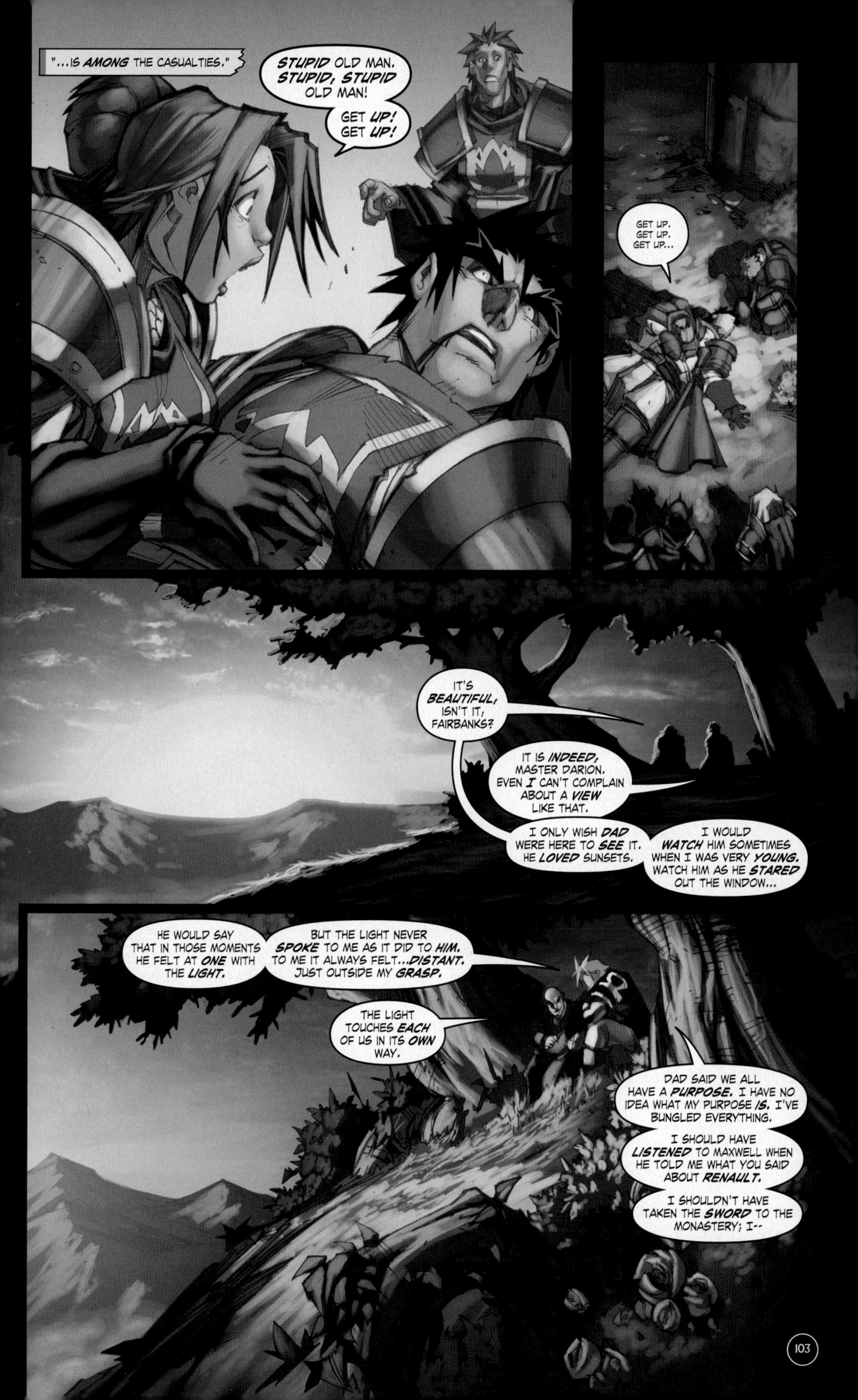

"...IS AMONG THE CASUALTIES."
STUPID OLD MAN. STUPID, STUPID OLD MAN!
GET UP! GET UP!
GET UP. GET UP. GET UP...
IT'S BEAUTIFUL, ISN'T IT, FAIRBANKS?
IT IS INDEED, MASTER DARION. EVEN I CAN'T COMPLAIN ABOUT A VIEW LIKE THAT.
I ONLY WISH DAD WERE HERE TO SEE IT. HE LOVED SUNSETS.
I WOULD WATCH HIM SOMETIMES WHEN I WAS VERY YOUNG. WATCH HIM AS HE STARED OUT THE WINDOW...
HE WOULD SAY THAT IN THOSE MOMENTS HE FELT AT ONE WITH THE LIGHT.
BUT THE LIGHT NEVER SPOKE TO ME AS IT DID TO HIM. TO ME IT ALWAYS FELT...DISTANT. JUST OUTSIDE MY GRASP.
THE LIGHT TOUCHES EACH OF US IN ITS OWN WAY.
DAD SAID WE ALL HAVE A PURPOSE. I HAVE NO IDEA WHAT MY PURPOSE IS. I'VE BUNGLED EVERYTHING.
I SHOULD HAVE LISTENED TO MAXWELL WHEN HE TOLD ME WHAT YOU SAID ABOUT RENAULT.
I SHOULDN'T HAVE TAKEN THE SWORD TO THE MONASTERY; I--

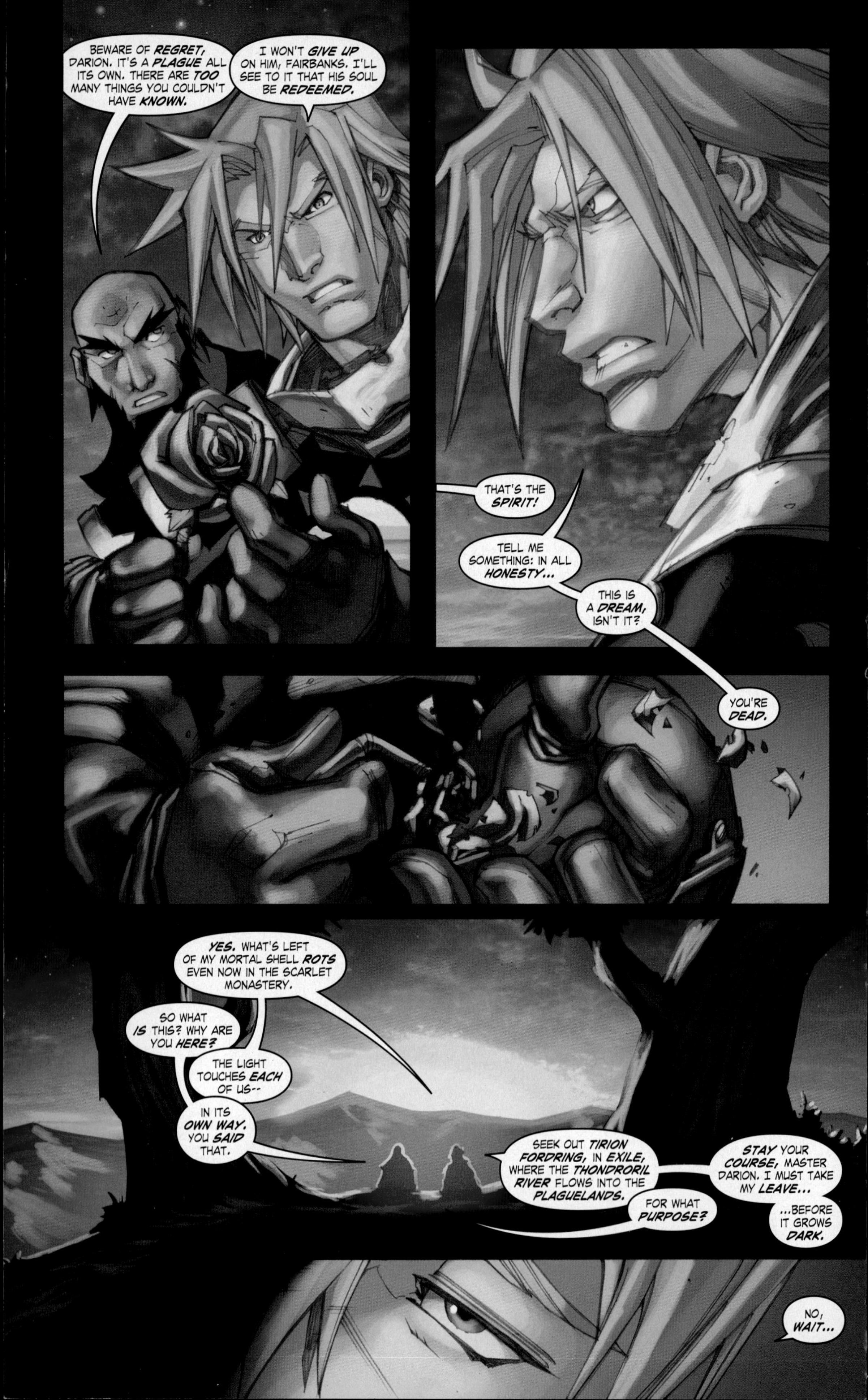
BEWARE OF REGRET, DARION. IT'S A PLAGUE ALL ITS OWN. THERE ARE TOO MANY THINGS YOU COULDN'T HAVE KNOWN.
I WON'T GIVE UP ON HIM, FAIRBANKS. I'LL SEE TO IT THAT HIS SOUL BE REDEEMED.
THAT'S THE SPIRIT!
TELL ME SOMETHING: IN ALL HONESTY...
THIS IS A DREAM, ISN'T IT?
YOU'RE DEAD.
YES. WHAT'S LEFT OF MY MORTAL SHELL ROTS EVEN NOW IN THE SCARLET MONASTERY.
SO WHAT IS THIS? WHY ARE YOU HERE?
THE LIGHT TOUCHES EACH OF US--
IN ITS OWN WAY. YOU SAID THAT.
SEEK OUT TIRION FORDRING, IN EXILE, WHERE THE THONDRORIL RIVER FLOWS INTO THE PLAGUELANDS.
FOR WHAT PURPOSE?
STAY YOUR COURSE, MASTER DARION. I MUST TAKE MY LEAVE...
...BEFORE IT GROWS DARK.
NO, WAIT...

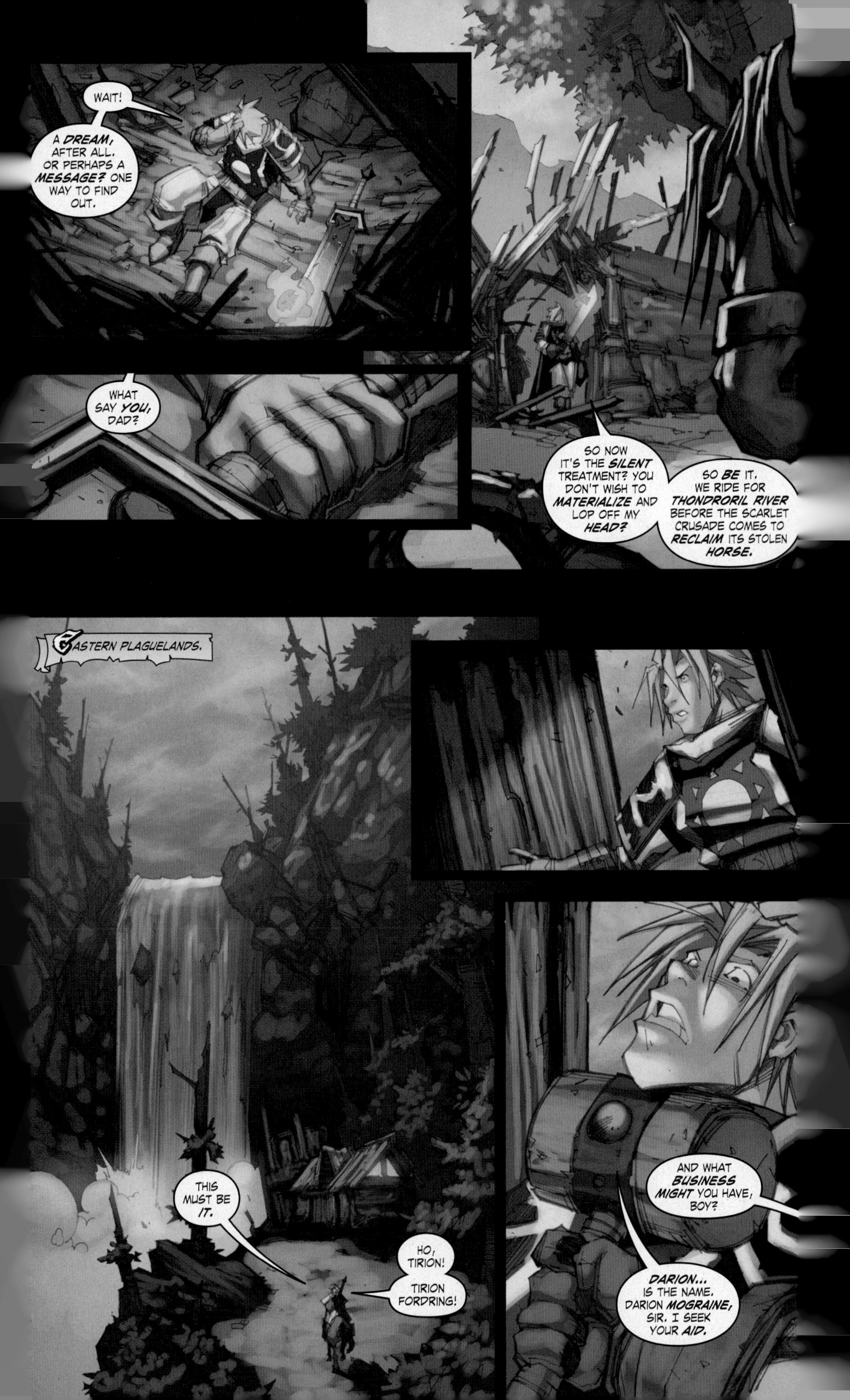
WAIT!
A DREAM, AFTER ALL. OR PERHAPS A MESSAGE? ONE WAY TO FIND OUT.
WHAT SAY YOU, DAD?
SO NOW IT'S THE SILENT TREATMENT? YOU DON'T WISH TO MATERIALIZE AND LOP OFF MY HEAD?
SO BE IT. WE RIDE FOR THONDRORIL RIVER BEFORE THE SCARLET CRUSADE COMES TO RECLAIM ITS STOLEN HORSE.
EASTERN PLAGUELANDS.
THIS MUST BE IT.
HO, TIRION!
TIRION FORDRING!
AND WHAT BUSINESS MIGHT YOU HAVE, BOY?
DARION... IS THE NAME. DARION MOGRAINE, SIR. I SEEK YOUR AID.

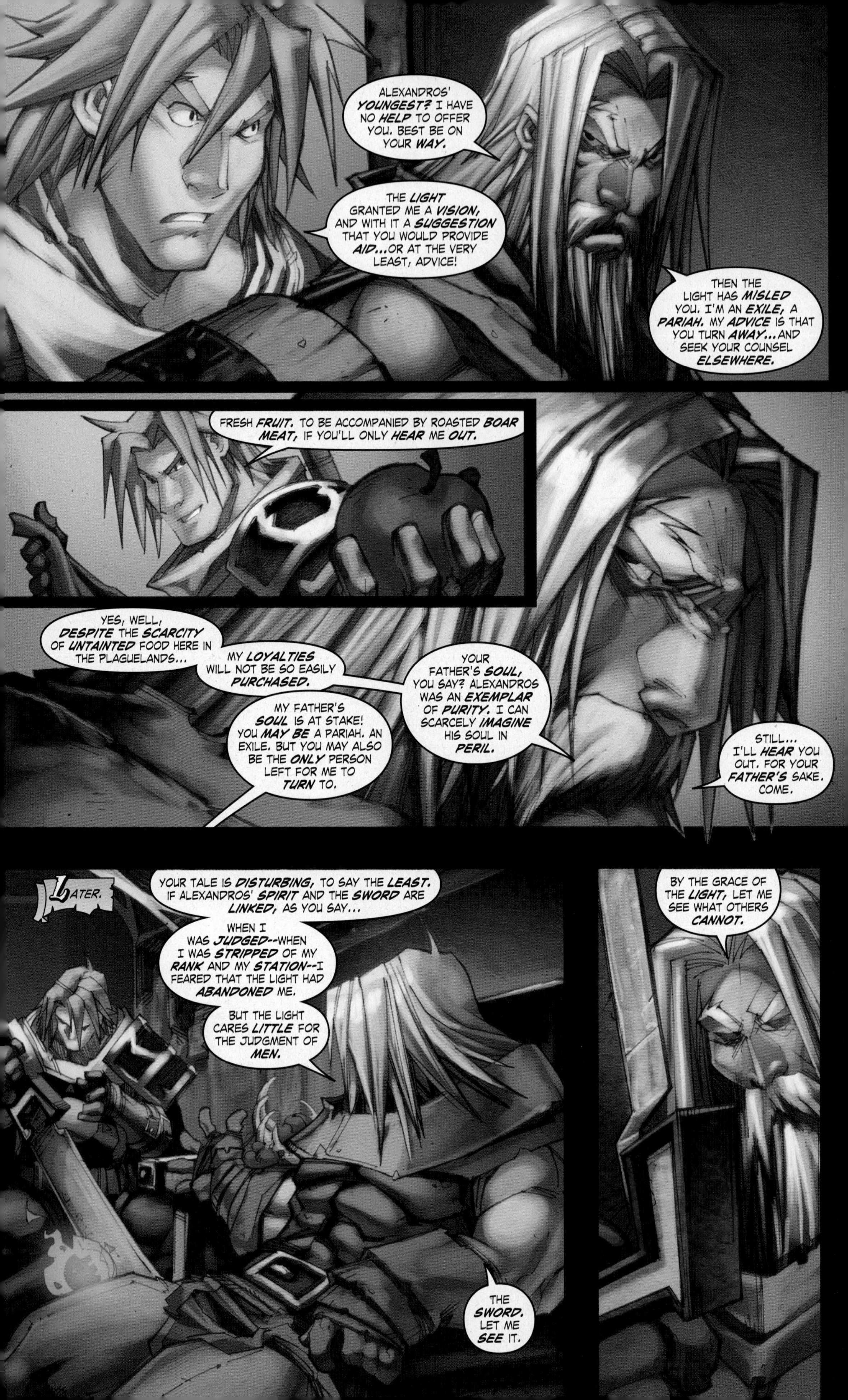

ALEXANDROS' YOUNGEST? I HAVE NO HELP TO OFFER YOU. BEST BE ON YOUR WAY.
THE LIGHT GRANTED ME A VISION, AND WITH IT A SUGGESTION THAT YOU WOULD PROVIDE AID...OR AT THE VERY LEAST, ADVICE!
THEN THE LIGHT HAS MISLED YOU. I'M AN EXILE, A PARIAH. MY ADVICE IS THAT YOU TURN AWAY...AND SEEK YOUR COUNSEL ELSEWHERE.
FRESH FRUIT. TO BE ACCOMPANIED BY ROASTED BOAR MEAT, IF YOU'LL ONLY HEAR ME OUT.
YES, WELL, DESPITE THE SCARCITY OF UNTAINTED FOOD HERE IN THE PLAGUELANDS...
MY LOYALTIES WILL NOT BE SO EASILY PURCHASED.
MY FATHER'S SOUL IS AT STAKE! YOU MAY BE A PARIAH. AN EXILE. BUT YOU MAY ALSO BE THE ONLY PERSON LEFT FOR ME TO TURN TO.
YOUR FATHER'S SOUL, YOU SAY? ALEXANDROS WAS AN EXEMPLAR OF PURITY. I CAN SCARCELY IMAGINE HIS SOUL IN PERIL.
STILL... I'LL HEAR YOU OUT. FOR YOUR FATHER'S SAKE. COME.
LATER.
YOUR TALE IS DISTURBING, TO SAY THE LEAST. IF ALEXANDROS' SPIRIT AND THE SWORD ARE LINKED, AS YOU SAY...
WHEN I WAS JUDGED--WHEN I WAS STRIPPED OF MY RANK AND MY STATION--I FEARED THAT THE LIGHT HAD ABANDONED ME.
BUT THE LIGHT CARES LITTLE FOR THE JUDGMENT OF MEN.
THE SWORD. LET ME SEE IT.
BY THE GRACE OF THE LIGHT, LET ME SEE WHAT OTHERS CANNOT.

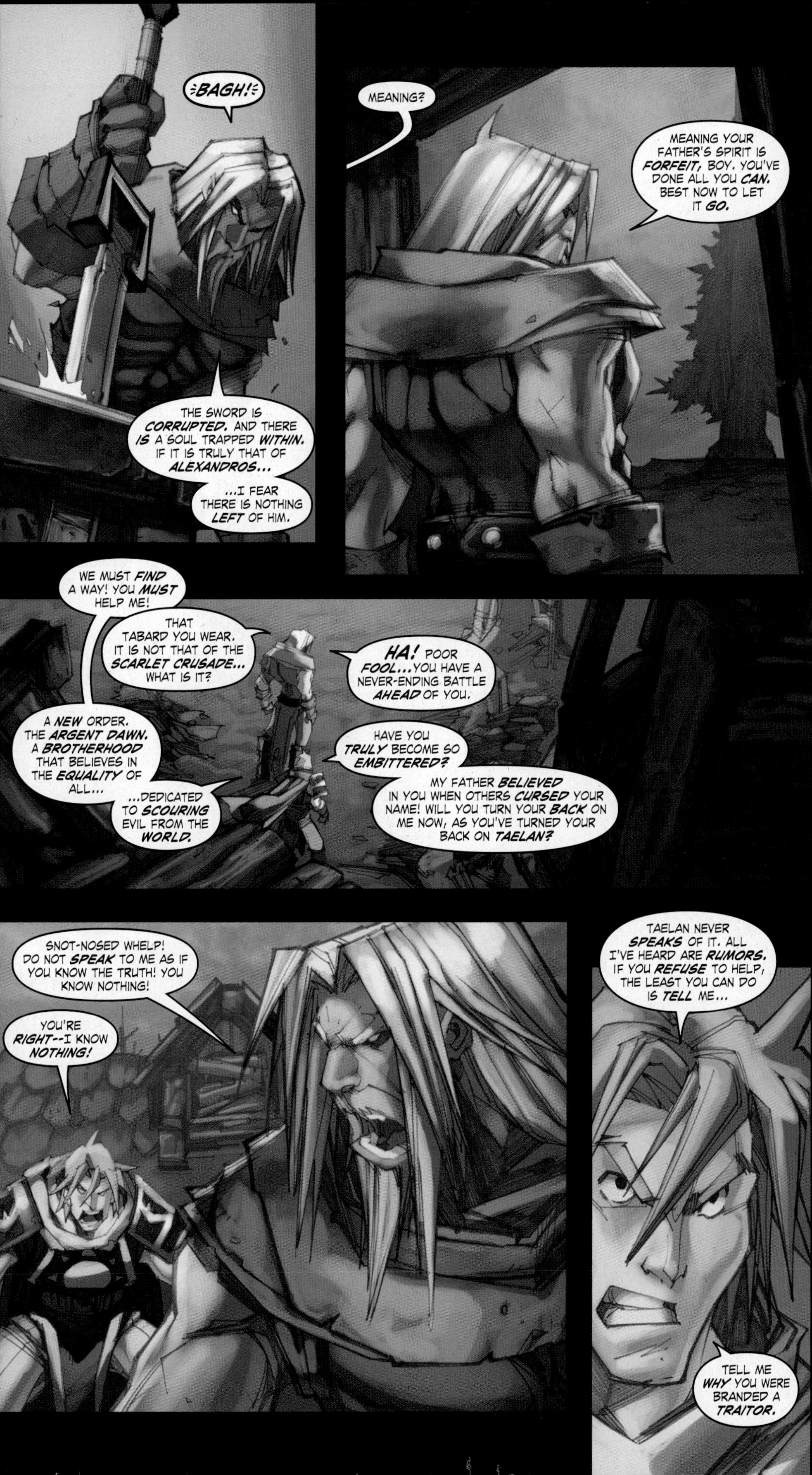
BAGH!
THE SWORD IS CORRUPTED. AND THERE IS A SOUL TRAPPED WITHIN. IF IT IS TRULY THAT OF ALEXANDROS...
...I FEAR THERE IS NOTHING LEFT OF HIM.
MEANING?
MEANING YOUR FATHER'S SPIRIT IS FORFEIT, BOY. YOU'VE DONE ALL YOU CAN. BEST NOW TO LET IT GO.
WE MUST FIND A WAY! YOU MUST HELP ME!
THAT TABARD YOU WEAR. IT IS NOT THAT OF THE SCARLET CRUSADE... WHAT IS IT?
A NEW ORDER. THE ARGENT DAWN. A BROTHERHOOD THAT BELIEVES IN THE EQUALITY OF ALL...
...DEDICATED TO SCOURING EVIL FROM THE WORLD.
HA! POOR FOOL...YOU HAVE A NEVER-ENDING BATTLE AHEAD OF YOU.
HAVE YOU TRULY BECOME SO EMBITTERED?
MY FATHER BELIEVED IN YOU WHEN OTHERS CURSED YOUR NAME! WILL YOU TURN YOUR BACK ON ME NOW, AS YOU'VE TURNED YOUR BACK ON TAELAN?
SNOT-NOSED WHELP! DO NOT SPEAK TO ME AS IF YOU KNOW THE TRUTH! YOU KNOW NOTHING!
YOU'RE RIGHT--I KNOW NOTHING!
TAELAN NEVER SPEAKS OF IT. ALL I'VE HEARD ARE RUMORS. IF YOU REFUSE TO HELP, THE LEAST YOU CAN DO IS TELL ME...
TELL ME WHY YOU WERE BRANDED A TRAITOR.

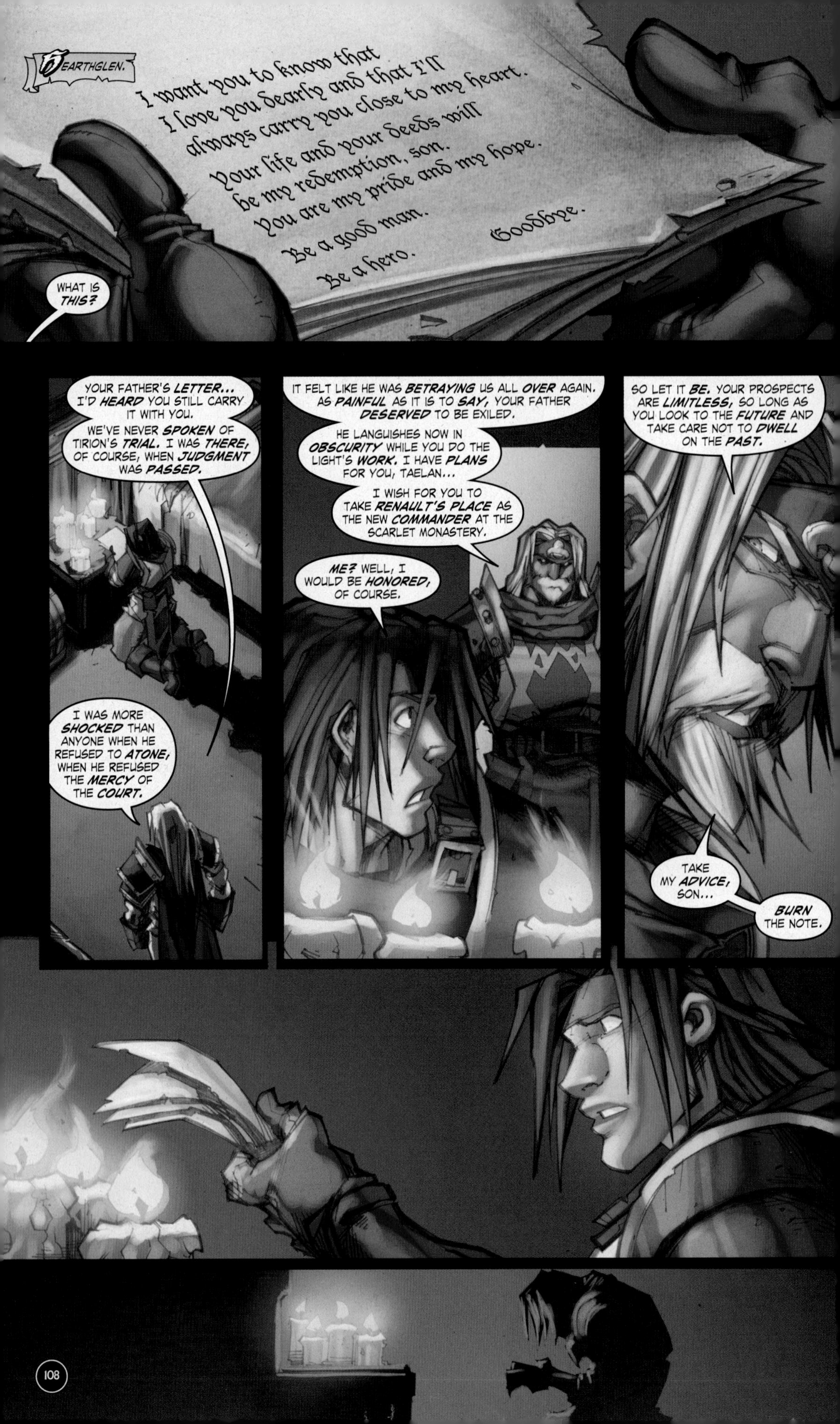

HEARTHGLEN.
I want you to know that I love you dearly and that I'll always carry you close to my heart.
Your life and your deeds will be my redemption, son.
You are my pride and my hope.
Be a good man.
Be a hero.
Goodbye.
WHAT IS THIS?
YOUR FATHER'S LETTER... I'D HEARD YOU STILL CARRY IT WITH YOU.
WE'VE NEVER SPOKEN OF TIRION'S TRIAL. I WAS THERE, OF COURSE, WHEN JUDGMENT WAS PASSED.
I WAS MORE SHOCKED THAN ANYONE WHEN HE REFUSED TO ATONE, WHEN HE REFUSED THE MERCY OF THE COURT.
IT FELT LIKE HE WAS BETRAYING US ALL OVER AGAIN. AS PAINFUL AS IT IS TO SAY, YOUR FATHER DESERVED TO BE EXILED.
HE LANGUISHES NOW IN OBSCURITY WHILE YOU DO THE LIGHT'S WORK. I HAVE PLANS FOR YOU, TAELAN...
I WISH FOR YOU TO TAKE RENAULT'S PLACE AS THE NEW COMMANDER AT THE SCARLET MONASTERY.
ME? WELL, I WOULD BE HONORED, OF COURSE.
SO LET IT BE. YOUR PROSPECTS ARE LIMITLESS, SO LONG AS YOU LOOK TO THE FUTURE AND TAKE CARE NOT TO DWELL ON THE PAST.
TAKE MY ADVICE, SON...
BURN THE NOTE.

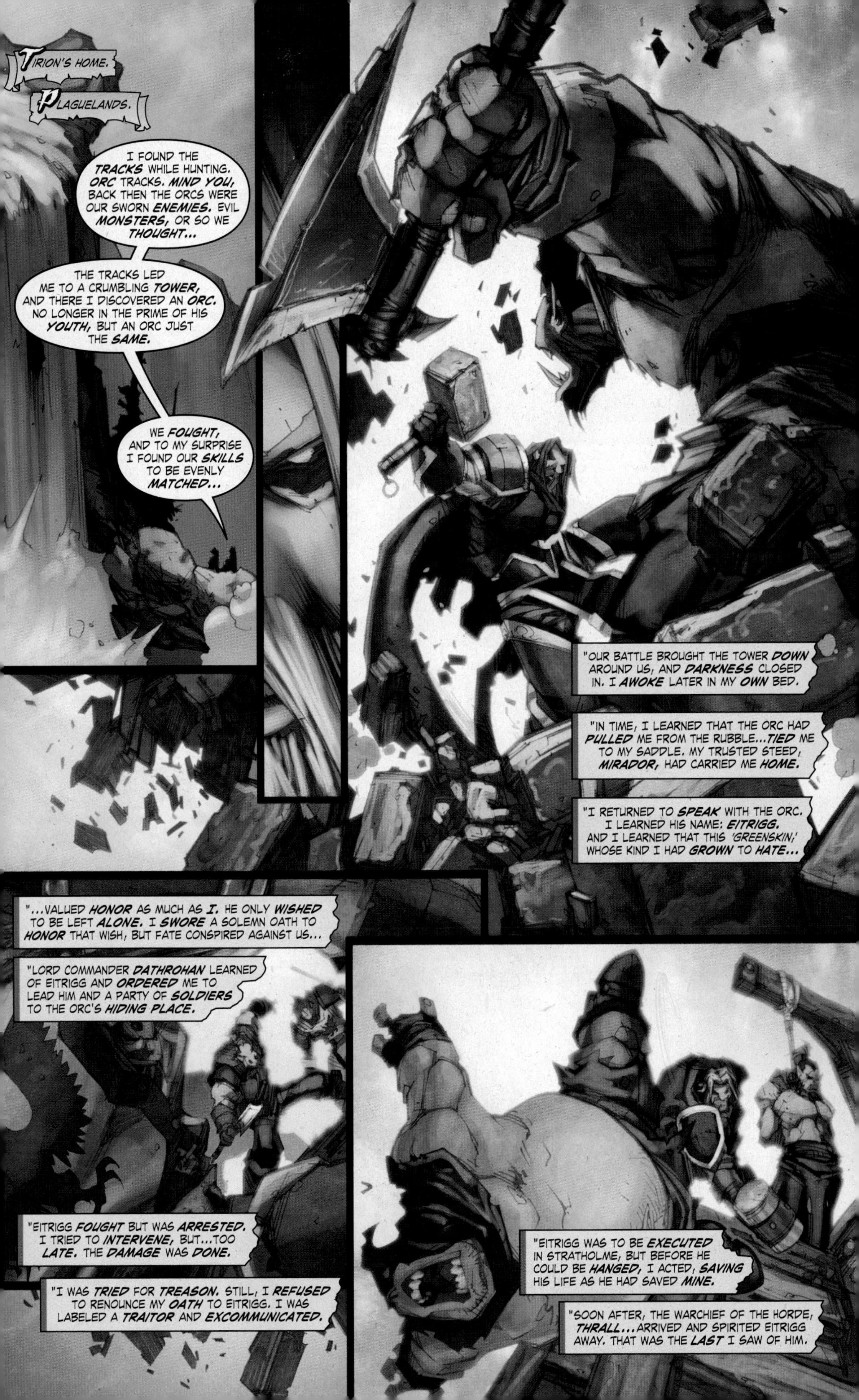

TIRION'S HOME.
PLAGUELANDS.
I FOUND THE TRACKS WHILE HUNTING. ORC TRACKS. MIND YOU, BACK THEN THE ORCS WERE OUR SWORN ENEMIES. EVIL MONSTERS, OR SO WE THOUGHT...
THE TRACKS LED ME TO A CRUMBLING TOWER, AND THERE I DISCOVERED AN ORC. NO LONGER IN THE PRIME OF HIS YOUTH, BUT AN ORC JUST THE SAME.
WE FOUGHT, AND TO MY SURPRISE I FOUND OUR SKILLS TO BE EVENLY MATCHED...
"OUR BATTLE BROUGHT THE TOWER DOWN AROUND US, AND DARKNESS CLOSED IN. I AWOKE LATER IN MY OWN BED.
"IN TIME, I LEARNED THAT THE ORC HAD PULLED ME FROM THE RUBBLE...TIED ME TO MY SADDLE. MY TRUSTED STEED, MIRADOR, HAD CARRIED ME HOME.
"I RETURNED TO SPEAK WITH THE ORC. I LEARNED HIS NAME: EITRIGG. AND I LEARNED THAT THIS 'GREENSKIN,' WHOSE KIND I HAD GROWN TO HATE...
"...VALUED HONOR AS MUCH AS I. HE ONLY WISHED TO BE LEFT ALONE. I SWORE A SOLEMN OATH TO HONOR THAT WISH, BUT FATE CONSPIRED AGAINST US...
"LORD COMMANDER DATHROHAN LEARNED OF EITRIGG AND ORDERED ME TO LEAD HIM AND A PARTY OF SOLDIERS TO THE ORC'S HIDING PLACE.
"EITRIGG FOUGHT BUT WAS ARRESTED. I TRIED TO INTERVENE, BUT...TOO LATE. THE DAMAGE WAS DONE.
"I WAS TRIED FOR TREASON. STILL, I REFUSED TO RENOUNCE MY OATH TO EITRIGG. I WAS LABELED A TRAITOR AND EXCOMMUNICATED.
"EITRIGG WAS TO BE EXECUTED IN STRATHOLME, BUT BEFORE HE COULD BE HANGED, I ACTED, SAVING HIS LIFE AS HE HAD SAVED MINE.
"SOON AFTER, THE WARCHIEF OF THE HORDE, THRALL... ARRIVED AND SPIRITED EITRIGG AWAY. THAT WAS THE LAST I SAW OF HIM.

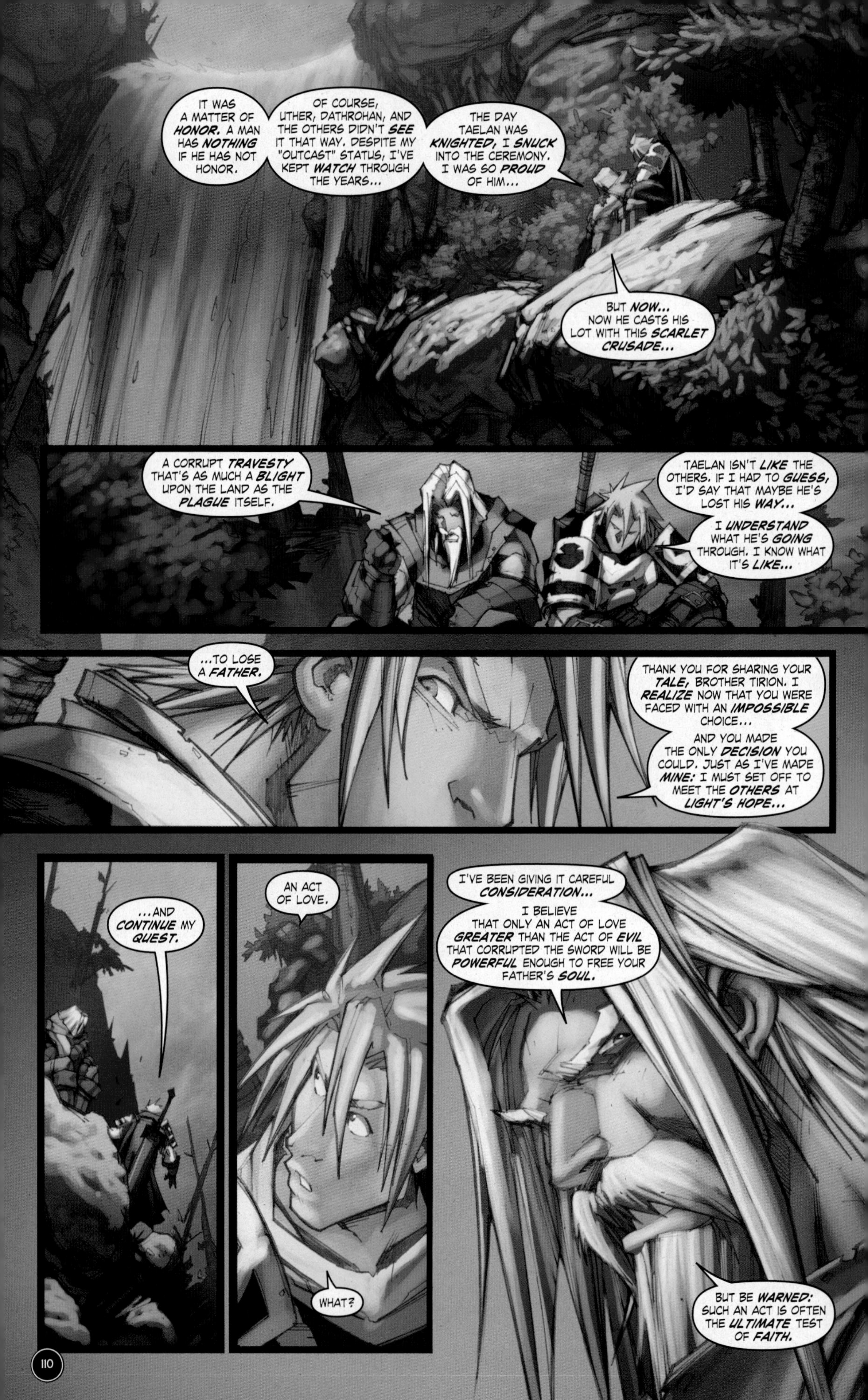
IT WAS A MATTER OF HONOR. A MAN HAS NOTHING IF HE HAS NOT HONOR.
OF COURSE, UTHER, DATHROHAN, AND THE OTHERS DIDN'T SEE IT THAT WAY. DESPITE MY "OUTCAST" STATUS, I'VE KEPT WATCH THROUGH THE YEARS...
THE DAY TAELAN WAS KNIGHTED, I SNUCK INTO THE CEREMONY. I WAS SO PROUD OF HIM...
BUT NOW... NOW HE CASTS HIS LOT WITH THIS SCARLET CRUSADE...
A CORRUPT TRAVESTY THAT'S AS MUCH A BLIGHT UPON THE LAND AS THE PLAGUE ITSELF.
TAELAN ISN'T LIKE THE OTHERS. IF I HAD TO GUESS, I'D SAY THAT MAYBE HE'S LOST HIS WAY...
I UNDERSTAND WHAT HE'S GOING THROUGH. I KNOW WHAT IT'S LIKE...
...TO LOSE A FATHER.
THANK YOU FOR SHARING YOUR TALE, BROTHER TIRION. I REALIZE NOW THAT YOU WERE FACED WITH AN IMPOSSIBLE CHOICE...
AND YOU MADE THE ONLY DECISION YOU COULD. JUST AS I'VE MADE MINE: I MUST SET OFF TO MEET THE OTHERS AT LIGHT'S HOPE...
...AND CONTINUE MY QUEST.
AN ACT OF LOVE.
WHAT?
I'VE BEEN GIVING IT CAREFUL CONSIDERATION...
I BELIEVE THAT ONLY AN ACT OF LOVE GREATER THAN THE ACT OF EVIL THAT CORRUPTED THE SWORD WILL BE POWERFUL ENOUGH TO FREE YOUR FATHER'S SOUL.
BUT BE WARNED: SUCH AN ACT IS OFTEN THE ULTIMATE TEST OF FAITH.

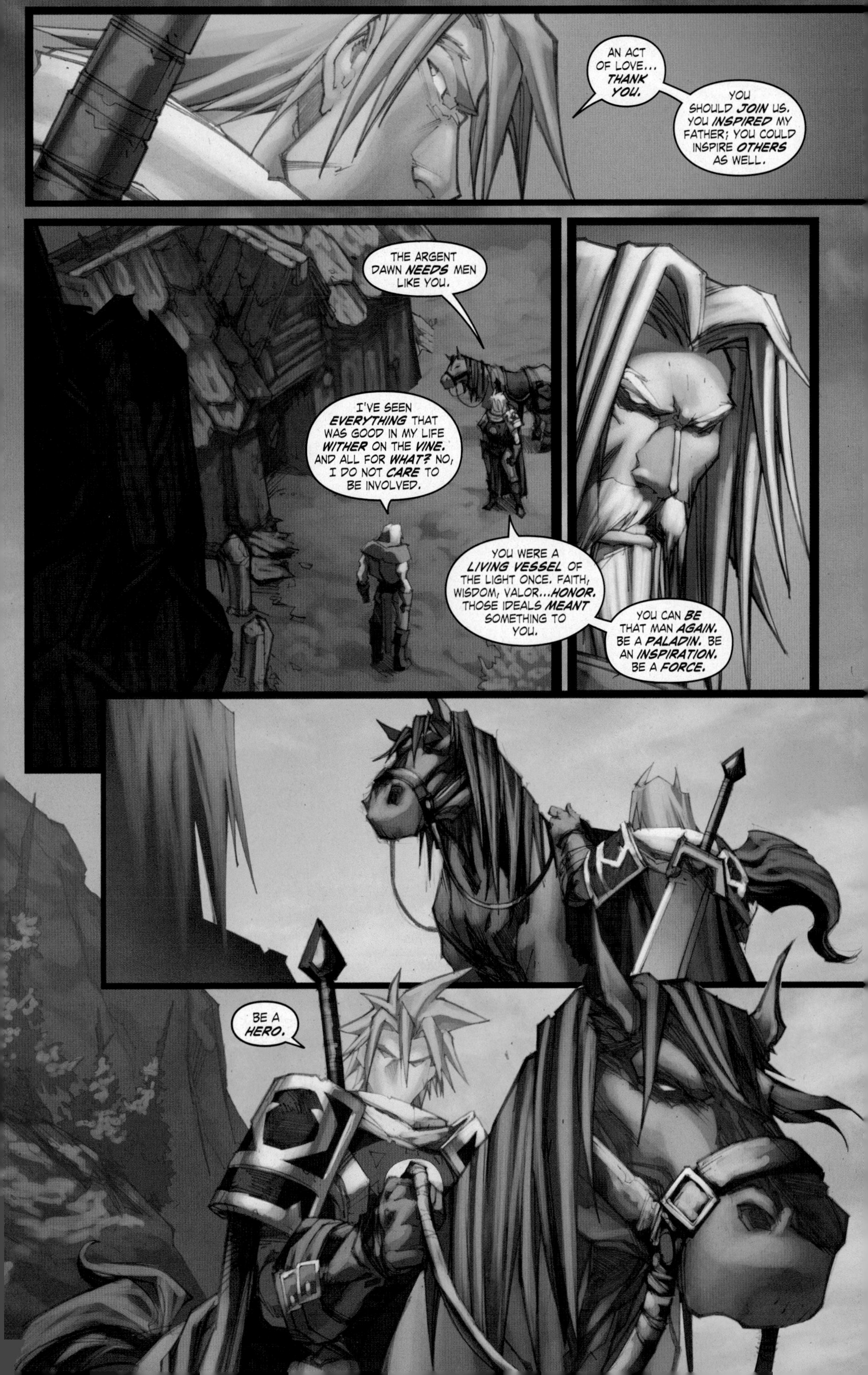
AN ACT OF LOVE... THANK YOU.
YOU SHOULD JOIN US. YOU INSPIRED MY FATHER; YOU COULD INSPIRE OTHERS AS WELL.
THE ARGENT DAWN NEEDS MEN LIKE YOU.
I'VE SEEN EVERYTHING THAT WAS GOOD IN MY LIFE WITHER ON THE VINE. AND ALL FOR WHAT? NO, I DO NOT CARE TO BE INVOLVED.
YOU WERE A LIVING VESSEL OF THE LIGHT ONCE. FAITH, WISDOM, VALOR...HONOR. THOSE IDEALS MEANT SOMETHING TO YOU.
YOU CAN BE THAT MAN AGAIN. BE A PALADIN. BE AN INSPIRATION. BE A FORCE.
BE A HERO.

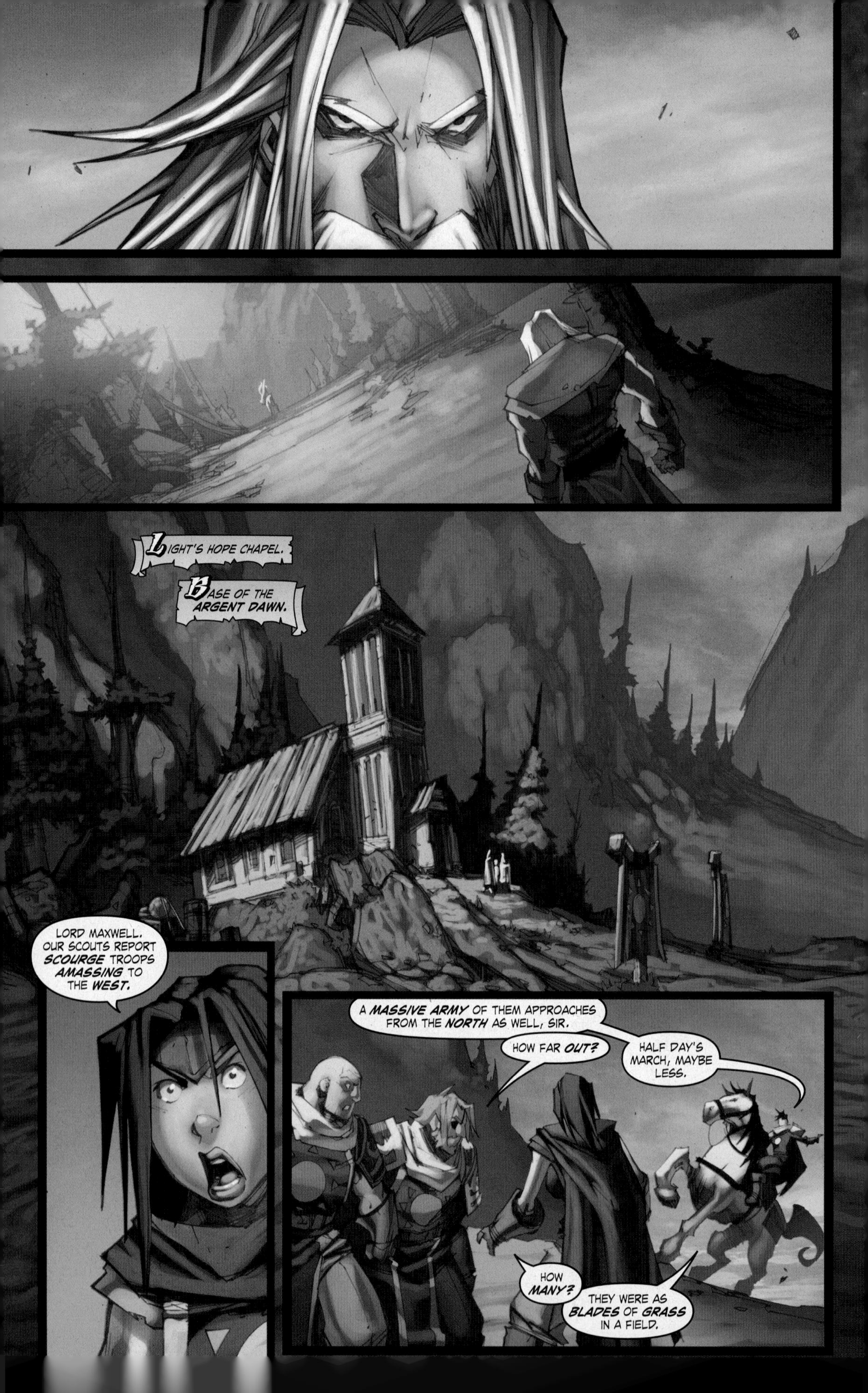
LIGHT'S HOPE CHAPEL.
BASE OF THE ARGENT DAWN.
LORD MAXWELL. OUR SCOUTS REPORT SCOURGE TROOPS AMASSING TO THE WEST.
A MASSIVE ARMY OF THEM APPROACHES FROM THE NORTH AS WELL, SIR.
HOW FAR OUT?
HALF DAY'S MARCH, MAYBE LESS.
HOW MANY?
THEY WERE AS BLADES OF GRASS IN A FIELD.

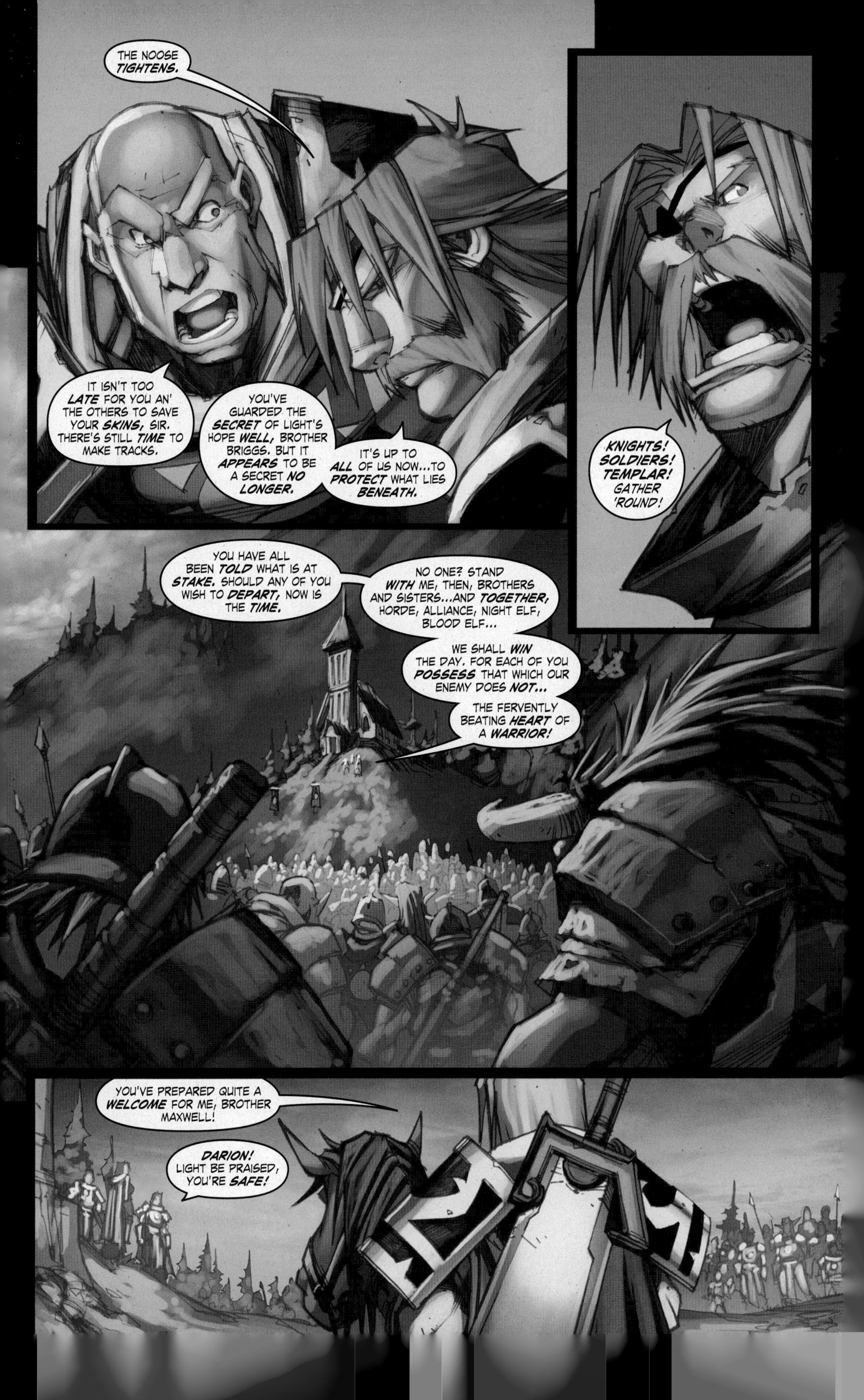
THE NOOSE TIGHTENS.
IT ISN'T TOO LATE FOR YOU AN' THE OTHERS TO SAVE YOUR SKINS, SIR. THERE'S STILL TIME TO MAKE TRACKS.
YOU'VE GUARDED THE SECRET OF LIGHT'S HOPE WELL, BROTHER BRIGGS. BUT IT APPEARS TO BE A SECRET NO LONGER.
IT'S UP TO ALL OF US NOW...TO PROTECT WHAT LIES BENEATH.
KNIGHTS! SOLDIERS! TEMPLAR! GATHER 'ROUND!
YOU HAVE ALL BEEN TOLD WHAT IS AT STAKE. SHOULD ANY OF YOU WISH TO DEPART, NOW IS THE TIME.
NO ONE? STAND WITH ME, THEN, BROTHERS AND SISTERS...AND TOGETHER, HORDE, ALLIANCE, NIGHT ELF, BLOOD ELF...
WE SHALL WIN THE DAY. FOR EACH OF YOU POSSESS THAT WHICH OUR ENEMY DOES NOT...
THE FERVENTLY BEATING HEART OF A WARRIOR!
YOU'VE PREPARED QUITE A WELCOME FOR ME, BROTHER MAXWELL!
DARION! LIGHT BE PRAISED, YOU'RE SAFE!

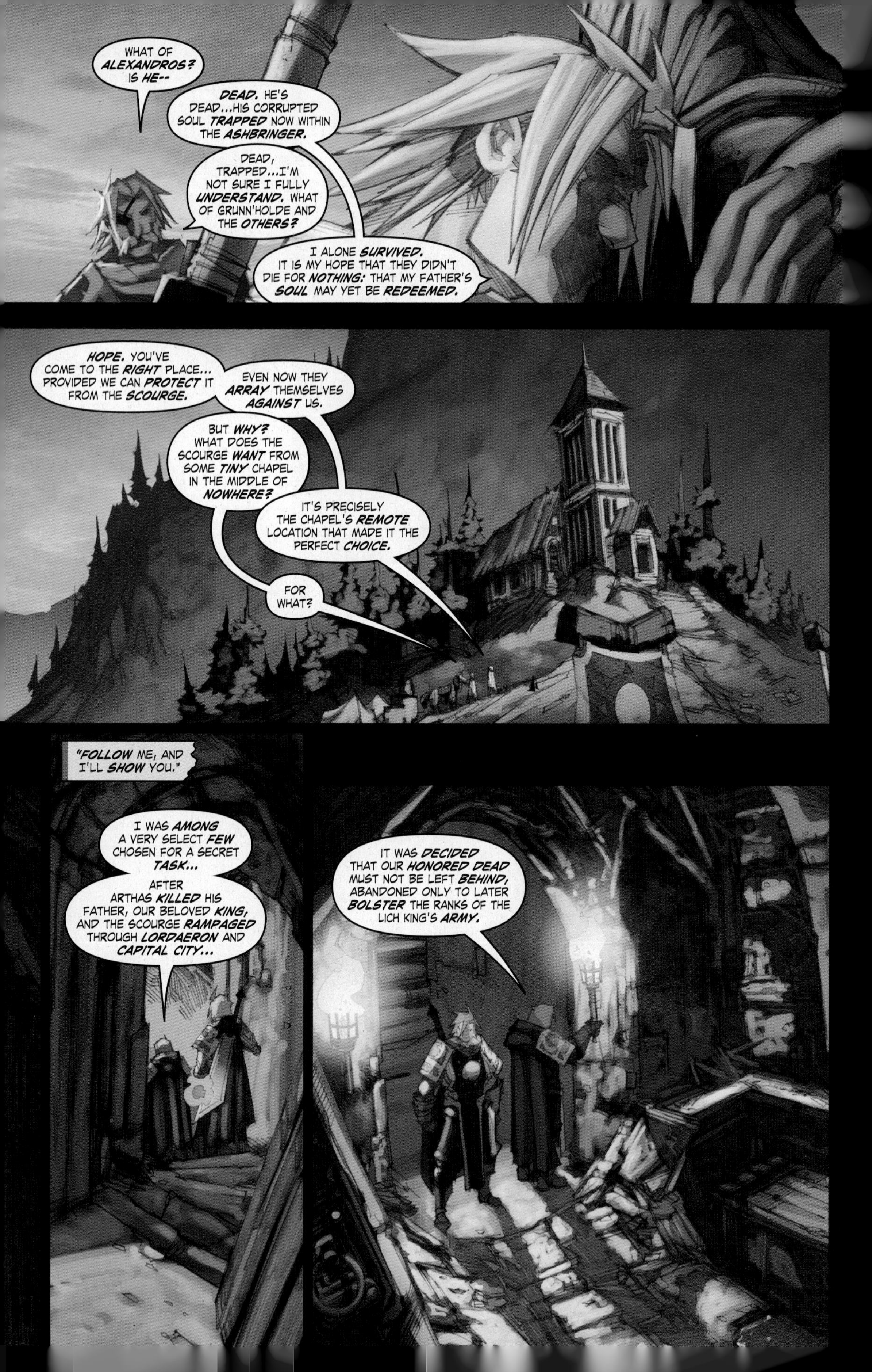
WHAT OF ALEXANDROS? IS HE--
DEAD. HE'S DEAD...HIS CORRUPTED SOUL TRAPPED NOW WITHIN THE ASHBRINGER.
DEAD, TRAPPED...I'M NOT SURE I FULLY UNDERSTAND. WHAT OF GRUNN'HOLDE AND THE OTHERS?
I ALONE SURVIVED. IT IS MY HOPE THAT THEY DIDN'T DIE FOR NOTHING: THAT MY FATHER'S SOUL MAY YET BE REDEEMED.
HOPE. YOU'VE COME TO THE RIGHT PLACE... PROVIDED WE CAN PROTECT IT FROM THE SCOURGE.
EVEN NOW THEY ARRAY THEMSELVES AGAINST US.
BUT WHY? WHAT DOES THE SCOURGE WANT FROM SOME TINY CHAPEL IN THE MIDDLE OF NOWHERE?
IT'S PRECISELY THE CHAPEL'S REMOTE LOCATION THAT MADE IT THE PERFECT CHOICE.
FOR WHAT?
"FOLLOW ME, AND I'LL SHOW YOU."
I WAS AMONG A VERY SELECT FEW CHOSEN FOR A SECRET TASK...
AFTER ARTHAS KILLED HIS FATHER, OUR BELOVED KING, AND THE SCOURGE RAMPAGED THROUGH LORDAERON AND CAPITAL CITY...
IT WAS DECIDED THAT OUR HONORED DEAD MUST NOT BE LEFT BEHIND, ABANDONED ONLY TO LATER BOLSTER THE RANKS OF THE LICH KING'S ARMY.

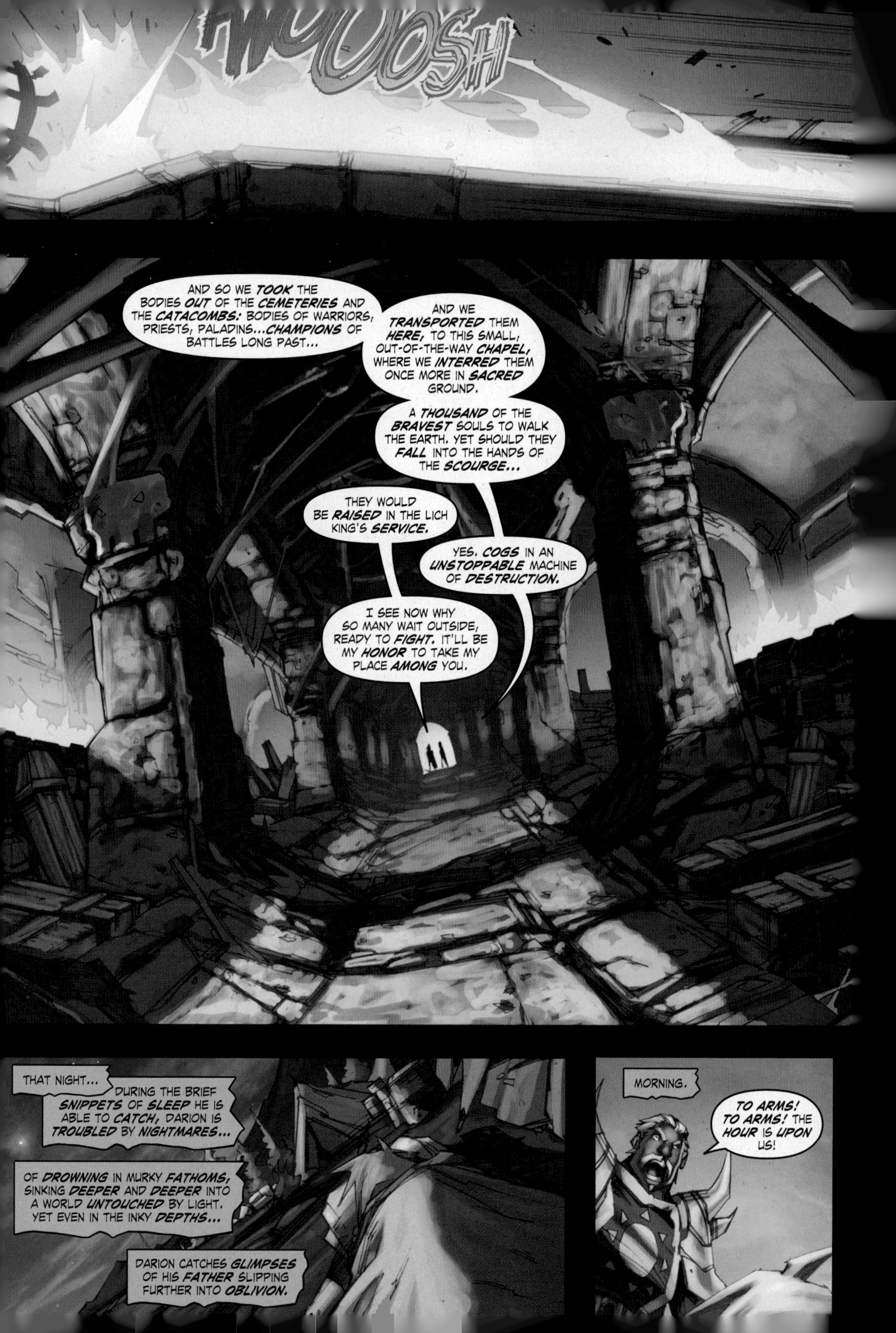
WOOSH
AND SO WE TOOK THE BODIES OUT OF THE CEMETERIES AND THE CATACOMBS: BODIES OF WARRIORS, PRIESTS, PALADINS...CHAMPIONS OF BATTLES LONG PAST...
AND WE TRANSPORTED THEM HERE, TO THIS SMALL, OUT-OF-THE-WAY CHAPEL, WHERE WE INTERRED THEM ONCE MORE IN SACRED GROUND.
A THOUSAND OF THE BRAVEST SOULS TO WALK THE EARTH. YET SHOULD THEY FALL INTO THE HANDS OF THE SCOURGE...
THEY WOULD BE RAISED IN THE LICH KING'S SERVICE.
YES. COGS IN AN UNSTOPPABLE MACHINE OF DESTRUCTION.
I SEE NOW WHY SO MANY WAIT OUTSIDE, READY TO FIGHT. IT'LL BE MY HONOR TO TAKE MY PLACE AMONG YOU.
THAT NIGHT...
DURING THE BRIEF SNIPPETS OF SLEEP HE IS ABLE TO CATCH, DARION IS TROUBLED BY NIGHTMARES...
OF DROWNING IN MURKY FATHOMS, SINKING DEEPER AND DEEPER INTO A WORLD UNTOUCHED BY LIGHT. YET EVEN IN THE INKY DEPTHS...
DARION CATCHES GLIMPSES OF HIS FATHER SLIPPING FURTHER INTO OBLIVION.
MORNING.
TO ARMS! TO ARMS! THE HOUR IS UPON US!

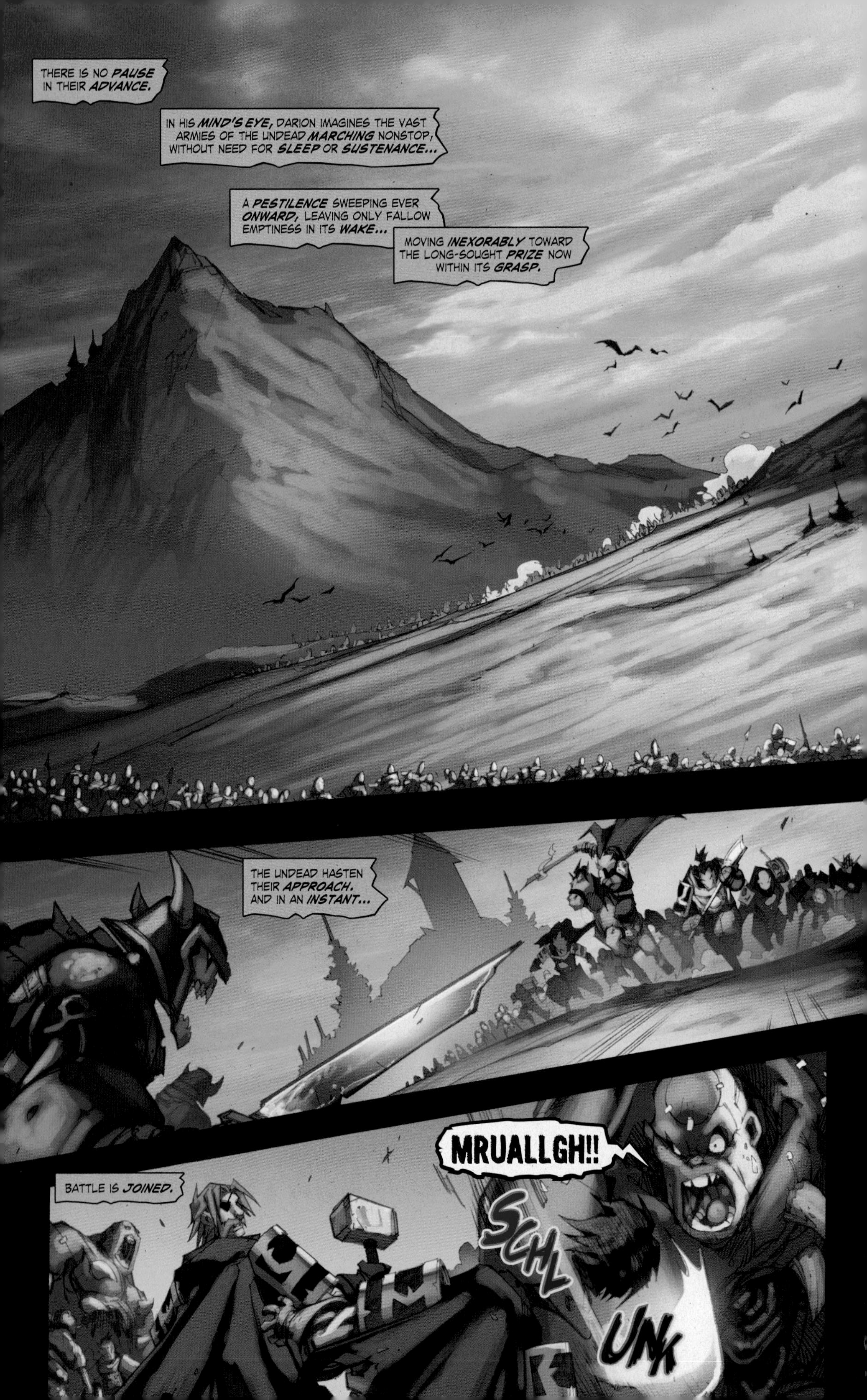
THERE IS NO PAUSE IN THEIR ADVANCE.
IN HIS MIND'S EYE, DARION IMAGINES THE VAST ARMIES OF THE UNDEAD MARCHING NONSTOP, WITHOUT NEED FOR SLEEP OR SUSTENANCE...
A PESTILENCE SWEEPING EVER ONWARD, LEAVING ONLY FALLOW EMPTINESS IN ITS WAKE...
MOVING INEXORABLY TOWARD THE LONG-SOUGHT PRIZE NOW WITHIN ITS GRASP.
THE UNDEAD HASTEN THEIR APPROACH. AND IN AN INSTANT...
MRUALLGH!!
BATTLE IS JOINED.
SCHL
UNK

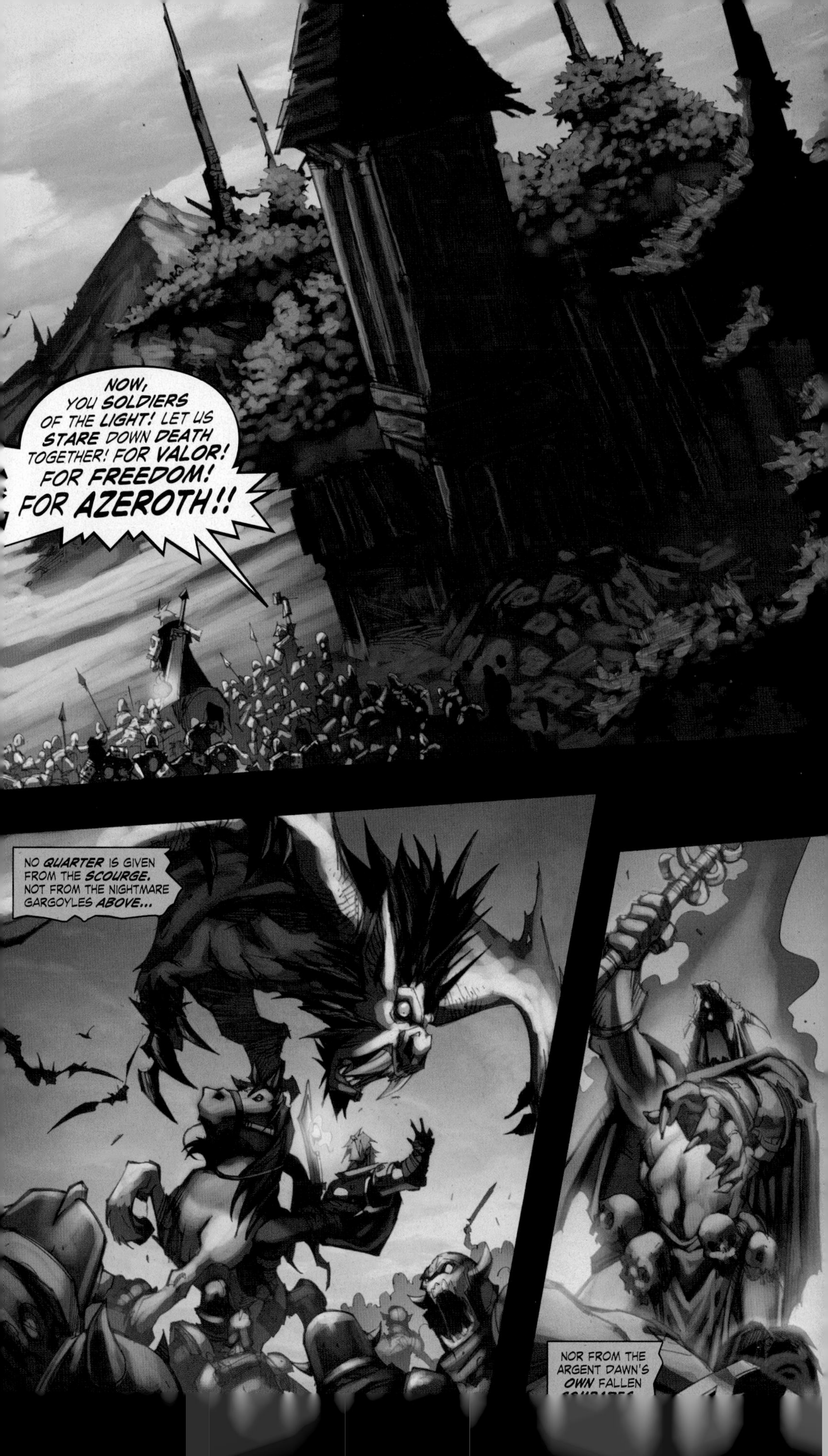
NOW, YOU SOLDIERS OF THE LIGHT! LET US STARE DOWN DEATH TOGETHER! FOR VALOR! FOR FREEDOM! FOR AZEROTH!!
NO QUARTER IS GIVEN FROM THE SCOURGE. NOT FROM THE NIGHTMARE GARGOYLES ABOVE...
NOR FROM THE ARGENT DAWN'S OWN FALLEN

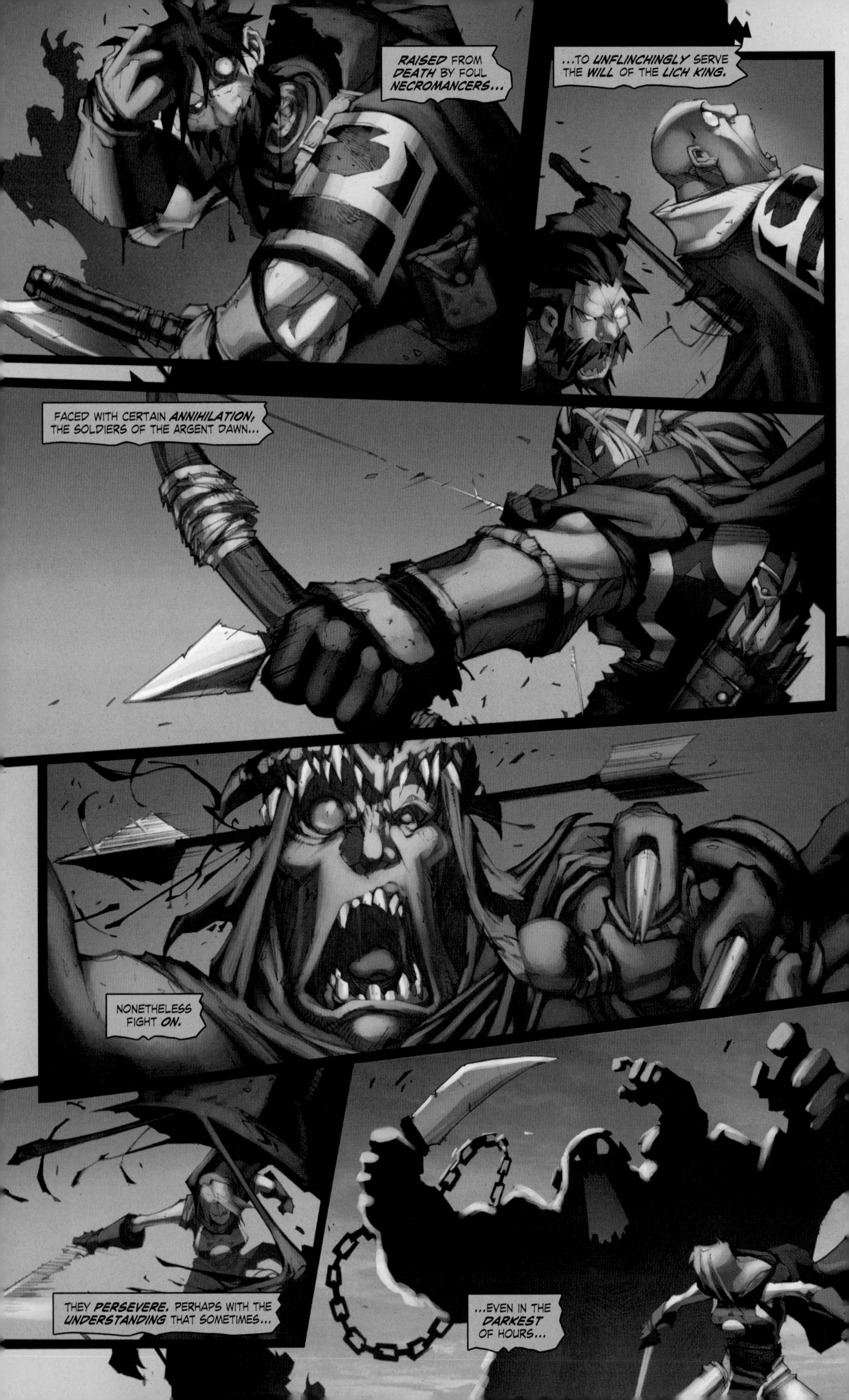
RAISED FROM DEATH BY FOUL NECROMANCERS...
...TO UNFLINCHINGLY SERVE THE WILL OF THE LICH KING.
FACED WITH CERTAIN ANNIHILATION, THE SOLDIERS OF THE ARGENT DAWN...
NONETHELESS FIGHT ON.
THEY PERSEVERE, PERHAPS WITH THE UNDERSTANDING THAT SOMETIMES...
...EVEN IN THE DARKEST OF HOURS...

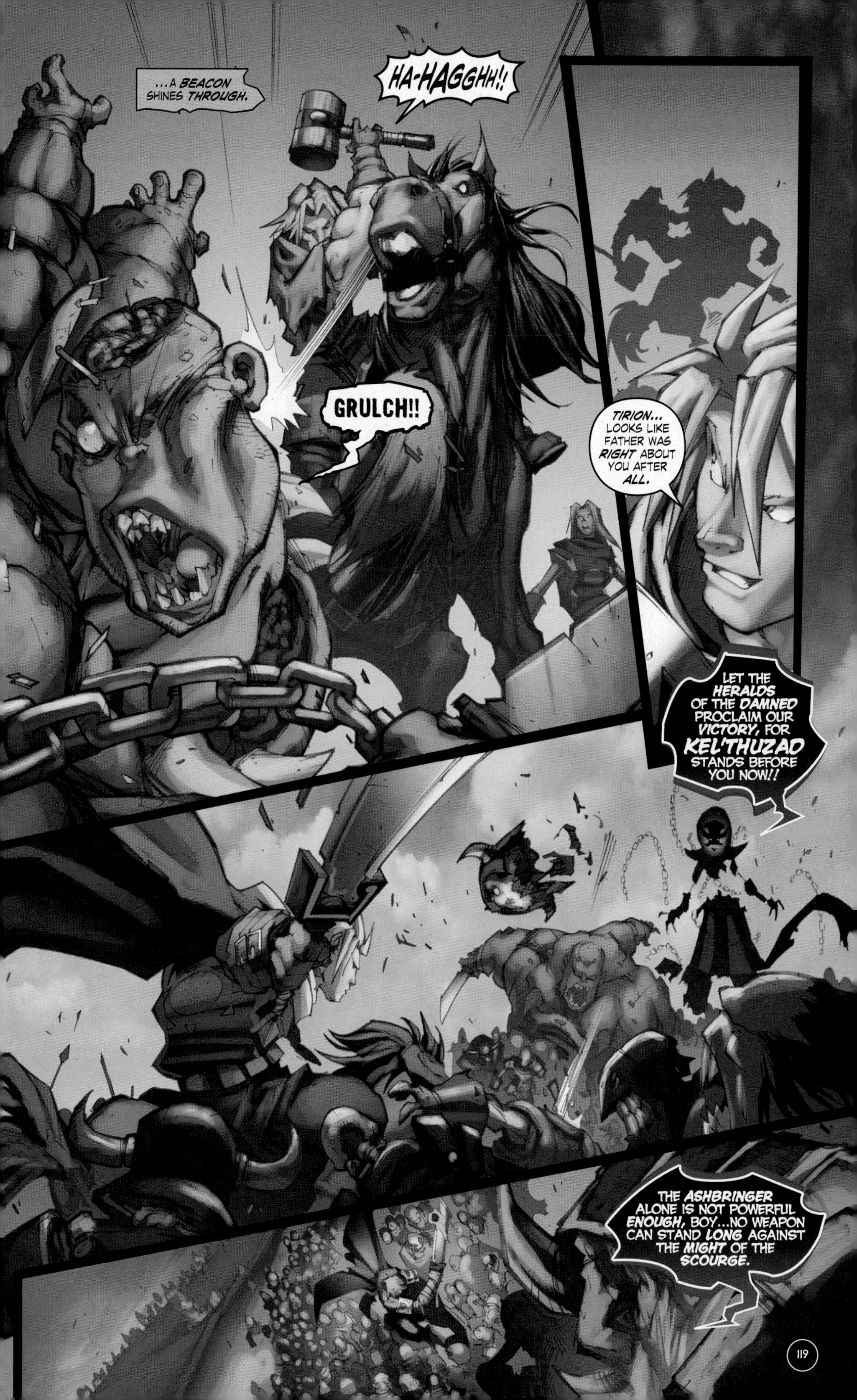
...A BEACON SHINES THROUGH.
HA-HAGGHH!!
GRULCH!!
TIRION... LOOKS LIKE FATHER WAS RIGHT ABOUT YOU AFTER ALL.
LET THE HERALDS OF THE DAMNED PROCLAIM OUR VICTORY, FOR KEL'THUZAD STANDS BEFORE YOU NOW!!
THE ASHBRINGER ALONE IS NOT POWERFUL ENOUGH, BOY...NO WEAPON CAN STAND LONG AGAINST THE MIGHT OF THE SCOURGE.

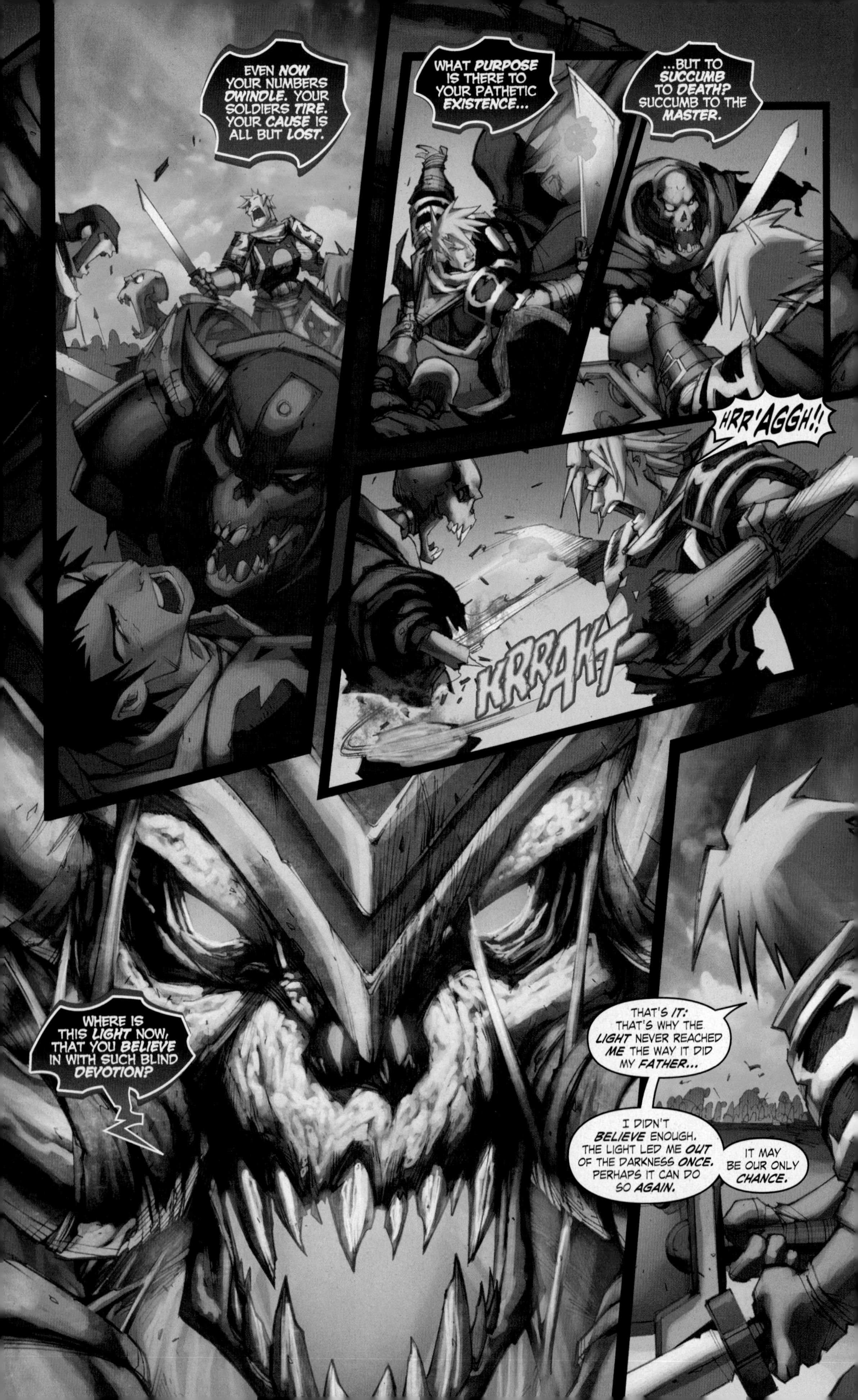
EVEN NOW YOUR NUMBERS DWINDLE. YOUR SOLDIERS TIRE. YOUR CAUSE IS ALL BUT LOST.
WHAT PURPOSE IS THERE TO YOUR PATHETIC EXISTENCE...
...BUT TO SUCCUMB TO DEATH? SUCCUMB TO THE MASTER.
HRR'AGGH!!
KRRAKT
WHERE IS THIS LIGHT NOW, THAT YOU BELIEVE IN WITH SUCH BLIND DEVOTION?
THAT'S IT: THAT'S WHY THE LIGHT NEVER REACHED ME THE WAY IT DID MY FATHER...
I DIDN'T BELIEVE ENOUGH. THE LIGHT LED ME OUT OF THE DARKNESS ONCE. PERHAPS IT CAN DO SO AGAIN.
IT MAY BE OUR ONLY CHANCE.

THE *ULTIMATE* TEST OF *FAITH...*
AN *ACT* OF *LOVE.*
DARION...
THIS IS MY *PURPOSE,* THEN. SO *BE* IT.
MY *SOUL* FOR *YOURS.*
I *LOVE* YOU, DAD.
SCHLUNKT
ONCE *AGAIN,* DARION IS OVERWHELMED BY A *SENSATION* OF SINKING BENEATH MURKY *FATHOMS,* OF *STRUGGLING* FOR *BREATH...*
YET EVEN AS OBLIVION *BECKONS,* HE IS ABLE TO CATCH A BRIEF *GLIMPSE...*

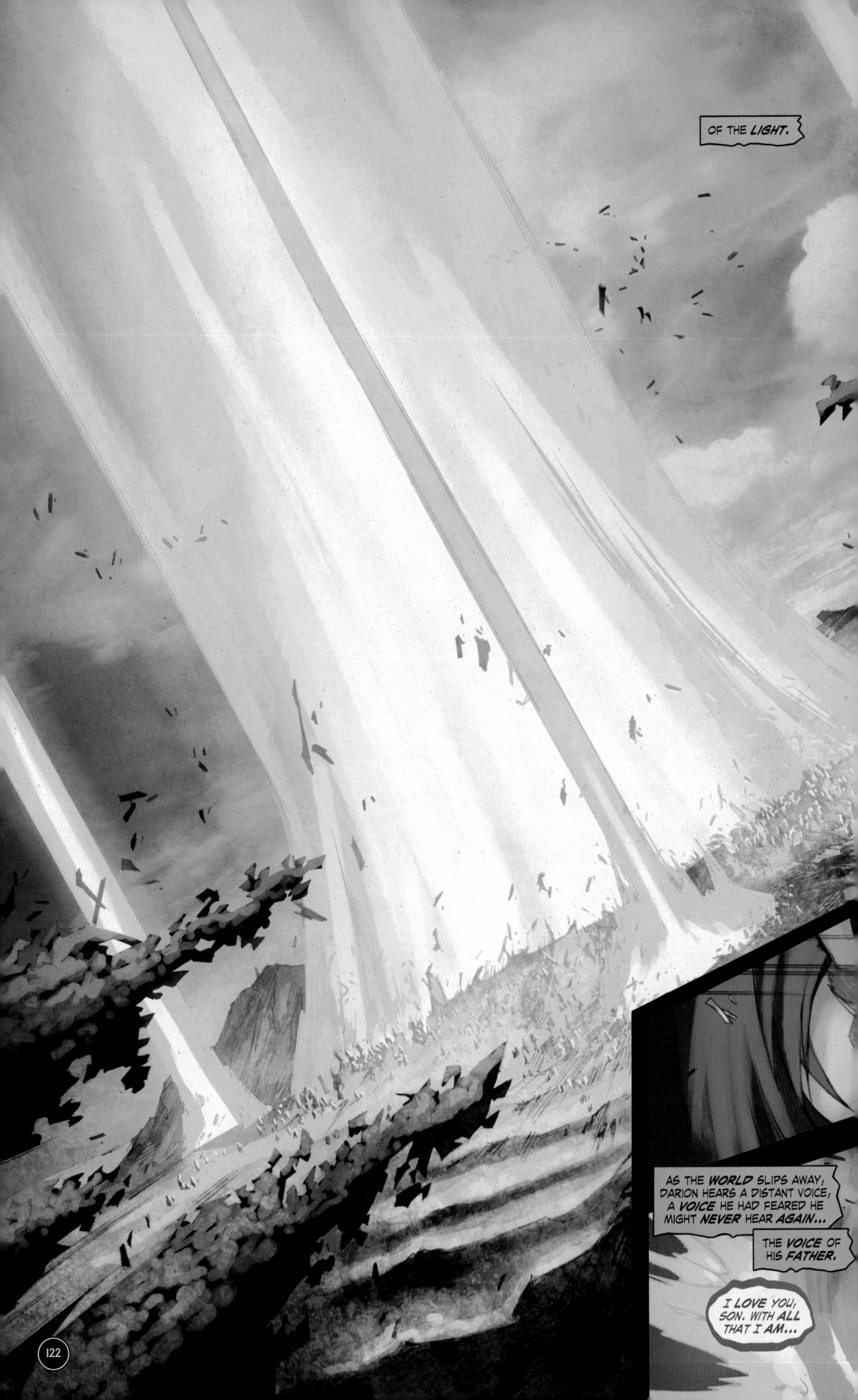
OF THE LIGHT.
AS THE WORLD SLIPS AWAY, DARION HEARS A DISTANT VOICE, A VOICE HE HAD FEARED HE MIGHT NEVER HEAR AGAIN...
THE VOICE OF HIS FATHER.
I LOVE YOU, SON. WITH ALL THAT I AM...

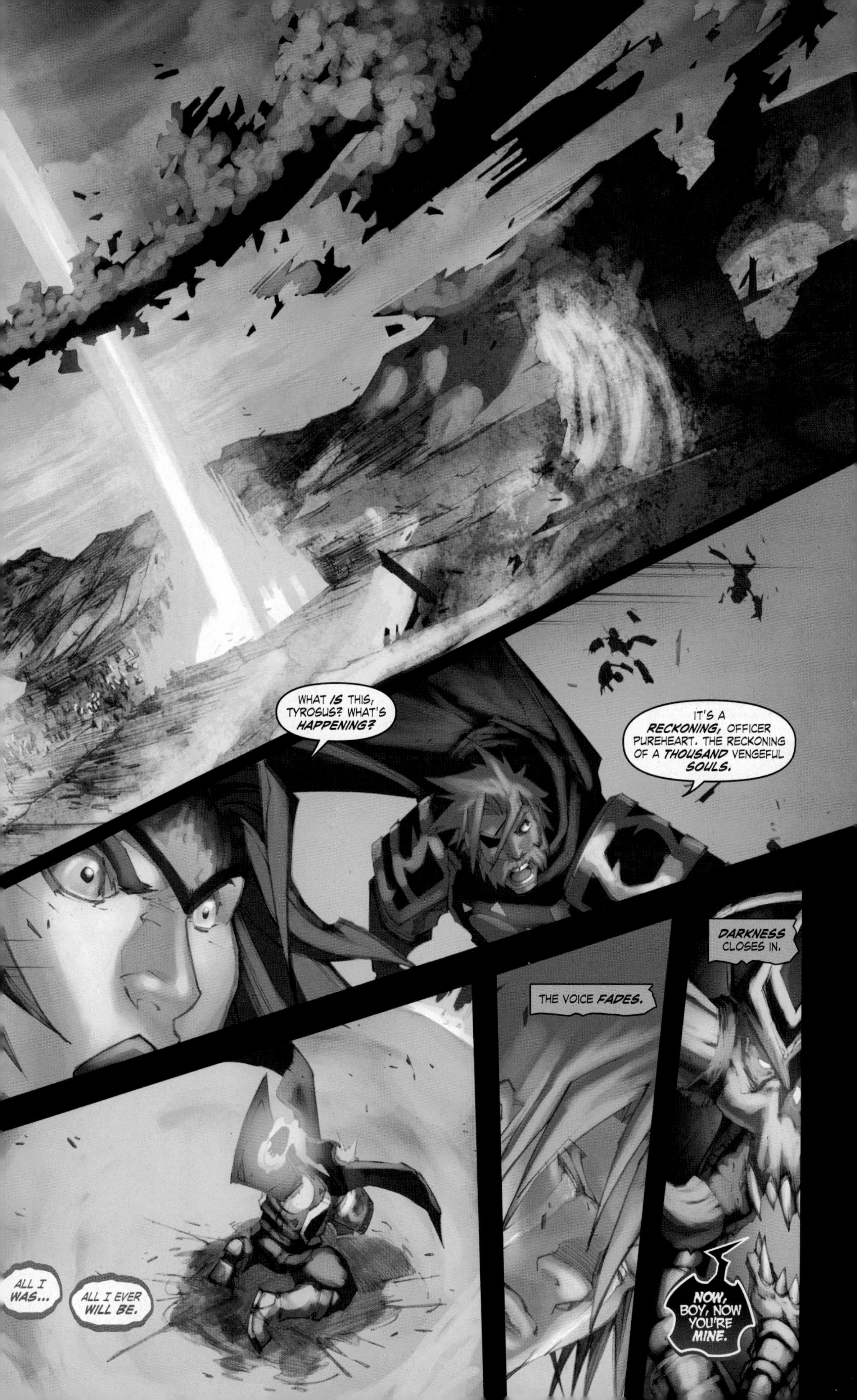
WHAT *IS* THIS, TYROSUS? WHAT'S *HAPPENING?*
IT'S A *RECKONING,* OFFICER PUREHEART. THE RECKONING OF A *THOUSAND* VENGEFUL *SOULS.*
ALL I *WAS...*
ALL I EVER *WILL BE.*
THE VOICE *FADES.*
DARKNESS CLOSES IN.
NOW, BOY, NOW YOU'RE *MINE.*

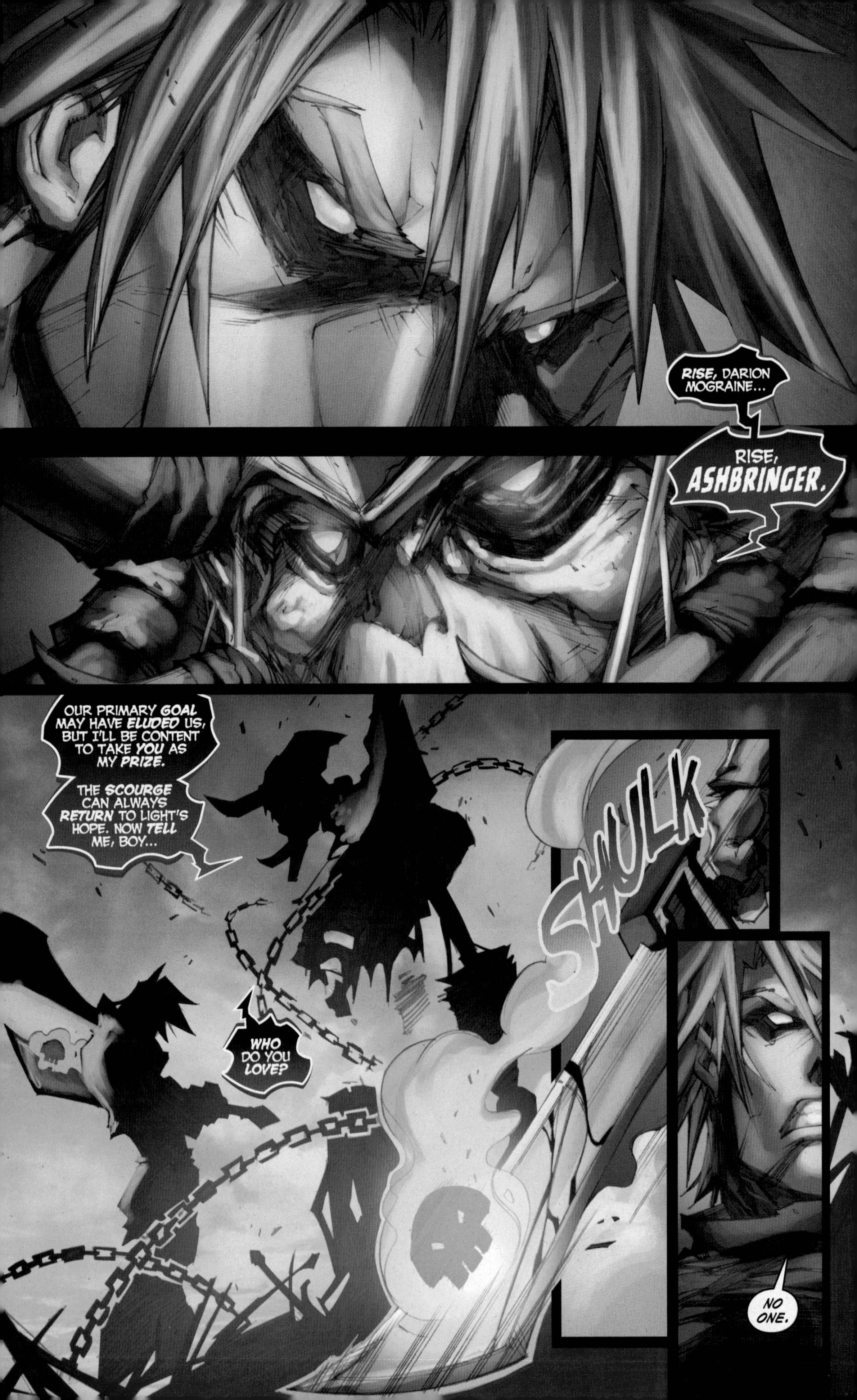
RISE, DARION MOGRAINE...
RISE, ASHBRINGER.
OUR PRIMARY GOAL MAY HAVE ELUDED US, BUT I'LL BE CONTENT TO TAKE YOU AS MY PRIZE.
THE SCOURGE CAN ALWAYS RETURN TO LIGHT'S HOPE. NOW TELL ME, BOY...
WHO DO YOU LOVE?
SHULK
NO ONE.

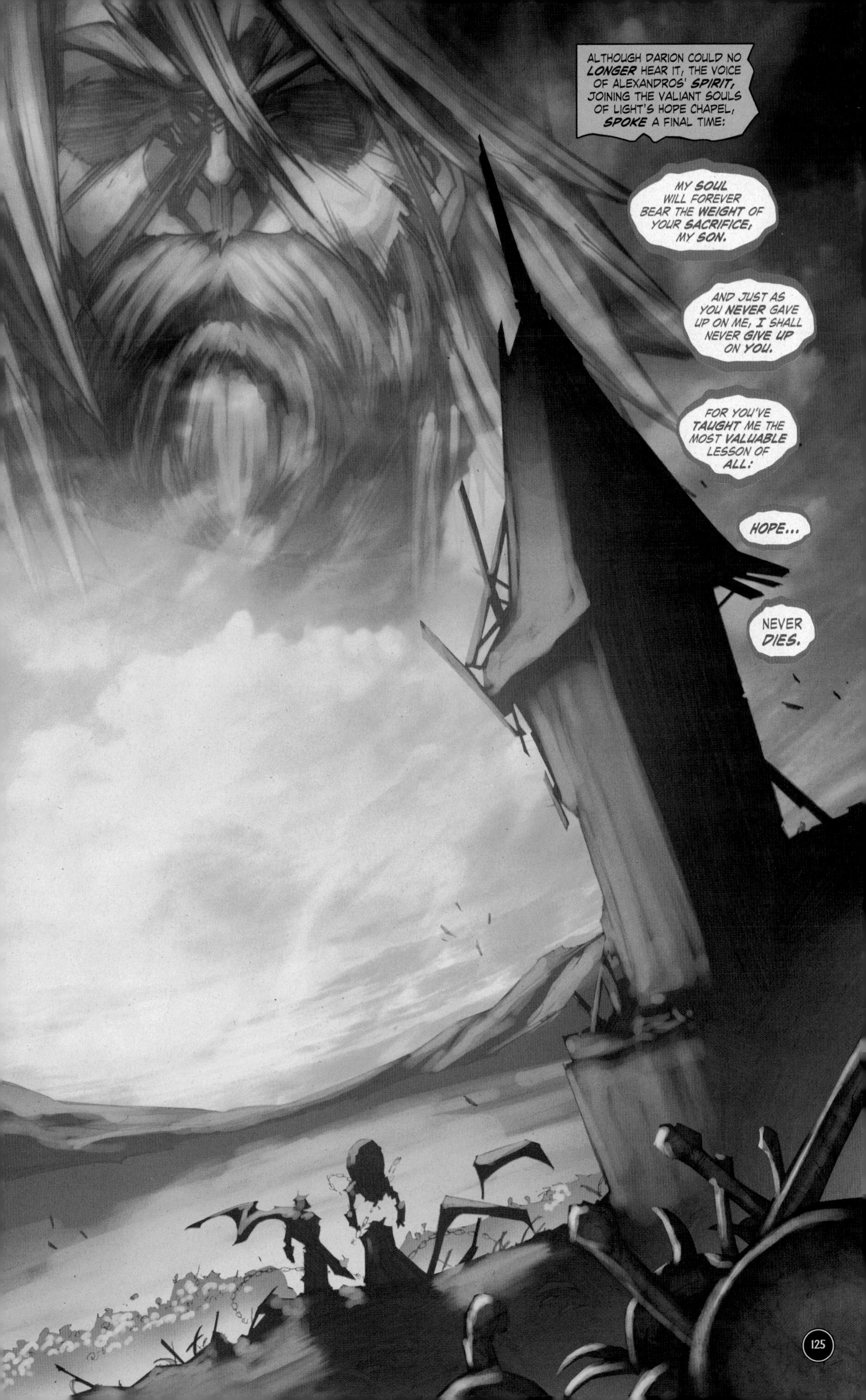
ALTHOUGH DARION COULD NO LONGER HEAR IT, THE VOICE OF ALEXANDROS' SPIRIT, JOINING THE VALIANT SOULS OF LIGHT'S HOPE CHAPEL, SPOKE A FINAL TIME:
MY SOUL WILL FOREVER BEAR THE WEIGHT OF YOUR SACRIFICE, MY SON.
AND JUST AS YOU NEVER GAVE UP ON ME, I SHALL NEVER GIVE UP ON YOU.
FOR YOU'VE TAUGHT ME THE MOST VALUABLE LESSON OF ALL:
HOPE...
NEVER DIES.

EPILOGUE

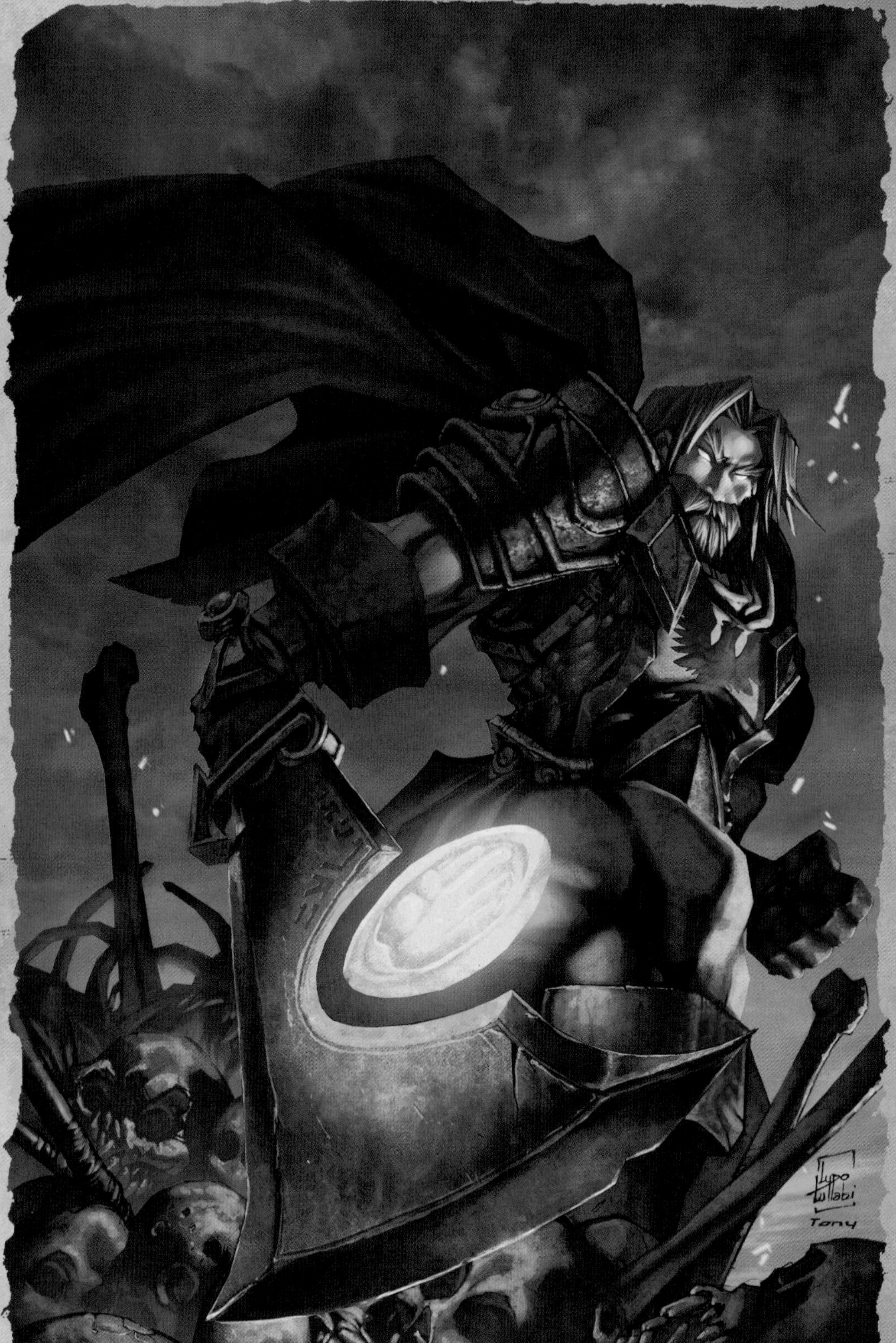

Cover #1 by Ludo Lullabi and Tony Washington

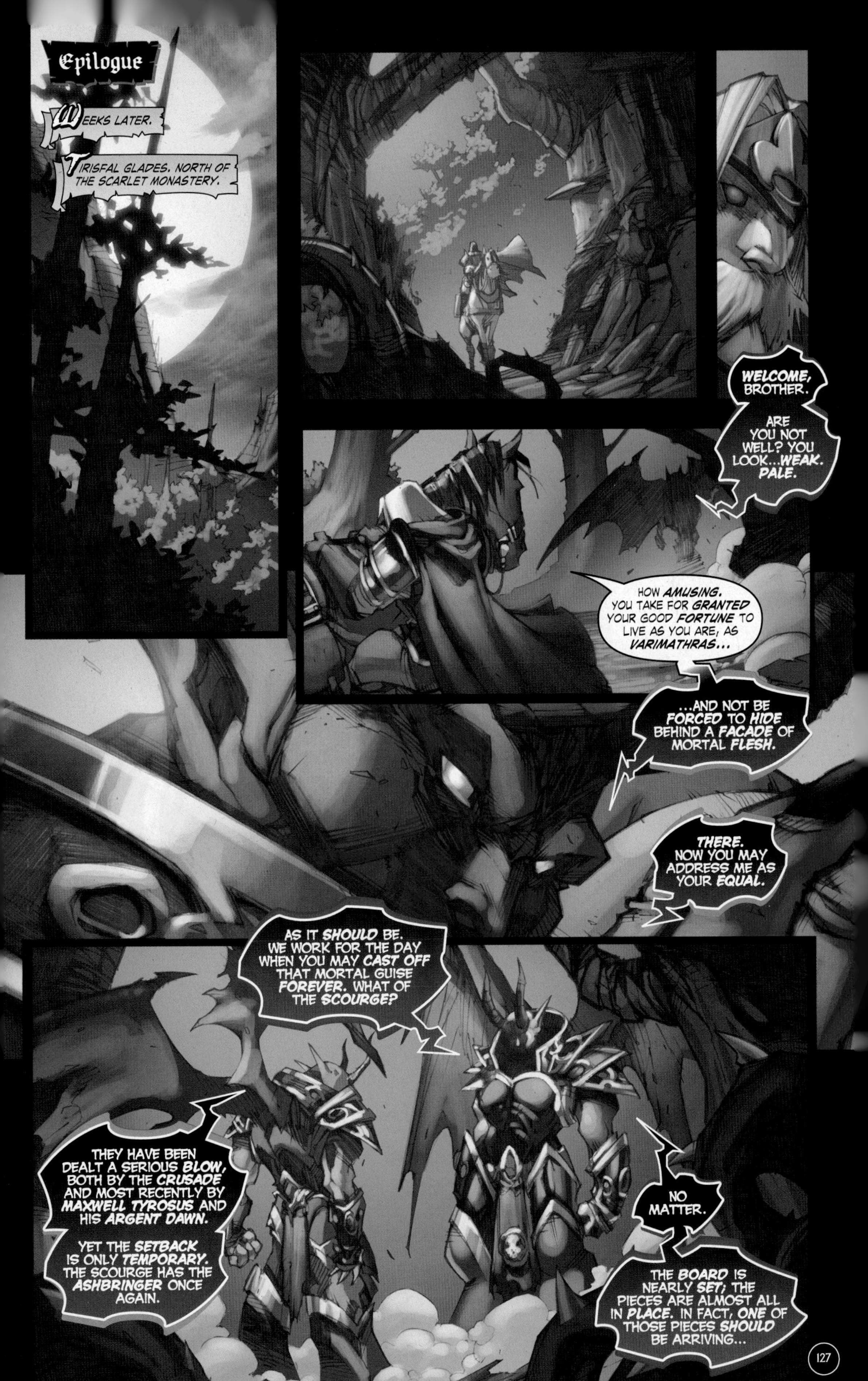
Epilogue
WEEKS LATER.
TIRISFAL GLADES. NORTH OF THE SCARLET MONASTERY.
WELCOME, BROTHER.
ARE YOU NOT WELL? YOU LOOK...WEAK. PALE.
HOW AMUSING. YOU TAKE FOR GRANTED YOUR GOOD FORTUNE TO LIVE AS YOU ARE; AS VARIMATHRAS...
...AND NOT BE FORCED TO HIDE BEHIND A FACADE OF MORTAL FLESH.
THERE. NOW YOU MAY ADDRESS ME AS YOUR EQUAL.
AS IT SHOULD BE. WE WORK FOR THE DAY WHEN YOU MAY CAST OFF THAT MORTAL GUISE FOREVER. WHAT OF THE SCOURGE?
THEY HAVE BEEN DEALT A SERIOUS BLOW, BOTH BY THE CRUSADE AND MOST RECENTLY BY MAXWELL TYROSUS AND HIS ARGENT DAWN.
YET THE SETBACK IS ONLY TEMPORARY. THE SCOURGE HAS THE ASHBRINGER ONCE AGAIN.
NO MATTER.
THE BOARD IS NEARLY SET; THE PIECES ARE ALMOST ALL IN PLACE. IN FACT, ONE OF THOSE PIECES SHOULD BE ARRIVING...

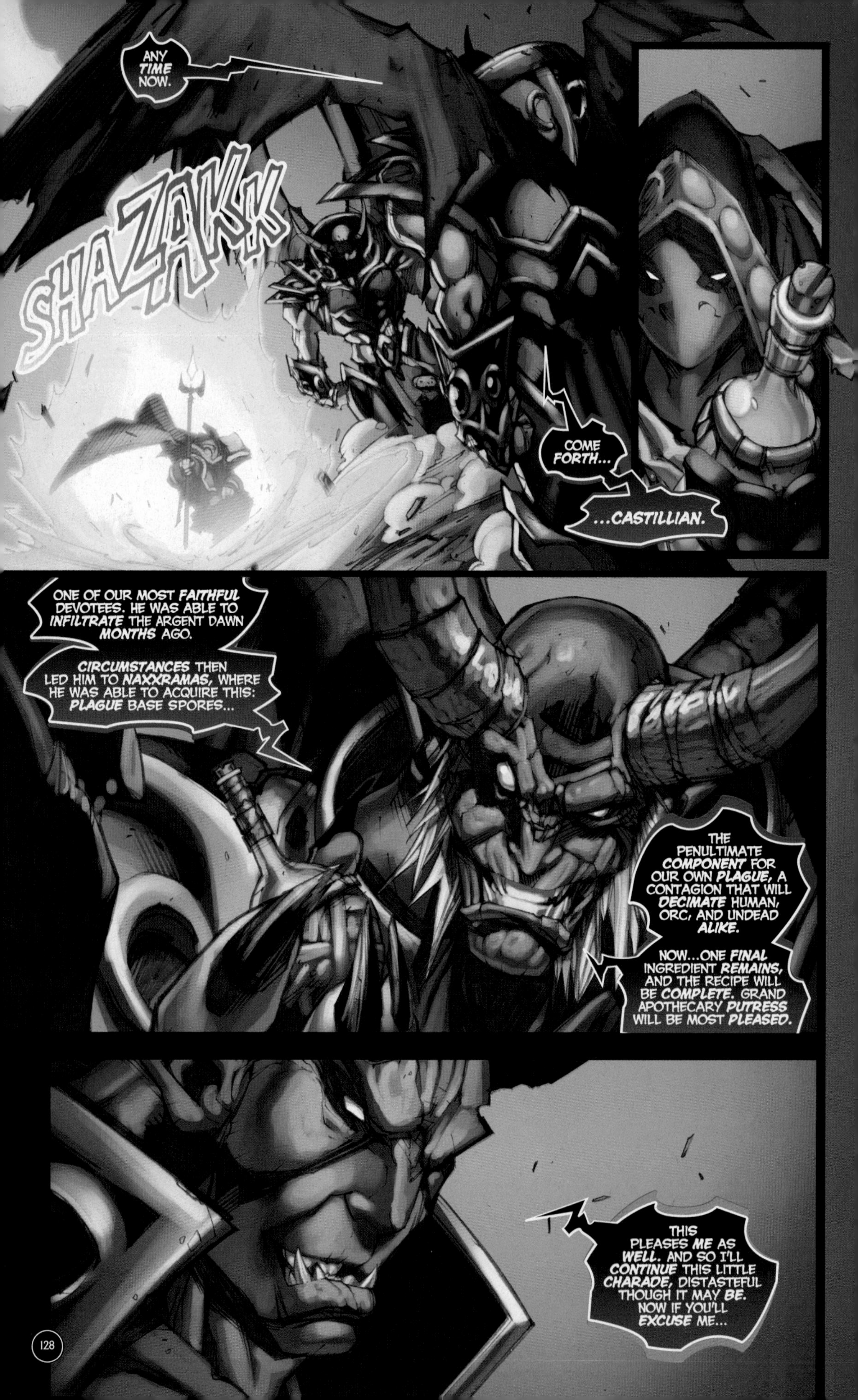
ANY TIME NOW.
SHAZAKK
COME FORTH...
...CASTILLIAN.
ONE OF OUR MOST FAITHFUL DEVOTEES. HE WAS ABLE TO INFILTRATE THE ARGENT DAWN MONTHS AGO.
CIRCUMSTANCES THEN LED HIM TO NAXXRAMAS, WHERE HE WAS ABLE TO ACQUIRE THIS: PLAGUE BASE SPORES...
THE PENULTIMATE COMPONENT FOR OUR OWN PLAGUE, A CONTAGION THAT WILL DECIMATE HUMAN, ORC, AND UNDEAD ALIKE.
NOW...ONE FINAL INGREDIENT REMAINS, AND THE RECIPE WILL BE COMPLETE. GRAND APOTHECARY PUTRESS WILL BE MOST PLEASED.
THIS PLEASES ME AS WELL. AND SO I'LL CONTINUE THIS LITTLE CHARADE, DISTASTEFUL THOUGH IT MAY BE. NOW IF YOU'LL EXCUSE ME...

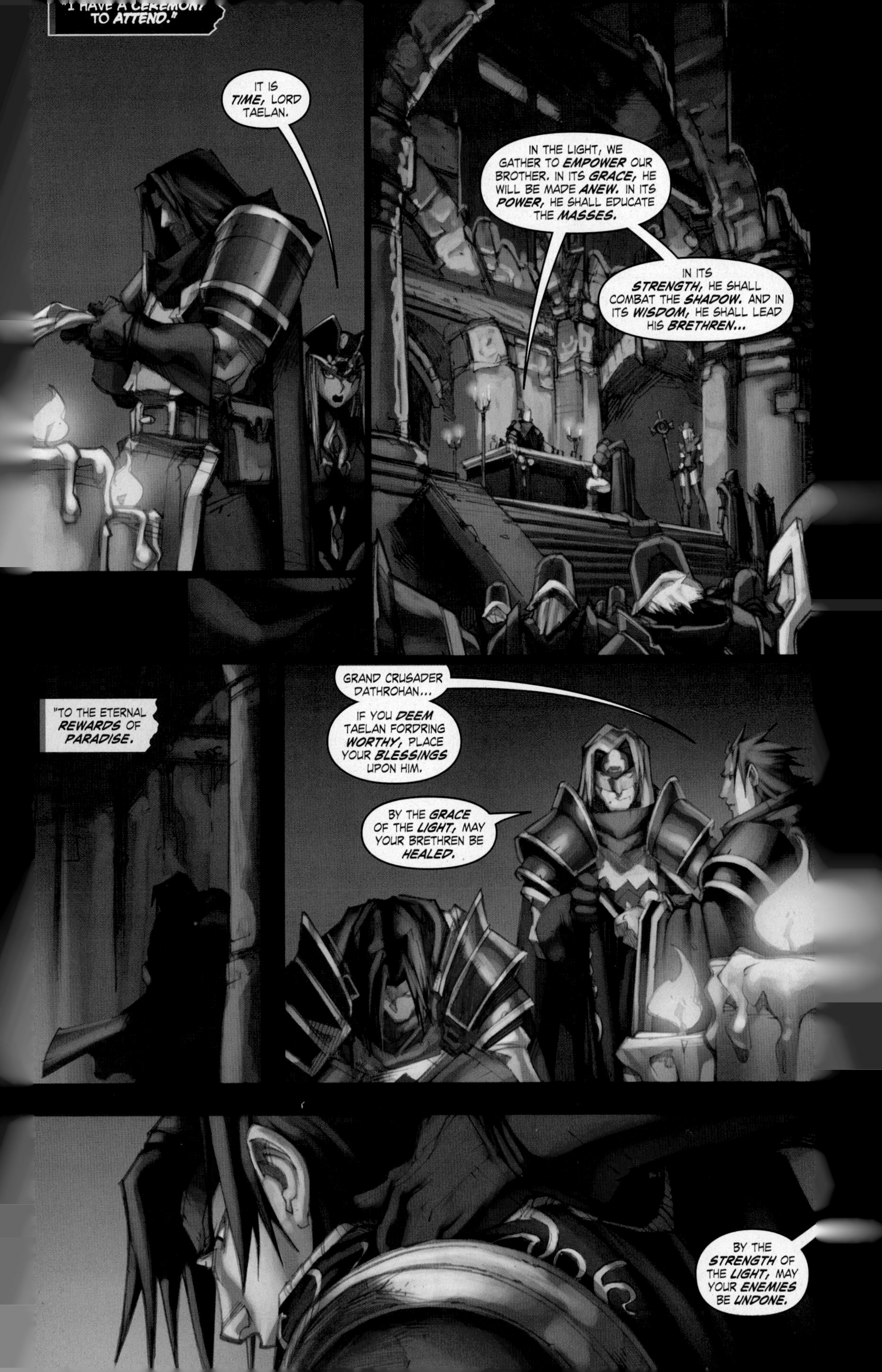
"I HAVE A CEREMONY TO ATTEND."
IT IS TIME, LORD TAELAN.
IN THE LIGHT, WE GATHER TO EMPOWER OUR BROTHER. IN ITS GRACE, HE WILL BE MADE ANEW. IN ITS POWER, HE SHALL EDUCATE THE MASSES.
IN ITS STRENGTH, HE SHALL COMBAT THE SHADOW. AND IN ITS WISDOM, HE SHALL LEAD HIS BRETHREN...
"TO THE ETERNAL REWARDS OF PARADISE.
GRAND CRUSADER DATHROHAN...
IF YOU DEEM TAELAN FORDRING WORTHY, PLACE YOUR BLESSINGS UPON HIM.
BY THE GRACE OF THE LIGHT, MAY YOUR BRETHREN BE HEALED.
BY THE STRENGTH OF THE LIGHT, MAY YOUR ENEMIES BE UNDONE.

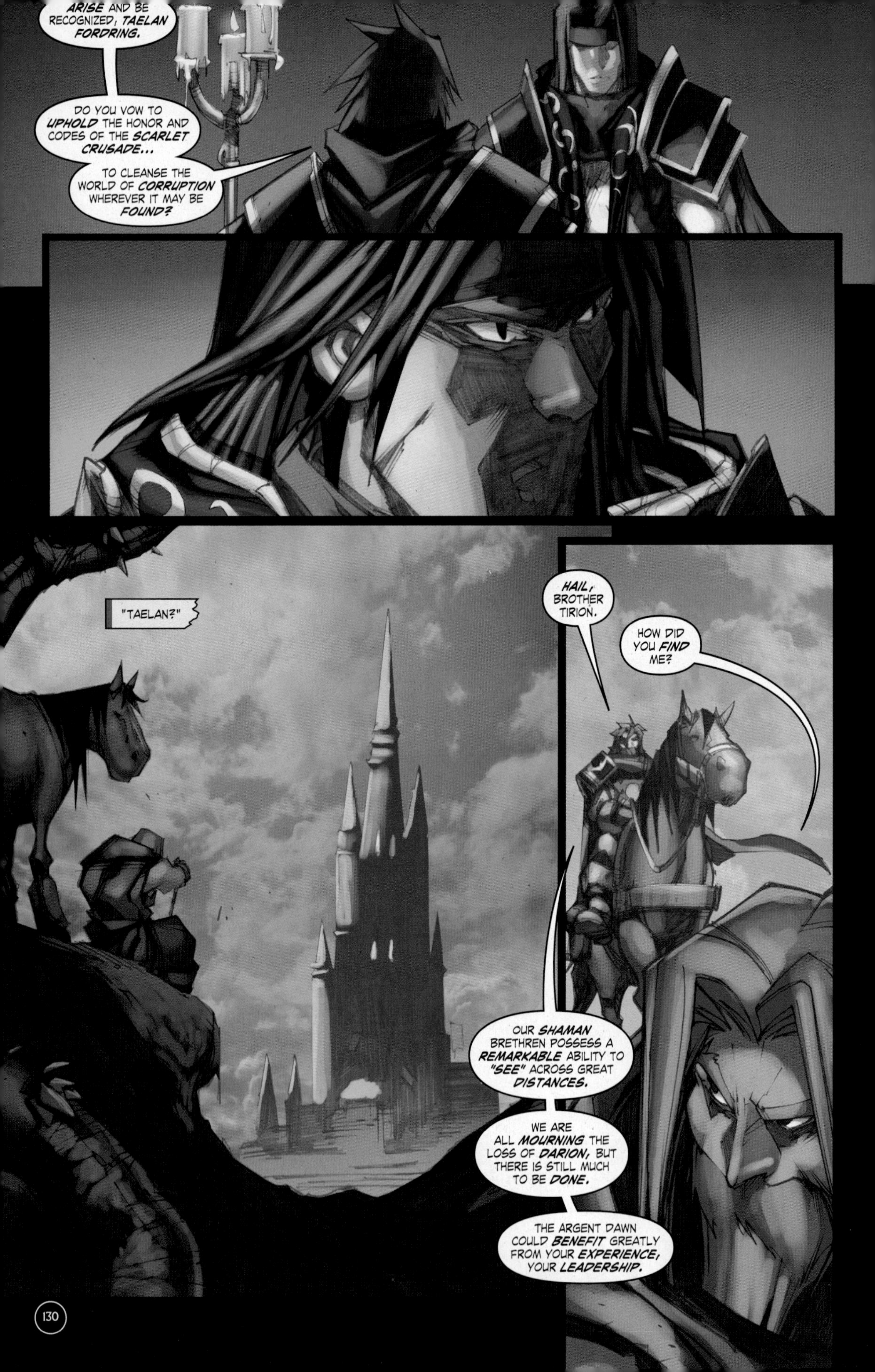
ARISE AND BE RECOGNIZED, TAELAN FORDRING.
DO YOU VOW TO UPHOLD THE HONOR AND CODES OF THE SCARLET CRUSADE...
TO CLEANSE THE WORLD OF CORRUPTION WHEREVER IT MAY BE FOUND?
"TAELAN?"
HAIL, BROTHER TIRION.
HOW DID YOU FIND ME?
OUR SHAMAN BRETHREN POSSESS A REMARKABLE ABILITY TO "SEE" ACROSS GREAT DISTANCES.
WE ARE ALL MOURNING THE LOSS OF DARION, BUT THERE IS STILL MUCH TO BE DONE.
THE ARGENT DAWN COULD BENEFIT GREATLY FROM YOUR EXPERIENCE, YOUR LEADERSHIP.

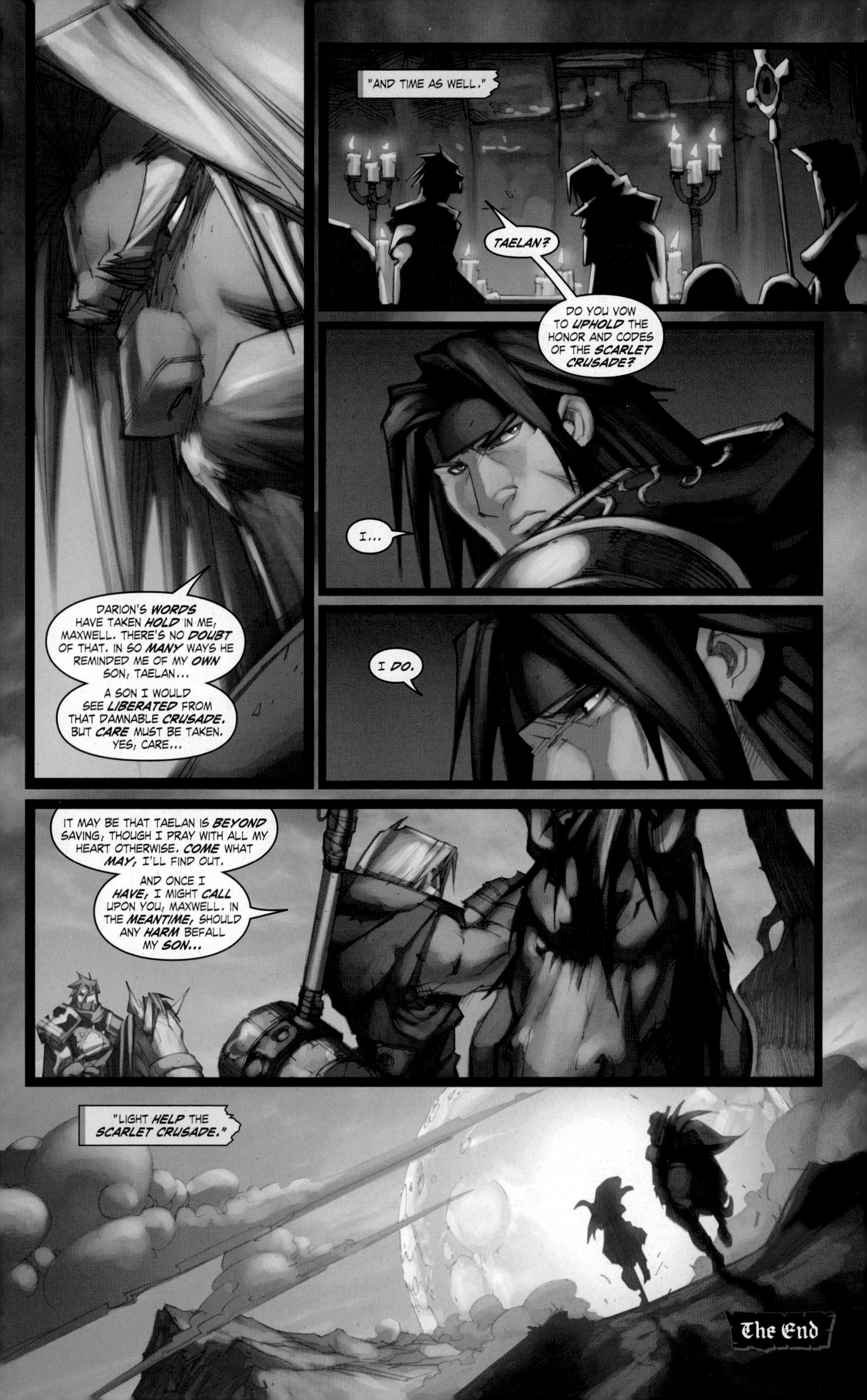

"AND TIME AS WELL."
TAELAN?
DO YOU VOW TO UPHOLD THE HONOR AND CODES OF THE SCARLET CRUSADE?
I...
DARION'S WORDS HAVE TAKEN HOLD IN ME, MAXWELL. THERE'S NO DOUBT OF THAT. IN SO MANY WAYS HE REMINDED ME OF MY OWN SON, TAELAN...
A SON I WOULD SEE LIBERATED FROM THAT DAMNABLE CRUSADE. BUT CARE MUST BE TAKEN. YES, CARE...
I DO.
IT MAY BE THAT TAELAN IS BEYOND SAVING, THOUGH I PRAY WITH ALL MY HEART OTHERWISE. COME WHAT MAY, I'LL FIND OUT.
AND ONCE I HAVE, I MIGHT CALL UPON YOU, MAXWELL. IN THE MEANTIME, SHOULD ANY HARM BEFALL MY SON...
"LIGHT HELP THE SCARLET CRUSADE."
The End

Creating A Page:
PENCILS

Stage 1: Roughed in
Ludo starts by breaking the page into panels, and laying out the figures. In page 1, panel 1, you can see that he's broken out the markers to place the trees against the moon.

Stage 2: Tightened Sketches
For these pages, Ludo chose to re-do the sketches and tighten them up before moving to the final boards with his pencils. Page 2, panel 2 is almost complete, but panel 3 shows that he's still working out how the shadows fall on Balnazzar's wings--gray markers this time!

Stage 3: Final Pencils
This is the final stage before we send them off to Tony. Pencils only, drawn on Strathmore art boards, working area approximately 11" x 17". Of course, Ludo has to draw on the reverse of our regular boards, so the scanner doesn't pick up the live area and crop lines.

PAGE ONE

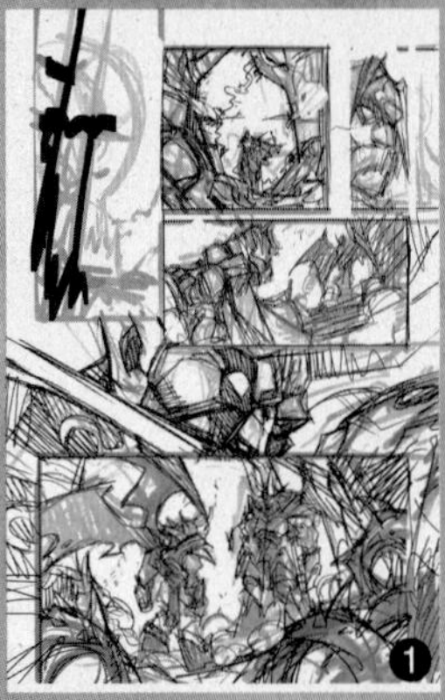
1

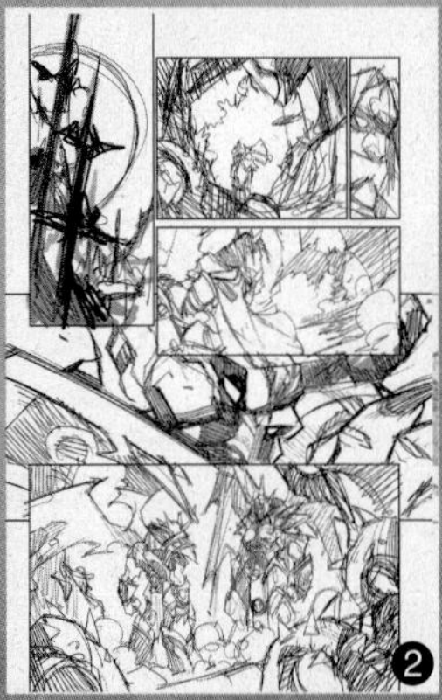
2

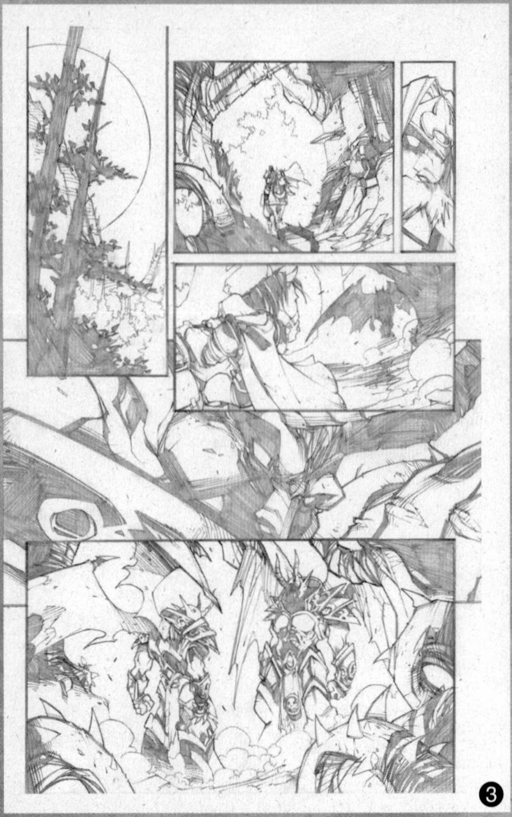
3

PAGE TWO

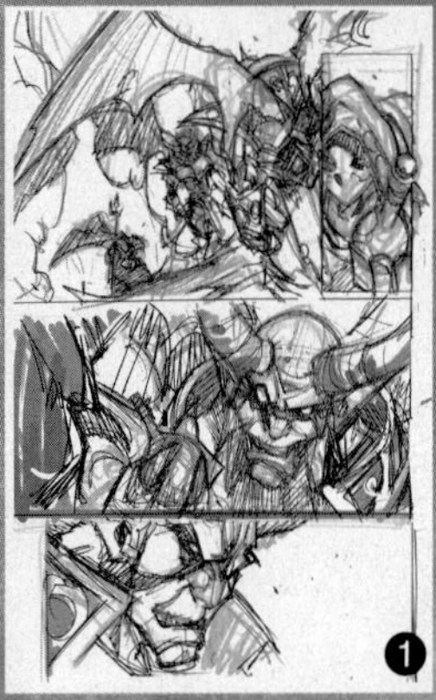
1

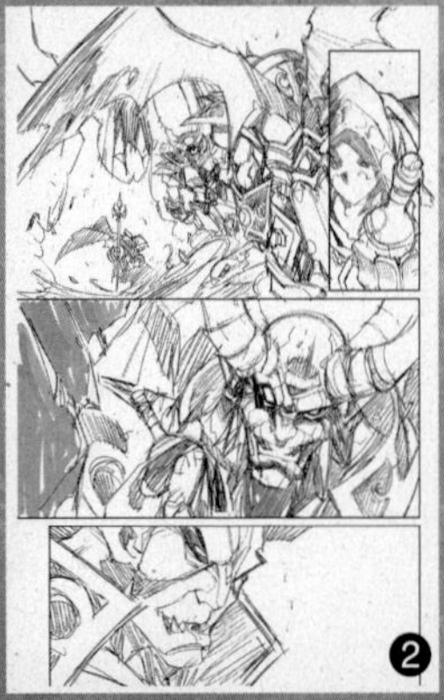
2

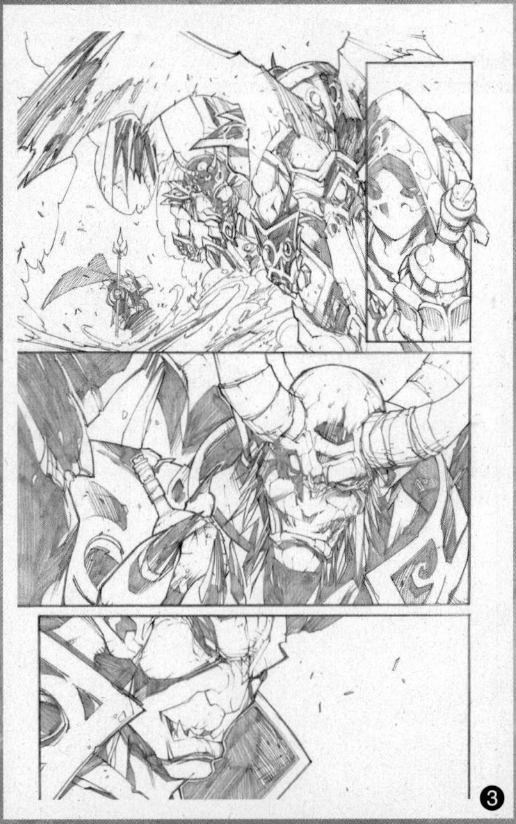
3

PAGE ONE

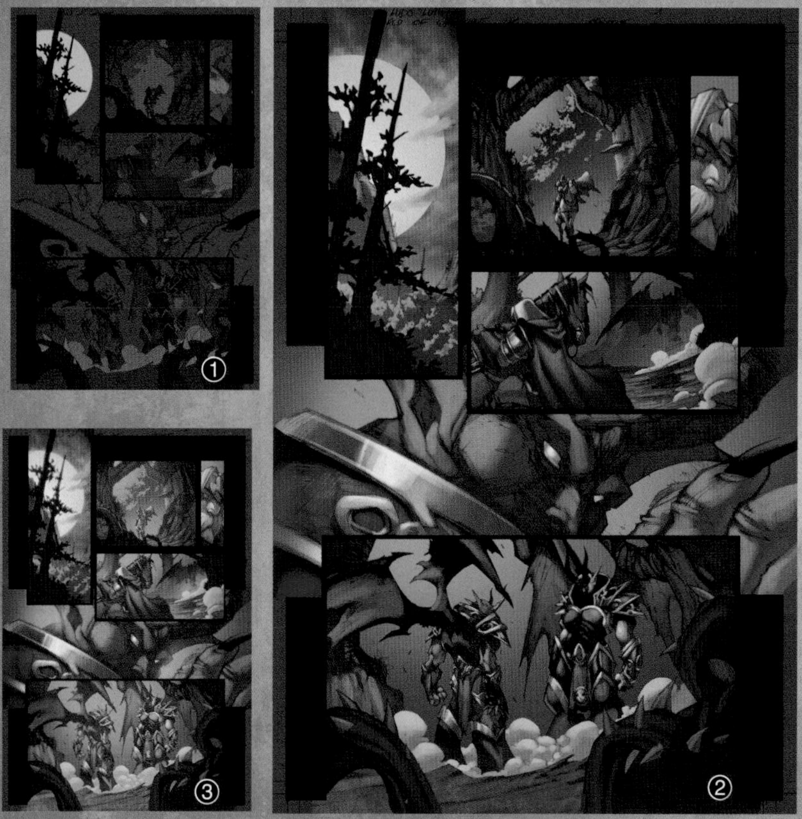

PAGE TWO

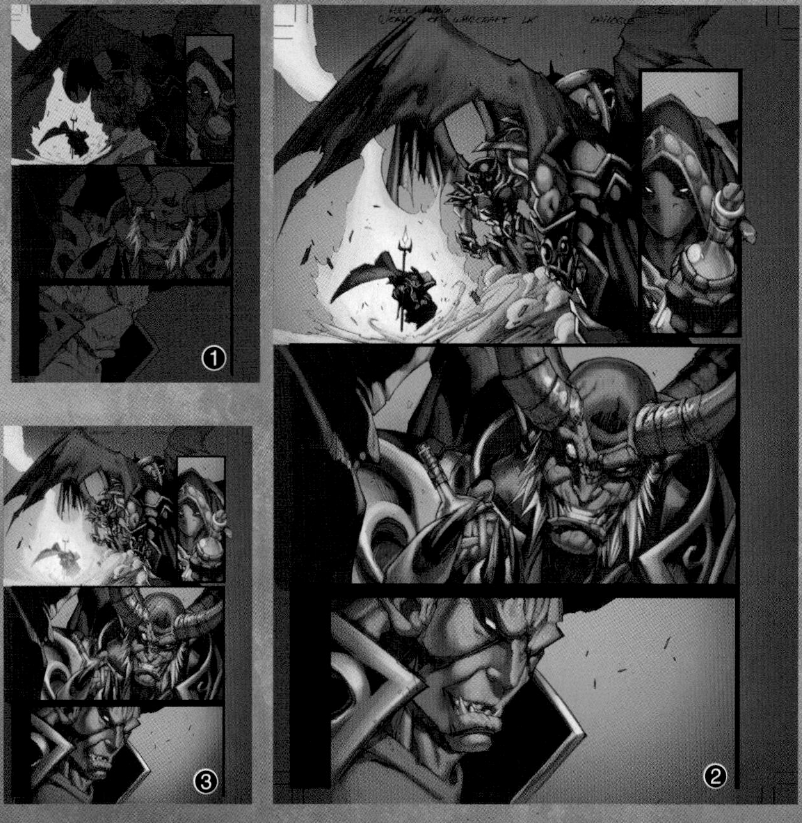

Creating A Page:
COLORS

Stage 1: Flats
The first step in digital coloring is flatting. You select the main shapes and assign them a color—but overall, the piece stays dark. Tony's a glutton for punishment and handles this himself, though a lot of pro colorists opt to have an assistant take care of this step.

Stage 2: Rendering
This is where you see most of the change happening. Background trees reappear in page 1, panel 2. Dathrohan's hair and skin tones are refined to match his regular appearance. Overall, this is where all the details take shape.

Stage 3: Effects
By this point, the changes are all subtle. Looking at page 2, panel 1, Castillian's arrival goes from a harsh tan blob in stage 1, to a fiery yellow-orange in stage 2, to a glowing fire-burst in stage 3. Suddenly, he's not "just" stepping out of a yellow glare. The light reflects off his cloak and staff, and the glow hits Balnazzar's wings—but not as obviously, increasing the distance between them, which is a nice trick when you're coloring on a flat plane.

Stage 4: Final colors
If you turn back to pages 127 and 128, you can see the final colors for these pages. There are changes, because while Tony's good, with this many characters in play, the editors occasionally do have to request tweaks to make sure we're consistent with previous appearances.

Stop Poking Me!

Lazy Peons

Quest

Orc Hero Required

Lazy Peons enters play exhausted.

Exhaust Lazy Peons to complete this quest.

Reward: Draw a card.

"Stop poking me!"

DARK PORTAL 303/319

Art by: Steve Ellis

©2007 UDC ©2007 Blizzard Entertainment, Inc.

World of WarCraft
TRADING CARD GAME

- Each set contains new Loot™ cards to enhance your online character.
- Today's premier fantasy artists present an exciting new look at the World of Warcraft®.
- Compete in tournaments for exclusive World of Warcraft® prizes!

For more info and events, visit:

WOWTCG.COM

WORLD OF WARCRAFT

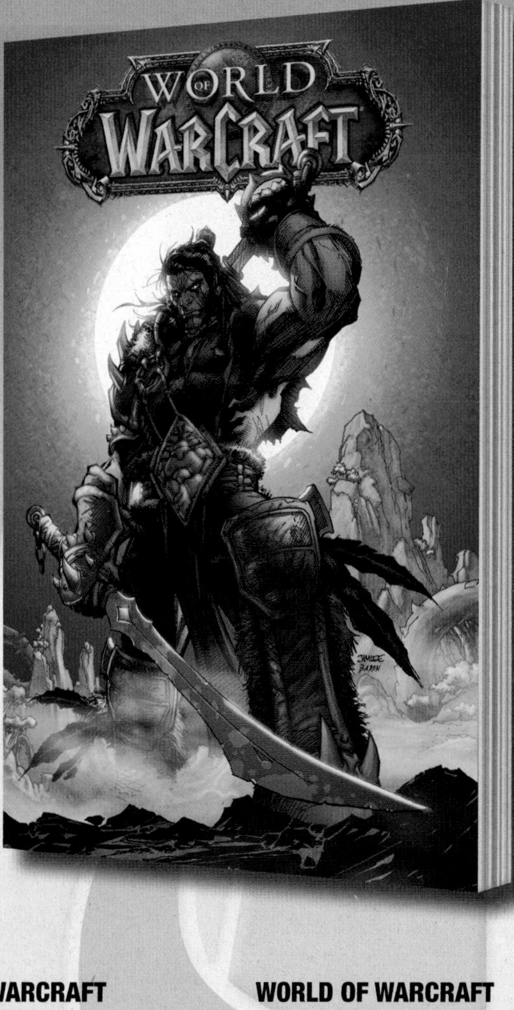
WORLD OF WARCRAFT

An amnesiac washes up on the shores of Kalimdor, starting the epic quest of the warrior Lo'Gosh, and his unlikely allies Broll Bearmantle and Valeera Sanguinar. Striking uneasy relationships with other races, as well as each other, they must fight both the Alliance and the Horde as they struggle to uncover the secrets of Lo'Gosh's past! Written by Walter Simonson (THE JUDAS COIN, *Thor*) and illustrated by Ludo Lullabi (*Lanfeust Quest*) and Sandra Hope (JUSTICE LEAGUE OF AMERICA), this is the latest saga set in the World of Warcraft!

WORLD OF WARCRAFT
BOOK TWO

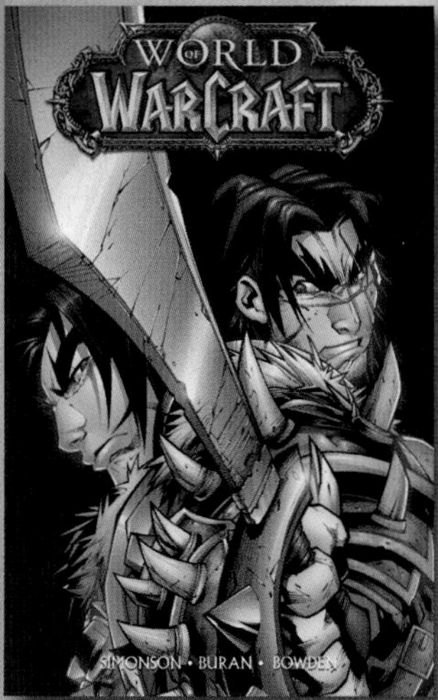
WORLD OF WARCRAFT
SIMONSON • BURAN • BOWDEN

Simonson
Buran • Bowden

WORLD OF WARCRAFT
BOOK THREE
COMING SUMMER 2010

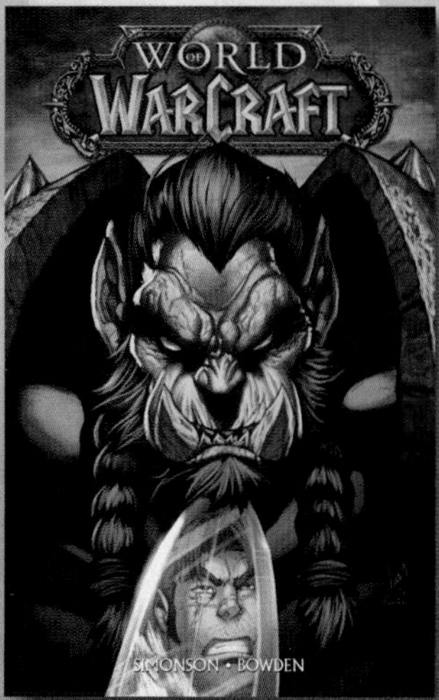
WORLD OF WARCRAFT
SIMONSON • BOWDEN

Simonson
Bowden

WORLD OF WARCRAFT
BOOK FOUR
COMING FALL 2010

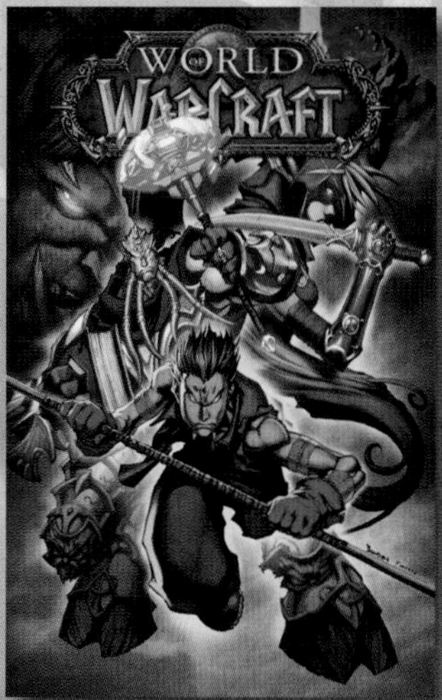
WORLD OF WARCRAFT

Simonson
Bowden

SEARCH THE **GRAPHIC NOVELS SECTION** OF
WILDSTORM.COM
FOR ART AND INFORMATION ON ALL OF OUR BOOKS!

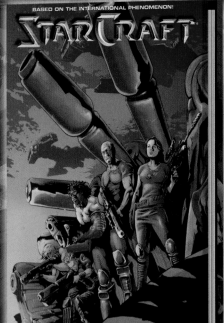